CW00568564

Gre

Horizons

Edna Hunneysett

chipmunkapublishing
the mental health publisher

Published by
Chipmunkapublishing
United Kingdom

http://www.chipmunkapublishing.com

ISBN   978-1-78382-6162

By the same Author

Our Suicidal Teenagers 'Where Are You God'?
Pastoral Care Mental Health
From The Heart Mental Health
Greener Beyond The Hill
Greener Pastures and Brown Blazers

Acknowledgements

I want to thank a special friend for giving her time and painstakingly proof-reading my manuscript and advising on corrections and improvements. My thanks to our son, Peter, who rescues me when I have blips with my computer. As always, I am very grateful to my husband for his support and technical help in displaying photographs.

About the Author

Edna Mary Hunneysett was born in 1940 near Stratford-on-Avon but in her infancy, the family moved to a small hillside farm on the North Yorkshire moors where Edna spent her early life with six siblings. After passing the eleven+ exams, she was a boarder at a Convent grammar school and on finishing school, worked in the Inland Revenue department of the Civil Service. Edna married in 1961 and has eight children, twenty-one grandchildren and three great grandchildren. From 1977 to 1991, she worked part-time as receptionist at a BBC local radio station. She gained a BA Hons (Divinity) in 1995 and an MA in 1998. Edna lives with her husband, a retired teacher, in Middlesbrough.

Summer 1957 / Autumn 1957

The early morning light filters through the flimsy, floral-patterned curtains. Emma is wide awake, listening to the cock crowing its dawn call. Gazing at the old, beamed ceiling in the draughty bedroom of the farmhouse, unable to get back to sleep, she lays still, thinking. She does not want to disturb her fourteen-year-old sister, Amy, at home from boarding-school and soundly asleep next to her. Bankside farm on the North Yorkshire moors has been home to Emma and her six siblings, for most of her life. When at boarding-school for six of those years, she returned each holiday. Although she has been working away for almost four years, the farm is always home to come back to.

'I will never experience this again as Emma Holmes,' she thinks. 'It is incredible. I'm getting married today and will become Mrs Harding, but my initials will remain the same.' This pleases her. As it is much too early to get ready for her wedding, Emma turns onto her side and snuggles down into the blankets. There is no heating in the farmhouse apart from the kitchen and the air is chilly this early April morning. Emma thinks back about the time when she left the convent grammar boarding-school in July, nineteen fifty-seven and with her friend, Faith, went into lodgings in Holmestown, an industrial town not far from Bradford, to start work.

The girls originally met at boarding-school and slowly formed a close friendship. Following the death of her mother in their second year at school, Faith became a frequent visitor to Emma's home on the isolated farm, usually in the long summer holidays. Although originally planning to leave school at sixteen, they'd both returned, after getting good General Certificate of Education (GCE) results, even though neither having an urge to take up a specific career. During the course of that year, they had agreed, after much discussion between themselves that they'd had enough, especially of bedtime at eight-thirty, but also of the strict routine and rigorous discipline. They wanted paid employment. As end of term approached, Faith came to a decision.

'I'll tell you what we'll do. I will go home for a week after we break up. Then I'll join you and we will apply for jobs,' she says to Emma.

A week into the summer holidays, Faith arrives at the farm, after spending time with her sister, Rose, and her three bachelor uncles with whom she lives.

'I'll be back to collect my things,' she tells them, on leaving the house, 'when we have found work.'

'Isn't this exciting,' says Emma, greeting her friend. They are delighted at the thought of no more school and instead, to be planning their move to a working life with money. Sharing the double bed downstairs in what is the farmhouse sitting-room, they talk quietly until the early hours. They consider different options from the information collected before leaving school. Next morning, Tom, Emma's dad, watches them walk into the kitchen. Both look animated and in high spirits.

'A pair of bonny lasses,' he thinks, looking at his daughter, tall and slim with a mass of black curls, and with her thick, black eyebrows, neatly plucked to give them a better shape; and her friend, equally as tall but with a fairer complexion, her wavy, auburn hair gently framing her freckled face. The girls sit down on the old, wooden, hard chairs and help themselves to bread and marmalade, still deep in conversation.

Pouring a second cup of almost colourless tea, having added more water from the kettle to the large, tin teapot, Emma speaks.

'I think we have gone over it all enough. I'm going to apply to the Civil Service. They offer a better wage than the banks which would be my other choice. They also help in finding suitable lodgings.' Her hazel eyes sparkle. Emma is exhilarated. 'Have you decided, Faith?' Her friend holds out her cup for more tea. She is used to it being weak. She takes her time answering, raising her voice above the noise and chatter of Emma's four younger siblings.

'I'm thinking of the Civil Service too, even though my sister told me that they're advertising vacancies at our local bank in Bartown. I want to move elsewhere. I think Rose feels responsible for my welfare since mam died. I told her that we are hoping to be together, to start with, anyway. She feels protective towards me but happy for me to go further afield if I'm with you.'

'That's settled, then. Let's do it. We will fill the forms in today and post them,' Emma says. 'Decision made. What a relief.'

Tom and Mary, Emma's parents, who have been listening intently to the girls discussing the pros and cons of applying for jobs, look at each other. Tom has been secretly hoping that Emma would continue her education and then maybe go to a Teacher Training College.

'She is certainly clever enough,' he thinks, but realises that it isn't going to happen. He can see that she's had enough of studying and boarding-school. Mary understands her daughter's eagerness to become independent. She, herself, left school at fourteen. Martha, Emma's sister and a year older, left school at fifteen and earns money, albeit a very small wage.

'It will also be one less mouth to feed,' Mary thinks. She deals with the family income which is mostly the monthly milk cheque. She counts the pennies every month, often struggling to make ends meet.

'I'll leave you to it. Must get on,' Tom says, standing up and making for the door. He doesn't want Emma picking up on his disappointment.

Within weeks, both girls are interviewed by officials at the Inland Revenue offices in Holmestown. Neither of them applied to this branch of the Civil Service, but an interviewer on the panel of two, explains to each of them, when being interviewed, that there are shortages of applicants to the Inland Revenue. Emma mentions that she would like to work in the same town as her friend so that they can share lodgings together. They are delighted to be offered positions as income tax officers and to start at the beginning of September.

'This is the name and address of a landlady who takes in boarders. I have known her for several years,' says the personnel officer, speaking to them after the interviews. He gives Faith the card. 'I have spoken to her and she can take you.' He is confident that these two young ladies will be well looked after. The girls walk out of the office, smiling at each other.

'We have done it,' says Emma, gleefully. They hurry along the streets. They have a bus to catch and a long journey home.

'All set then, Emma?' queries Tom, as he enters the farmhouse kitchen one morning, a few weeks later. Tom is tall and lean. He has been cleaning out the calf shed. His ragged working-jacket is tied with binder band; his working-cap covers most of his dark hair; and patched trousers are tucked inside his black wellington boots, still gleaming and wet because of Tom having swilled the muck off them at the water trough. Recently, he has become the proud owner of a little van, a step up from the tractor that has been their means of transport for years. There is a minor road into Moorbeck, the hamlet where they live, often referred to as the new road and it is a big improvement on the cart track over the moor that they've used for years. Tom has promised his daughter that he will take her to the main road to catch a bus into Whitby. From there, her plan is to change buses to continue her journey to York to meet with her friend who is travelling by bus from Bartown. Faith returned home a few days earlier to sort out her clothes and say goodbye to her uncles and her older sister.

'You are meeting Faith at York railway station?' Tom asks. Emma nods.

'Yes, we have arranged the travelling, Dad. We want to turn up at our lodgings together.' There are hugs all around. 'Don't worry,' Emma says to her siblings. 'I will be back for a visit and I'll write. I will miss you all.' Little three-year-old Miriam, looking watery-eyed, her black fringe hanging low and almost into her deep-set brown eyes, gazes up at Emma. She is a bright little girl and very articulate for her age.

'I'll miss you,' she whispers. At this, Emma reaches down and picks her up.

'Don't cry,' she says. 'You'll set me off. That goes for you, too, Jacob,' she adds, looking at her eight-year-old youngest brother. 'I will come home soon for a weekend. I promise.' She puts Miriam down and gives Jacob a big hug and another one to her mam.

'Right, Dad, let's go.'

Some hours later, Faith and Emma are on the train heading for Holmestown. As the train speeds through the countryside, stopping on route at various stations, the two girls chat, excitedly.

'I see you are wearing your Flash Harry coat,' Faith comments, with a twinkle in her eye.

'It still fits and it's not school uniform,' Emma says, smiling at her friend. 'Remember that day when we were in the vestry putting on our outdoor shoes, ready for the daily excursion walking in pairs in a crocodile through the streets of Scarborough?' They both giggle. 'I can still see Mother Colette's face when you were doing your twirl, showing off your coat,' Faith adds. She walked in when we were egging you on. We weren't even allowed to talk in there and we were chatting and laughing. She listened when you explained that your mam had just had another baby and couldn't afford a school uniform coat.'

'Yes, mam bought it in a sale and hoped it was passable.' The boarders had seen the film *St Trinians* with Flash Harry in it and Emma's coat resembled his long mackintosh, with padded shoulders, a broad belt and a pleat at the back. It was a slightly lighter brown than the uniform standard colour. The boarders nick-named Emma *Flash Harry* from then on. 'I can just see her when she replied *I see* and then she went into the chapel, probably to pray for us all,' Emma replies, grinning at her friend. 'She never mentioned it again though. She was really decent about it, I thought.' The girls are silent for a few moments as the train passes through a tunnel.

'Just think, Emma,' says Faith, as the train pulls out into the sunshine, 'no more bedtimes at half-eight; no more studying; and no more rules and regulations and all the silences. There is no-one to insist that we go to church. We can choose for ourselves.'

'I won't have to do the Saturday baking, milk cows, help clean out pigsty and suchlike,' Emma replies. 'Not that I minded helping as it's what we all do on the farm to help dad and mam, but being on our own, it will be great. Your coat is very smart, Faith. A lovely colour,' Emma adds, changing the subject.

'My uncles gave me some money and Rose went shopping with me. I love the bluey-grey shade and the deep pockets. I can button it right up if it's cold. It has a narrow belt with a buckle. It's much nicer than my school brown one.' Emma has never been to her friend's home, but she knows about the three uncles she lives with and her older sister. 'I bought a couple of jumpers too. In fact, I had a lovely day shopping with Rose and she helped me choose makeup and underwear. It's such fun now we've left school,' Faith continues. 'Rose told me that she is planning to move out very shortly, but will keep in touch by letter. She says to make sure I write back and tell her how I'm getting on. Being a few years older than me, I guess she tries to watch over me.' She becomes silent, thinking about what life might have been like had her mother not died. She misses her so much especially at a time like this when wanting to tell her about their plans.

The train pulls into Holmestown station and the girls pick up their cases and make their way along the platform.

'I hope Mrs Mackey is nice,' says Faith. 'Stop a minute. I have a map here of the streets. I bought it in Smiths, at home. I thought it might be useful.' The girls scrutinise the map to plan their route.

'It's not too far to walk,' says Emma. 'Look. It is also a short walk from there to the tax office, too, according to this map. That's great.' After walking along the streets, checking each name and pausing occasionally to look at the map, they finally turn into St Mary's Road. The terraced houses are of the old Victorian style, tall and narrow. Halfway down the street, they stop in front of number thirty-one. Faith presses a button at the side of the green painted door. Nothing happens. After a short wait, she presses it again. They look at each other, each wondering what they will do if no one responds.

'Down here, girls,' a voice calls out. A well-rounded, middle-aged lady, her greying hair tucked behind her ears, is walking up the stone steps from the basement. 'This is the door we use. I'm Mrs Mackey. You must be the two ladies starting work in the tax office. I have been expecting you.' Faith and Emma follow her down the well-worn steps and into a large kitchen. 'Have you had a good journey?' she asks politely, with a trace of an Irish accent. 'Tell me who is who,' she requests, smiling at them. The girls introduce themselves. 'Take off your coats and hang them through here in the scullery,' she says, walking into a small room off the kitchen. 'That's the washing-machine,' she states, pointing to a white object along one wall. 'It is a twin-tub. One tub is for washing and the other for spinning and draining. You will each have a night when you do your own laundry. Mabel, our daughter, is at work, but you will meet her later. She will show you how to use it if you are unsure and I'm not around. I don't suppose either of you have used one.' The girls shake their heads. They smile at each other. 'There is a toilet through here too.' The girls take off their coats and hang them on the coat-pegs before following Mrs Mackey back into the kitchen. 'I'll show you your bedroom. Bring your cases and follow me upstairs,' she instructs, while making her way to another door.

On the first floor, Emma, trailing behind Faith, pauses at an open door. She takes a quick glance inside, spying a polished, dark oak, dining-room table and carved-back chairs to match.
'So beautifully decorated, unlike our distempered walls at the farm,' she thinks. There is a glass cabinet in one corner filled with glassware and china. She turns to follow Faith. Another door is ajar. She peeps inside. 'Very posh,' she thinks, looking at the crimson-coloured, plush settees and thick, velvet curtains. She hurries up the next flight of stairs just as Mrs Mackey is pointing out that on this floor are bedrooms for her own family, plus a

bathroom and toilet that the girls can use. After climbing a further narrower staircase, they reach the attic.

'You sleep in here,' Mrs Mackey states, walking into a large room with low eaves at one end. 'You share the wardrobe. I'll leave you to unpack and then we'll have dinner in half-an-hour. I will ask that you are prompt for meals, please. Let me know if you have any food allergies. Please ask me if you have any queries. I've given accommodation to many lasses over the years and I've never had any trouble. I want you to be happy with us,' she concludes, her light-blue eyes twinkling, as she smiles at them. She turns away and disappears through the door, closing it behind her.

Emma and Faith gaze around. There are two single beds, each covered with a cream counterpane, plus two small brown bedside cabinets and a matching dresser with mirror. Emma puts down her case and sits on a bed, thrilled with thoughts of starting work and earning her own money.

'Very efficient, isn't she,' says Faith, 'but she seems nice enough. It's all clean and tastefully decorated. I like this cream wall-paper with the small, coloured flowers it.'

'This bed is comfy, too,' Emma adds, giving a little bounce on it.

Later in the evening, the girls are introduced to Mabel, a tall, well-built lady, with shoulder-length, brown hair. They discover that she is some years older than they are. She is pleasant and informative, telling them about the shops, dance-halls and places of interest. Mr Mackey shows his face briefly. He is slightly built and narrow-faced, with receding grey hair and a moustache. He nods at them in acknowledgement but doesn't say anything.

'He's a bit dour,' Emma thinks, 'but hopefully we won't have much to do with him.' The evening passes with gentle conversation. It is ten o'clock when Emma gets up from her chair. She is tired. 'I think I will go to bed. It has been a long day. I'm very happy to be here,' she says to Mrs Mackey. 'Thank you for taking us.'

'I am sure we'll get along, just fine,' the landlady says, smiling at the girls. 'Let me know if there is any particular food that you don't like. Otherwise, I'll cook what I always do. Have you an alarm to get you up?'

'I have,' replies Faith. 'It's a small, travelling clock with an alarm, a gift from my sister.'

'I'll see you both in the morning, then. Goodnight and God bless.'

'She's quite motherly, isn't she,' Faith states to Emma, on the way upstairs. Her friend nods, before replying.

'Mabel seems a pleasant person, too. Not sure about him, but I think we will be fine here. I am glad that you are with me. It is so different to our home in Moorbeck. Having a washing-machine is amazing.'

Over the next weeks, the girls become accustomed to a weekday routine of walking to the tax office and returning to their lodgings. On one particular street, there is a strong smell of beer as they walk past and Emma realises that it must be where the beer is made: a local brewery. She has never really thought about how it is made, until now. They look forward to their meals after work as Mrs Mackey provides delicious dinners. She is a good cook and fusses over the girls, making sure they eat well. They soon learn to take turns at washing the pots and remembering which night to do their weekly laundry.

Settling in at the office takes longer. There is so much to learn. Each new employee is given a week on various sections in order to gain some understanding of the run of the place.

'I've never seen anything like this,' says Emma to her colleague, Janet, who is overseeing her. 'Answering a call and then plugging it in to transfer it to someone. It is fascinating. I'm not used to taking telephone calls.'

'This is why we give you a week, helping on the switchboard,' Janet explains, pushing her wire-framed glasses up. 'I must get these tightened. They are new and keep sliding.' The mail intrigues Emma, too. Each day, a large hessian sack, full of letters, is delivered. It is taken to the sorting room and emptied onto a table. All the letters are opened and put into piles to be taken to the different sections.

'What's schedule D again?' Emma questions, while sorting the post and trying to memorise all that is being explained to her.

'It is where income tax is calculated on those people who are self-employed as in the professions. The system for paying income tax for most people is under Schedule E, known as Pay As You Earn and generally referred to as PAYE,' her colleague replies, naming the letters. 'You will learn a lot more about it when you are working on the Section, especially about these,' she adds, holding up a form. 'This is a blank P45. It has different parts. When a person leaves a firm for another job, they are given a P45 in duplicate, showing their gross pay and income tax deducted, code number and the reference number of the employer, et cetera. The two copies are handed in to their new employer, one of which is sent to the income tax office that deals with that firm. That tax office can then link it up with their previous employment. This ensures a continuation of pay and tax details. Don't try and remember everything as it will be easier to understand over the weeks when you are dealing with them. You will have training sessions and a week away at some point.' Emma thinks it sounds so complicated but she guesses that she will grasp it in time. She continues sorting the letters into the numerous piles, ready for delivery to the various departments. She is enjoying this whole new way of learning.

'And I'm getting paid for it,' is her happy thinking.

The girls don't go out on weekday evenings during the first weeks. They are tired after long hours at the tax office. Weekends are different. There are lots of attractions in the town for them to discover. Mabel tells them where to find the Catholic churches. Emma has contemplated for a while about the church thing, before deciding that she wants to continue. One Saturday afternoon, while Faith is out window-shopping, she takes a long walk through the streets to St Mary's Catholic Church. She notes the time before setting off on her walk. She needs to find out how long it will take her to get there on a Sunday morning. The Mackey family attends a church further afield and Emma isn't sure what Faith's plans are. 'I can please myself where I go,' she thinks, enjoying the feeling of making her own choices.

St Mary's is a very old church. Emma arrives to find the wooden doors slightly ajar. She pushes one further open and wanders inside to an inner porch. Looking around, she can see lots of hymn books on a table and a glass-fronted cabinet with holy objects on display: crucifixes; prayers books; boxed rosary beads; and small statues. She opens the inner door and finds herself in the large, gloomy interior of the church. There are no lights on. Dipping her fingers into the holy water stoup and crossing herself, she looks around. There are rows of wooden benches with a centre aisle and smaller benches to the sides, plus two confessional boxes on the left-hand side. One is a double: the priest using the centre door, with walk-in doors at either end for penitents. The other is a single confessional box like the one in St Peter's back home. The Stations of the Cross, comprising pictures depicting Christ's journey on the road to Calvary and His crucifixion, are also familiar. She can see candles flickering on a stand to the side of the church, at the front.

At the far end of one of the benches, Emma notices an old man, leaning forward from a sitting position with his head in his hands, resting them on the bench in front. She studies him from a distance. His dark coat looks shabby and his uncombed, grey, straggly hair is hanging over the collar.

'He is probably having a quiet pray or he has recently lost someone and needs to grieve and finds it comforting to sit awhile in here. Maybe he is a tramp wandering the streets and he comes in for somewhere to go. There are lots of possible reasons for his visit,' she thinks, pensively. She wonders if she should speak to him but thinks better of it. She can see at the front of the church, a couple of ladies watering the flowers that decorate the altar. 'The flower ladies,' she muses, 'like the women who take turns to see to the flowers in the church at home.' She walks down the centre aisle and genuflecting, steps inside a bench to kneel and say a prayer, but her mind wanders. She drifts far away to the convent chapel at her old school. Then to St Peter's in Windrush, where her family goes each Sunday. This leads her to thinking about her siblings and she realises that she is missing them. 'Maybe one weekend I will go on the bus and have a night at home to see everyone and tell them about my job.'

On leaving the bench, she wanders over to the candle-stand that is in front of a statue of Mary holding baby Jesus in her arms. Emma drops some pennies in the money-box and lights a candle and whispers a prayer. The familiarity of such an action pleases her; she feels connected to her family.

'Tonight, I'll write home. Tomorrow, I will come to Mass,' she thinks. Before leaving the church, she approaches one of the women on the altar. 'Have you the time, please?'

'It is almost three-thirty,' the lady replies, after looking at her watch. Emma thanks her and genuflecting, walks down the aisle and out of the church back along the streets to the lodgings.

'I now know how long it takes,' she thinks, feeling happy.

'Did you find it easily enough?' asks Mabel, as Emma walks into the kitchen. Removing her coat, Emma nods.

'I did. It is a good distance but I think I'll walk there tomorrow. I enjoy walking.'

'If you like, after you get paid, we can go to the wool shop one Saturday,' suggests Mabel. 'It's a bit of a walk too, but they have a great selection of wool and lots of knitting patterns.' Emma is pleased that Mabel is a knitter and delighted to hear that there is a well-stocked wool shop in Holmestown.

'Did you knit the cardigan you are wearing?' she asks, admiring the lacy panels running down the front of it. 'It looks very intricate.'

'Yes, I did, but that was some time ago. I am going to start knitting for Christmas. My dad likes a knitted waistcoat. I have a pattern but need the wool.' Emma wants to knit a cardigan to wear at work. Her wardrobe is very sparse. She has already dyed black, a brown school cardigan that her mam knitted. The first one her mam made was a cabled, patterned one, beautifully knitted but totally inappropriate for school. This one is very plain and was more in keeping with the official uniform cardigans. Now dyed black, being the only possible colour to cover the brown, Emma doesn't mind wearing it for work as she no longer feels it is school uniform.

At the end of the month, the girls receive their first salary. Faith and Emma walk out together on the Friday afternoon, as they are allowed half-an-hour in which to go and collect their wages in cash from the bank.

'Our very first earnings,' says Emma, happily.

'I don't think I have ever handled so much money in one go,' her friend replies. 'I can't wait to go shopping.' After work, on arriving at the lodgings, they are surprised to see Mrs Mackey standing at the bottom of the basement steps with a huge grin on her face.

'Payday, I believe,' she says, laughing at them. 'I love it when I get my month's money from my girls.' The girls descend the steps, joining in with her hilarity and all walk into the kitchen. 'Right, ladies,' she continues, holding out her hand. The money is handed over. 'Now use yours wisely,' she advises, in her motherly way. 'Remember that it has to last a whole month.'

'She is lovely, isn't she,' Faith says to Emma, later on when they are undressing for bed. 'We are so lucky to have her.'

The following day, Faith is up early and breakfasted, even before the shops open.

'Now I can go and buy that skirt that I have been looking at,' she says. 'It is so exciting, buying our own clothes with money we have earned.' Emma agrees.

'You don't mind going on your own, do you?' she asks. 'It's just that I've arranged to go with Mabel to the wool shop.'

'I'll be fine. I have often shopped on my own since my mam died. I am used to it.' A little later, when on their way to the shop, Emma discusses her plan with Mabel.

'As well as wool for a cardigan, I also want some very fine wool and a pattern, to knit a top that I can wear for dancing.' They arrive. The shop is large with three aisles to walk down and a great array of wools in a multitude of thicknesses and shades. There is a section with many large folders filled with knitting patterns and labelled accordingly. Further down the aisle from the patterns are knitting needles of every size imaginable. Next to those are stands with containers filled with buttons, all colours of the rainbow, some glittery while other are shaped in tiny animals or stars or hearts. After a gentle stroll around the shop, Emma takes her time wading through patterns before deciding which one to buy.

'This is the cardigan. I love the diamond pattern and it is in double knitting wool which is perfect. This is a lacy cap-sleeved pattern for my dancing top,' she explains, showing them both to Mabel. 'It is in three ply wool. It will be very fine and delicate when I've made it and I'm buying white wool to go with my black taffeta skirt.' After further deliberation, she chooses emerald-green wool for the cardigan, counting out the number of balls of wool, as stated in the pattern for her size. She picks up the required balls of white wool needed and collects the pairs of knitting needles specified in each of the patterns. 'I will come back for the buttons when I have finished the items,' she says to the assistant at the till.

'Very sensible,' replies the middle-aged, well-built lady; her brown hair, sprinkled with grey, surrounding her chubby face. 'You will be able to pick the correct size when you have finished your garment.'

'It's a great shop,' Emma comments, while handing over her money. Mabel is waiting patiently outside, having finished her shopping rather more quickly than Emma.

Arriving back at the lodgings, Emma shows Faith the green wool and the very complex diamond cardigan pattern.

'I'm excited about doing this,' she says. 'When I have finished this one, I am going to knit this fancy top as I can wear it for dancing.

How did you get on? Did you get the skirt that you went shopping for?' Faith nods. Picking up her shopping bag that she'd placed on a chair, she takes out the skirt and holds it up for all to see.
'That is a lovely skirt,' Mrs Mackey exclaims, walking into the kitchen. 'I love those autumn russet colours.' Both Mabel and Emma enthuse over the skirt.
'It looks really good quality, Faith,' Emma says, thinking that she ought to buy a new one too. 'Maybe next weekend,' she decides, 'although better to wait for next payday,' she muses. The girls are learning to budget, knowing that the money has to last a month.
'It was expensive, but I couldn't resist it,' Faith replies. 'It's a great feeling being able to buy my own clothes. Next month, I will buy something else. I'll take it upstairs,' she adds, delighted with the responses.

During the week, Emma receives a letter. She doesn't recognise the writing. Tearing it open, she unfolds the paper and glances at the ending. It is from Greg. He wants to come and see her.
'Fancy that,' she says to Faith, as they are walking to work the next day, well wrapped up from the bitingly cold wind. 'He must have been to our farm to get the address from mam. I haven't seen him for a while. It isn't as if we were serious, but he is fun to be with and I especially liked the rides on his motor-bike.' She'd met him at a local village dance and had been seeing him regularly when at home on holiday from boarding-school. 'It might be good to meet up again and get the latest gossip, if there is any.' Over dinner, after work, Emma approaches the subject with Mrs Mackey and asks her if she knows of anywhere close by where he can stay overnight.
'If it is just for one night, he can sleep in the box-room. There is a bed in there but little else,' her landlady replies.
'Thank you. That's very kind of you. I'll write and tell him.'

Emma goes to their bedroom early that night and not only does she write to Greg but also composes a long letter home, remembering her resolve to go for a weekend. She is looking forward to seeing Greg. He arrives one Saturday afternoon, having journeyed by bus. She is surprised to find that she struggles a little when coming face to face with him in such different circumstances. There isn't quite the same spontaneity. They go to the pictures and have a drink afterwards at a local pub. Conversation is somewhat strained.
'Maybe next time, it will be easier,' thinks Emma, lying in bed,

going back over the evening.

'He is a fine-looking lad; tall and dark; and a real good-looker, as they say,' Mrs Mackey comments, after Greg leaves on the Sunday afternoon. 'He is quiet and polite. He can come anytime.'

'Thank you,' replies Emma, even though not sure how she is feeling about Greg.

The following Saturday, the girls decide to go dancing. The first time they go, Emma spends most of the evening taking in the surroundings. She is fascinated by the brightly flashing lights moving around the room, as the couples are rocking and rolling, swinging and jiving: rock and roll, especially, being the current craze. The style of dancing intrigues her, so unlike the ballroom dances that she's learnt. There are a few slower dances where the couple actually hold each other, one known as a creep, she finds out, which seems to her, like a slow shuffle. She studies the young women in their swirling knee-length skirts and skimpy tops. Many of the lads are wearing high-waist drainpipe trousers and drape jackets with dark-coloured pocket-flaps: some jackets are even trimmed with velvet collars. Their white shirts are high-necked and buttoned-up but loose-collared. She is surprised when noticing their brightly-coloured socks. Finally, the lads sport very thin ties in bright greens, blues and shocking pinks which she discovers are labelled Slim Jims, with many finishing in a square instead of a point. Their shoes are black suede with crepe soles, going by the name of creepers, unlike her dad's plain, black, patent-leather shoes that he keeps for best and wears for dancing.

'It's all quite bizarre,' she thinks. The young men with this particular attire are known as Teddy Boys and are part of a modern trend like the rock and roll dancing. She is fascinated by some of their hair styles too: long and greased-up with a quiff in front but sides combed back. There are other lads dressed in standard suits or smart trousers with shirt and jacket, obviously not classing themselves as Teddy Boys.

After going for a number of weeks, the girls are finding the dances great fun. It is Saturday night again. The band belts out the music and Emma's feet are tapping to *All Shook Up* followed by *Jailhouse Rock*, both Elvis Presley chart toppers for weeks at a time and being improvised by a local singer. The band continue with a Jerry Lee Lewis favourite, *Great Balls of Fire*, a song that encourages the dancers to go wild in displaying the dancing moves. Sometimes, records are played such as The Diamonds with *Little Darling* or Tab Hunter singing *Young Love* and Emma is already memorising the lyrics. She is asked a few times to dance and makes an effort at rock and roll.

'It will get easier,' one young man says to her, realising that she is new to it. 'You just need more practice.'

Early in November, Emma carries out her plan to return to Moorbeck to see her family. On the Friday morning, she takes her overnight small travelling case into work with her. She is planning to catch a bus immediately afterwards, having written earlier in the week to tell her mam that she is coming home for two nights. If the buses run on time, she knows she can make the last connection from Whitby. She invites Faith to come with her, her family being Faith's second home after losing her mam.

'You go. I'm fine here with Mrs Mackey. I am planning to go dancing on Saturday night as I am hoping to see Rory again.' Rory is a young man who is showing an interest in Faith at the dances and she is enjoying his attention. She has also settled in well in Holmestown, soaking up the kindness shown by Mabel and Mrs Mackey. 'Give your family my love, though,' she insists.

After work, Emma walks to the bus station. It is a windy evening with gentle rain starting to come down. She shelters in the waiting-room until the bus pulls up. The bus is nearly full when she steps on. She walks up the aisle, finds an empty seat and settles herself down, keeping her small case on her knee. Opening it, she takes out a couple of sandwiches that she made the previous evening; she has no drink.

'I can last until I get home. I'll have a cup of tea, then,' she thinks. 'I hope the little ones like the sweets that I've bought for them. I can't wait to see them. I won't be milking cows this time. Well, I hope not, anyway. It seems strange going home as a working girl. I feel different, but how they will find me?'

Autumn 1957 / Spring 1958

After what seems a long journey to Emma, she finally steps down
from the bus at Windrush signpost. The bus disappears over the
horizon. As she crosses the road, she is surprised at how dark it is.
'No street lights around here, but it is not raining, thank goodness,'
she tells herself.' She shines her torch onto the rough moor track
and although it seems pitch black at first, her eyes soon adjust to
the dim light from the stars and a half moon shining. It is a mile
over the dirt track before she finally arrives back at Bankside farm.
When entering the farmhouse kitchen, she is met with brief smiles
as Tom and Mary are engrossed in a game of whist with Mark and
Tim. They finish their game and then Mary makes Emma
sandwiches, which she enjoys with a cup of tea.
'You can sleep in Amy's bed,' says Mary, 'with Miriam. That
okay?' Emma nods and smiles. She is tired after a full day at work
and the long journey.
'I'll go up now,' she says, on finishing her second sandwich. 'We
can talk tomorrow.'

Things are a little different at Bankside farm. Martha, who married
a few months earlier, lives in a nearby farmhouse with her husband
Joe. It was a bit of a whirl-wind romance and they married before
Emma left school. He is some years older than Martha, but a
pleasant man who originates from Newcastle and with his training
in forestry, was working on one of the estates, before they moved
onto the farm. The exciting news is that Martha is now pregnant
and baby's due date is early next May. Amy, having passed her
eleven plus exam earlier in the year, is away at the convent
boarding-school, the one Emma attended. Tim, her older brother,
still living at home, is working on a local farm. He is spending this
Saturday evening out with one of his friends as they meet up
regularly to play their guitars. Her younger brother Mark, now
fourteen and attending the grammar school in Middlesburn, tells
her how much he hates it and is hoping that he'll be allowed to
leave when he turns fifteen. He wants to farm and has no desire to
stay on at school to take exams.

Emma's particular joy is in seeing her youngest brother, Jacob,
plus her baby sister, three-year-old Miriam. She spends time with
them, playing cards and board games. Miriam, with her beautiful,
deep brown, expressive eyes peering out from under the black

fringe of her straight, black hair, is delighted to have someone who will play with her. Emma accompanies Jacob while he feeds the calves, and is amused by his cheeky, lop-sided grin. His black hair, she notices, is very straight, just like hers was before she started having it permed. Mary has been regularly perming her older daughters' hair since their early teens. In the evening, Mary and Tom, after a chat about her lodgings and work, play whist with Emma and Mark, the foursome required for the card game. It is fun although, having not played for a while, she is corrected when making a mistake or two. Sunday afternoon comes all too quickly and it is time for her to leave.

'I will be home for Christmas,' are her parting words. On the return journey, she mulls over her visit. 'It is still home,' she thinks, 'but in some ways, not quite the same. A part of me felt like a visitor and I suppose that's what I am.'

Back in Holmestown, Emma is keen to continue knitting her cardigan, spending the evenings with Faith in the basement kitchen and sometimes joined by Mabel or Mrs Mackey. She finds it a novelty to sit watching different programmes and the news on the television. Rarely do they see Mr Mackey and they don't like to ask of his whereabouts. He occasionally wanders into the kitchen for a late-night drink. Emma surmises that he watches another television in the posh sitting-room on the next floor.

A couple of weeks later, Greg returns for a short visit. This time Emma realises that, although she likes him as a friend, she is no longer interested in him as a boyfriend and doesn't want him building up false hopes.

'I've moved on,' she thinks. 'I think even our friendship is slowly falling apart.' She plucks up the courage to tell him, while they are having a drink together, that she is calling it a day. Although they part on amicable terms, Greg is saddened about their finishing, but Emma is comforted knowing that he is occupied with his studying at Askham Bryan college, finding it both challenging and enjoyable. She is sure that he will soon find another girlfriend. She is feeling light-hearted having made this decision, knowing she is free to accept invitations, without feeling guilty, from other interested boys that she meets at the regular Saturday night dance.

'He is getting really interested in you,' Emma says, teasingly, one Saturday evening, as the girls are sitting together watching the couples piling onto the dance floor. 'Here he comes again,' she adds, watching Rory approaching with a big grin on his face. Faith blushes. Rory is a pleasant, young Irish lad with a shock of fair hair swept to one side. He grins and holds his hand out to Faith who leaves her seat and joins him. The band is playing very loudly. At the start of the next dance, Emma, gazing at the dancers, suddenly realises that a tall, blond-haired man is in front of her, asking her for a dance. She stands up and smiles. Together they move in among the dancers to the music of Pat Boone and *Love Letters in the Sands*. Emma likes this one, as it is more slow-moving, with couples gliding gently across the floor.

'You are new here, aren't you?' he enquires, after they each introduce themselves. They talk quietly as they move around the floor. Later in the evening as Rory accompanies the girls back to their lodgings, Faith comments on the bloke, having seen him have several dances with Emma.

'He seems somewhat older than many of the lads.'

'You mean Colin. I didn't ask his age, but I think you are right,' Emma replies. 'He is more mature than the other lads that I've been dancing with, but I like him.'

Saturday evenings continue in a similar fashion with Colin appearing irregularly, but always giving Emma several dances when he does attend. He is taking their friendship very slowly and not forthcoming about his life but Emma is happy with the situation. Faith is quickly becoming attached to Rory, which helps Emma to grow in confidence by venturing out more on her own.

'Colin is not pushy, you know,' she explains to Faith, as they are preparing for bed, one evening, 'but he has asked if he can pick me up during the week, after work, for a run out on his motor-bike. I have told Mrs Markey and she is fine about it. I'll have my dinner before I go. I am really looking forward to it.'

The following Wednesday evening, Colin pulls up on his motor-bike outside their lodgings. Emma is already waiting, wearing a pair of small-checked, brown trousers and her beige, thick jumper, for warmth. She'd bought these with some of her second month's salary. Colin passes Emma a helmet to wear, as a pillion passenger.

'Thank you. I haven't used one of these before.'

'It is safer if we wear them. They will pass a law eventually making them obligatory.' Emma loves the thought of a ride on a

motor-bike again. As soon as they are on the outskirts of Holmestown, Colin pulls up onto a grass verge and parks the bike. 'I think we'll venture further afield to a cinema and then have a bite to eat at a wayside café on the way back. What do you think?' 'Sounds great to me,' Emma replies, smiling at him.
'You may want to put this on over your clothes as it will feel quite chilly when I speed up on the main roads,' Colin states, taking a stylish, grey jumpsuit with yellow trimmings, from the pannier at the back of the bike and handing it to Emma.
'Thank you. That's very thoughtful of you.' She smiles again, thinking what a decent sort of bloke he is.

After a thrilling ride, they pull up at a cinema on the outskirts of a built-up area. Emma loves the pictures and soon is totally involved in the plot. *High Society* has a mixture of music and romance and a happy ending and is exactly the kind of story that Emma enjoys. It lasts longer than anticipated and after a light bite at a nearby café, they climb back onto the motor-bike and set off home. It seems a long way, but Emma is glowing. She has had a wonderful evening. They say goodnight as Colin drops her off at the end of the street so as not to disturb the occupants at her lodgings with the noise of the motor-bike. He gives her a gentle peck on the cheek and, mounting his bike, roars off into the night. Emma's heart is singing as she turns the key in the lock and creeps quietly into the kitchen. 'Maybe we will do it again,' she thinks, hopefully. There is a dim light on. A figure emerges from the chair in the corner.
'What time do you think this is, to be coming in?' Mr Mackey says angrily, as he approaches her.
'I'm sorry it's a bit late but we've just got back.'
'Gadding around the countryside at this time of night with a fellow you hardly know,' he states. 'Well, you listen to me, young lady. My girls were always in by eleven and it was good enough for them. If you aren't in by that time, any evening, you'll be out of here for good.' He turns his back and goes upstairs. Emma is dumfounded. Her heart sinks. Her happy feelings dissipate.
'Still with rules and regulations, even after leaving school,' she thinks, feeling very chastened. She puts the light out and creeps quietly up to the attic and quickly undressing, crawls into bed. It is some time before she falls asleep, chewing over her confrontation with Mr Mackey. She realises she will have to face Mrs Mackey the next day and hopes that she will be more sympathetic.

The bombshell comes next morning but not from Mrs Mackey who is tolerant and understanding.

'He is okay. His bark is worse than his bite,' she says, reassuringly, to Emma over breakfast, 'but you will have to be in by eleven. He will be on the look-out from now on. He considers it is best for your welfare and he feels responsible for you.' Relieved that Mrs Mackey is sympathetic, Emma leaves for work feeling happier about the incident until Faith gives her the information.

'He is married, you know,' she states. 'I happened to mention his name to a colleague at work and they know him. I have been meaning to tell you but it is really none of my business but I thought you'd like to know. I didn't think you'd be going out with him if you'd known.' Emma is dumfounded.

'Are you sure?'

'It seemed pretty definite to me from what William said at work and he has no reason to make it up.' Emma remains quiet, thinking.

'That jumpsuit I wore. Why did he have that in the pannier? It suddenly makes sense. It will be his wife's.' Emma feels sick. 'I can't believe it, me getting interested in a married man.' Later in the morning, a colleague calls Emma over.

'There is a phone call for you.' Emma's heart sinks.

'I will just tell him,' she thinks, determinedly, and she does. She makes it clear that she does not go out with married men. Colin is apologetic, claiming that it is just a friendship with no hidden agenda, before hanging up. 'I hope he doesn't turn up at the dances,' Emma thinks. 'I don't want to see him again.' She is angry, upset and confused, but tries to put her feelings to one side and concentrate on her work.

After a short visit to their homes for Christmas, the girls are back at their lodgings and work. Emma is knitting again. The emerald-green cardigan is a success and she wears it frequently at work but she has a disaster with her finely-knit, cap-sleeved top.

'It is so pretty,' she exclaims, when trying it on. Mabel, the only one at home, as Faith is out with Rory and Mrs Mackey is visiting a friend, agrees with her. 'I am just going into the scullery to give it a quick wash in the sink as it is a little scruffy. White gets dirty so quickly.' Emma washes the garment in suds in warm water but thinks nothing about rinsing it in cold water. As she is doing this, she senses something is wrong. Squeezing it out, she holds it up and exclaims loudly. Mabel appears. 'Look. It has shrunk,' she

states. She is devastated. 'What have I done?' She wants to cry.
'Did you rinse it in cold water?' asks Mabel. Emma nods, on the
verge of tears. 'Don't you know that you need to rinse wool in
warm water? Woollen garments shrink in cold water.' Emma
shakes her head. She hadn't known that.

'All that painstakingly hard work. It was so lovely.' A tear trickles
down her cheek and she wipes it away. Then she pulls herself
together. 'I'll just have to knit another one but I will get a different
pattern, one that is a bit easier and on thicker needles. I'll post this
to Miriam. It will fit one of her dolls. She will love that.' Mabel is
most sympathetic and Emma gives her a teary smile. 'Another
lesson learnt,' she thinks.

One Saturday evening, in mid-January, another young man whom
she hasn't seen before, approaches Emma for a dance. He
introduces himself as Harry. Barely taller than her, he is a little
stocky with light-brown, wavy hair and pale-blue eyes under his
bushy eyebrows. Emma chats about her work and where she lives.
Harry says very little at first. When he opens up, he talks a lot
about music and that he sings in an operatic society, telling her of
concerts that he has taken part in.

'His dancing is okay,' thinks Emma. 'He does a lot of jiving
around but he doesn't seem to do the slow ones. He doesn't dress
like the Teddy Boys although he dances like them.' He is wearing
brown slacks with a white shirt and plain beige jumper. The
following Saturday evening, he is at the dance again and is
persistent in his attention towards her. She is flattered by this.
'I'll take you to the operatic society next week,' he says. 'You can
come as a guest. Next Sunday, we'll have a run out as I have a
motor-bike. It's old but it gets me around.'

'That sounds fun,' she replies. 'I've been on motor-bikes before. I
love riding them.' In bed that night, Emma chews over their
conversations. She isn't sure about him. 'He is a bit full of himself
when he talks,' she thinks, 'but he hasn't mentioned work. He just
goes on about his singing and his bike.' Falling asleep, she decides
she will keep her word and go with him to the operatic society.

True to his word, Harry meets up with her, as arranged. Emma has
never heard of Gilbert and Sullivan. The music is new to her and
she enjoys the lyrics and the way they sing them. Harry is
confident and at ease with the others in the room and, when
singing, has a deep, baritone voice which impresses her. She goes

for a short ride with him on the Sunday afternoon and enjoys being on a motor-bike again, but unlike Colin, Harry doesn't have a crash-helmet and Emma isn't bothered about one either. They finish their ride in a rundown area that Emma doesn't know but, on being told that his mam has invited her to tea, realises it is where he lives. He drives down a back alley that is scruffy with empty bottles and bits of paper lying around plus a sodden mattress and a broken chair. Half-way down the alleyway, Harry pulls up at the back entrance of a terraced house and wheels his bike into a backyard. They walk in through a tiny kitchen to a living-room, sparsely furnished. Harry introduces her to his mother who fusses over Emma and makes her welcome. She has a mop of shoulder-length, untidy black hair sprinkled with grey, framing her round face. As she smiles, Emma notices her uneven teeth with a gap at the front. A small table in the living-room is set for the two of them and sandwiches are on the table. Emma surmises that there isn't much money around, but his mam is friendly.

'You must come to the club next Sunday evening,' she says to Emma, as she pours out a cup of tea from a chipped teapot. 'We will sign you in. We'll have a table to ourselves.'

'Thank you,' answers Emma, thinking it impolite to refuse but isn't sure about spending an evening with Harry's parents as she assumes his dad will be there. She feels it is all too soon and that she needs to back off a bit.

'We're going now, Mam,' Harry tells his mother. 'We are off to the pictures.'

On arriving at the picture-house, Emma offers to pay for herself, an offer Harry accepts. She'd contributed earlier towards the petrol.

'I bet he's the type that wants a snog in the back row,' she thinks, 'but if I am going to see a film, I want to watch it.' She is pleased that the back rows are full. They end up sitting nearer the front.

'Where do you work?' she finally asks him, while waiting for the picture to start and thinking that he doesn't seem to have much money. Harry hesitates.

'At present, I work on a butcher's stall at the market, twice a week. If you come down next Saturday, you will see me in my apron,' he says, laughing as he speaks. She guesses he is embarrassed, considering he knows that she works in a tax office. 'I am trying to get an apprenticeship but not having much luck,' he adds.

Emma becomes engrossed in the picture *Love Me Tender* starring Elvis Presley. She already knows the lyrics to the song of the same title as it is often played at the dances on Saturday evenings. She follows the story of this Western musical with total concentration. Elvis is the youngest of four sons and while his three older brothers are away at war, he looks after the family farm. There is intrigue with girlfriends but sadly he dies young at the end, much to Emma's dismay as she liked films with happy endings.

'Next time, I will check the story before agreeing to go,' she thinks. 'A picture with a sad ending isn't my idea of a night out.' On leaving the cinema, she explains to Harry that she has to dash to be in on time, adding that she will see him on Saturday at the market stall. It is a little after eleven o'clock when she quietly lets herself in but no-one is waiting for her. She goes stealthily up to the attic bedroom.

'You're a bit late,' her friend mumbles from under the bed clothes. I heard Mrs Mackey tell her husband that she'd given you permission, as the pictures finish late. You need to be careful.'

'She is good to me, isn't she,' Emma states. 'I will thank her tomorrow.'

The following Saturday, Emma wraps up warmly before making her way through the streets to the large market. It is early in February and a sharp wind is blowing as she wanders up and down the many stalls looking for a butcher's stand. Then she spots Harry, who, true to his word, is wearing a butcher's blue and white striped apron. He is hanging around the stall, trying to look busy. She walks up to him and says hello. She can hear the small wireless at the side of the stall.

'Have you heard?' is his greeting.

'Heard what?' she replies, wondering at this strange question.

'Manchester United. There's been a crash. You know. Matt Busby is the manager. They are a really big football team. They've crashed at Munich on take-off. I'll just see if anyone has an update.' He walks up to another bloke and they converse at length. Another guy joins them. The talking continues. Emma waits patiently, tapping her feet up and down to keep the circulation going. It is cold standing about. She doesn't know anything about football except for her parents filling in the football coupon every week and listening to the scores on a Saturday tea-time. 'Sorry about that,' Harry says, as he approaches her. 'They don't know much more but it is a major accident. I can't talk now but I'll see you tomorrow. I will meet you outside the club. You know where it is, don't you?' Emma nods and watches him disappear around the back of the stall.

'Well, that was a bit of a waste of time,' she thinks, glumly, as she saunters through the market looking at anything to buy.

'You seem to be seeing a lot of him,' comments Faith, when Emma tells her that she is going to a club on Sunday evening.

'I'm meeting his parents again. I don't know how to refuse but it is a bit soon, I think, to be going out with them.'

'Getting keen, is he?' Emma pulls a face.

'He is. I will have to watch him. You and Rory seem great.'

'Yes, he is really easy going and doesn't push me. I enjoy his company.' Much later in the evening, after a very noisy time at the social club, trying to be polite and make small talk with his parents, Emma, with Harry, say goodnight to them and set off home. On arriving at the end of her street, they part company.

'I will pick you up next Sunday and go for a spin,' Harry says, pulling her to one side and kissing her. Emma tries to make it brief, before running down the pavement, as it is after eleven o'clock. She is breathless by the time she arrives at the house, hoping that Mr Mackey is in bed. She quietly opens the kitchen door. The light is on. Her heart sinks, but it is Mrs Mackey who is watching late television. She gets up from her chair and speaks.

'It's all right. I told him I'd given you permission to be late but you will have to try harder to be back on time. I can't keep covering for you like this.' This is the second time that she has placated her husband over Emma's late nights.

'I'm sorry,' Emma whispers, panting as she speaks. 'You are so kind. Thank you.'

'Was it a good night, then?' her landlady asks.

'It was noisy. I found it difficult to talk. It was a bit strained.' She pauses and catches her breath. 'His dad is a big, broad fellow, with a shock of brown hair. He bought me a port and lemon drink; a couple actually. The parents are pleasant enough and they make a real effort to put me at ease. Harry is picking me up on his motor-bike on Sunday for another run out. I find him a bit too forward, like introducing me to his parents. I hardly know him. I'll sleep on it,' she says. 'I am thinking of missing the dances for a week or two. It is very cold being out at this time of year. I'll do some knitting and watch television.'

'Well, goodnight then. God bless,' Mrs Mackey says, as Emma turns to go upstairs.

It is a bright day for February, the following Sunday, when Harry pulls up at the lodgings. Emma is well wrapped-up, as she knows it will be cold on the motor-bike. They speed off up the street and out onto a main road, heading for some hills. They pull up at a beauty spot and after parking the motor-bike, go for a walk and it isn't long before Harry stops and kisses her. Emma isn't used to such attention from a boy and gently eases off. On the way home, Harry picks up speed and soon they are racing along, both enjoying the fun ride, until a police car flashes them to stop. It pulls up behind and a policeman gets out and walks over to them. 'Speeding a bit, you know, son,' he says, in a deep, gruff voice. 'How old are you?'
'Sixteen, but I'm seventeen next month.' The policeman looks at him, suspiciously.
'Have you your insurance, road tax certificate and licence with you?' Harry shakes his head.
'They're at home.'
'Well, you need to show them to your local police station within ten days. Okay?' Harry nods but says nothing. 'Now, be on your way and don't forget. I've taken your registration number and I will report it. Watch your speed as well.' The policeman returns to his car and drives away. Emma looks at Harry.
'I didn't realise you were just sixteen. I thought you were older. You seemed so confident at the operatic society meeting. Have you really got all the papers at home?' Harry looks crestfallen.
'I have a licence but I never got around to getting insurance or road tax. I haven't any money to pay for it. Now they'll probably fine me or take away my licence.'
'What about asking your dad or mam?'
'I can't do that. They will be furious.' He climbs onto his bike and Emma gets on behind him. He drives more carefully as he doesn't want to be stopped again. Emma is thinking. She knows what it is like to have no money and feels sympathy for him and realises that she is seeing his more vulnerable side, as opposed to his apparent self-assurance and cockiness.
'I'll tell you what,' she says, after dismounting from the bike at the top of her road. 'I have some savings, a prize I won for a competition in writing a story. I can draw the money out and give it to you. You can use it for a deposit for the insurance and also

pay the first month's road tax. After that, you can pay both monthly. I will get the money out tomorrow, in my dinner-hour, while you sort out your insurance and get a quote.'

'Are you sure?' Harry questions, his eyes lighting up. She nods, pleased that he is looking happier. He kisses her. 'What would I do without you? Thanks,' he says, before driving off.

Emma plans to spend another Saturday evening staying in, as Harry told her, when he called mid-week to pick up the money, that he won't be going dancing. She guesses he can't afford to. She doesn't mention the money to anyone but tells Mrs Mackey that he only called to let her know about Saturday night, as she senses there would be disapproval at what she has done. She buys some soft, white wool and a layette pattern at the shop on the Saturday, thinking that white is an ideal colour for a baby as it can be worn by a boy or a girl.

'It's for my sister Martha's baby,' Emma explains to Mabel. On the Sunday, the weather is cold and wet. Emma wonders how Harry is doing, sorting out his bike. 'No doubt, he'll be in touch,' she thinks.

The following Saturday, Faith, while drying her hair in the kitchen, speaks to Emma.

'Are you coming tonight? You've missed a few and you enjoy the dances.'

'Yes, I am coming. I do enjoy the dancing and I love the music too.' They walk to the dance-hall together and no sooner has she set foot inside the door, than Harry saunters up to her.

'I've been waiting for you. I wanted to tell you that I have sorted the bike out. I took the paperwork to the police station and they were okay about it. That policeman wasn't there. I guess they thought it was a routine check. I didn't tell them why I'd been told to bring it or anything.' This time, Emma realises that she is happy to see him. She feels that she is getting to know the real person and not a show-off that he appears to be.

'Let's dance,' he says, holding her close. 'It's a good weather forecast tomorrow. I will pick you up after dinner.'

Over the next weeks, Harry and Emma see more and more of each other. After helping him out financially, she feels closer to him and loves the rides on his motor-bike. Sometimes they go to his house but she prefers being out somewhere because, if his parents are out, he gets overly romantic and she keeps remembering that he is not quite seventeen yet. When she tells her friend his age, Faith is very surprised.

'He acts older than that,' she says to Emma. 'By the way, Mrs Mackey mentioned the other night that you don't buy many new clothes and she wonders where your money goes or maybe that you are saving it. I told her that you probably send some home to your family. You buy little presents for them, don't you? That dress you bought for Miriam was so pretty.' Faith waits expectantly for Emma to comment but, for once, Emma doesn't reveal anything to her friend as she feels uncomfortable about her knowing that she more than pays her way when out with Harry.

Easter creeps up and Emma decides to have a long weekend at home. It is early April and even though the sun is shining, there is a bitingly cold northerly wind blowing as she walks over the moors to Moorbeck. Over the next few days, she has conversations with her parents who are keen to know about her social life.

'You haven't written much lately,' Mary comments. 'Too occupied with him, are you?'

'Yes, we do see each other a lot,' Emma replies, smiling to herself.

'I'd like to meet him,' says Tom. 'Invite him over one weekend.' They are both concerned on hearing that although he hasn't a fulltime job, he has a motor-bike. Knowing their daughter's impulsive nature at times, they are wondering what is going on.

Towards the end April, Emma and Harry take the bus journey to Moorbeck so that Harry can meet her parents. It is not the best of weekends as Tom is becoming more and more concerned about their relationship. He can see that Emma is infatuated with Harry and that he is besotted with her.

'I suppose you help him a bit with money, do you?' he says, cautiously, to Emma, when Harry is out of earshot. Emma is honest with her dad and explains about the road tax and insurance and that she helps with petrol and pays her way at the pictures. Tom is very angry. 'You used that money that we suggested you keep for when you are older and you spent it on him,' he says.

'Well, it's what you do, isn't it,' she replies. 'You know, when someone is struggling, you help them.'

'He should get himself a proper job. I'm sure there's plenty if he looks hard enough.' He goes out, deeply troubled about his daughter and this lad. Tom left school at fourteen and has made his way in the world ever since and he cannot comprehend any bloke taking money like that, from a lass.

Later in the evening, after the youngsters have left, Emma's parents have a long chat.
'Did you know he was sixteen when she met him? He only turned seventeen a week ago,' Mary tells her husband. Tom didn't know and this knowledge adds to his worry. 'I don't know what our Emma is thinking of,' Mary continues. 'Bright and clever, she is. She could have anybody.'
'There's no telling her when her mind is made up but I am not having this,' Tom retorts. 'She is only seventeen and just out of boarding-school. I can see her turning up in a few years with kids around her ankles if it goes on. I need to do something about it. She is getting carried away with him and his bike.' Next morning, Tom chews it over while milking. Mary brings him his mug of tea to the cowshed. She can see that he is troubled. Over breakfast, he tells her of his decision. 'I'm going to ring that Mr Maguire, the personnel officer and talk to him. I'm not letting this go on.' Tom cares deeply about his daughter and realises that he can change things and even though it will cause a lot of upset, he feels it is for the best.
'What did he say?' Mary asks, when Tom returns an hour later, having been to Windrush and made what was a very lengthy phone call from the public, red telephone box in the village.
'He was very understanding as he has teenage daughters. What is going to happen is that he will get Emma transferred to Middlesburn. It will take a few weeks but she'll be nearer home. She can take what holiday is due and then unpaid leave until she can start. He said that they will be very disappointed to lose her as she is a good worker with great potential. I am going to give that lad an ultimatum. He can see her again in six months, provided he has sorted his life out and got a proper paid job. If they are serious, they'll survive.' After a lengthy pause, Tom continues. 'Emma intends booking a holiday in early May to look after Martha when she has her baby. When she arrives, I'll tell her. He will, no doubt, turn up to see her and I will tell him. It's best done, face to face. I'll take her back to pick up her clothes and make sure her landlady is paid to date.' Tom goes out to get on with his farm work leaving Mary very troubled. She knows this will upset Emma. She hates family strife. She doesn't feel like eating. It is all so worrying. She knows Tom has their daughter's best interests at heart but it seems

very tough on Emma and she wonders how her daughter will take it.

A few days into the month of May, Emma decides to book the week's holiday as the baby is overdue and Martha expects to give birth at any time. When seeing Harry on the Saturday night, she tells him what is happening.

'I can always come and see you,' he says. 'I'll surprise you and just turn up.' They have a lingering farewell after the dance as Emma has asked permission to be in later than eleven o'clock. The following morning, she goes to church and after dinner, leaves for Moorbeck. She is delighted to be having a break and looking forward to spending time with Martha, unaware of the bombshell that is about to explode.

On arrival, Martha greets her.

'This is good timing,' she says. 'I've just had a show but it will be hours yet. Probably arrive in the night or even tomorrow.'

'I'll go home and say hello, but I will sleep here if that's all right.'

'Of course, it is. Joe is expecting you to stay with us.' It is a lovely balmy evening with stillness in the air as Emma makes her way along the track to Bankside farm. She sings as she walks.

'Life is good,' she thinks. Walking up the cobbled-stone path to the coals door, as it is known because of all the coal stacked around the corner, she goes inside to find Tom and Mary having a cup of tea. They look up as she enters the kitchen. Tom is tired and can't face telling his daughter immediately, of his decisions. Emma doesn't stay long as she knows that she can see them over the next week. She thinks both her parents seem subdued.

'I'll walk over tomorrow,' she says, on leaving.

'Aye, do that, lass,' Tom replies. 'I want a talk with you.'

After a restless night, Martha is up early, drinking tea. Joe has already left to go to Windrush village to phone the midwife. Emma busies herself washing the breakfast pots and chatting with Martha who is restless, struggling with labour pains. Joe returns to say that Nurse Readman is on her way. It isn't long before she arrives; a buxom, tall, middle-aged woman with her brown hair tied back in a bun. Nurse Readman delivers all the babies for miles around and is well known in the villages. Although a bit blunt in speech, she is a warm-hearted, caring nurse, who is excellent at her professions of both midwife and health visitor.

'We'll have you upstairs and see what the progress is,' she says to Martha. A little later, she comes back down. 'I'll be back. It will be a while yet. I have a few visits to do.' Emma makes dinner but Martha isn't hungry. Time drags. Nurse Readman returns. 'Making progress, now,' she says, watching Martha pace the floor and then lean on the back of a chair as the pain engulfs her.

'You go on home if you like,' Martha says to Emma. 'Joe and Nurse Readman will be with me. You said dad wanted to see you.'

'I'm going to be an aunty. How exciting is that,' Emma thinks, walking along the track to Bankside farm. She is bubbling over with joy.

Tom is seated at the kitchen table when she walks in. Mary, having seen her daughter walking up the track and not wanting to be around when Tom gives Emma the news, has gone for a walk up the fields.

'Mam not here?' says Emma, sitting down opposite her dad.

'No. She's gone for a walk. Still seeing that lad, are you?' Emma nods. 'Has he got a job yet?' Emma shakes her head. 'Now listen to me. He is only just turned seventeen, far too young to be serious with a lass, especially when he has no money and no prospects. I've spoken to Mr McGuire.'

'What?' Emma interrupts, in surprise. 'You mean, at work?'

'Yes. We had a long conversation. You are not going back. You are being transferred to Middlesburn. It will take a few weeks. After your holiday, you will be on unpaid leave until they get a starting date. If Harry turns up, I'll be telling him that you can't see each other for six months to give him time to get himself sorted with a job and all that, to prove his worth. It's for the best.' Tom continues in the same vein, trying to convince his daughter that he has her welfare at heart. Emma doesn't speak. She gets up and walks out. She ambles along the track, kicking mud clots and pebbles. She is stunned. She is angry. She knows she needs to compose herself for Martha's sake as she doesn't want to upset her.

'It is my life,' she thinks. 'How can they do this to me? What about Faith? How will she feel when I give her this news? It is so unfair.'

Luckily, the newly-born baby girl diverts attention from Emma's dilemma. She doesn't tell Martha immediately and tries to put on a smile and be enthusiastic about the baby. Martha is tired and is happy to be left to sleep. Over the next days, Emma mooches around trying to be helpful and having turns at nursing the baby. She takes Martha her meals and sees to the washing as there are plenty of nappies to wash, both muslin and terry ones. Joe flits in and out, busy on the farm. All the while, she mulls over the conversation with her dad. Her life has been turned upside down.

'That's a letter for you,' says Jacob, later in the week, as he troops into the kitchen with his little sister and gives Emma an envelope. 'Mam said to bring it.' He is wearing a pair of hand-me-down shorts and a well-worn tee-shirt, a bit ripped on one short sleeve. 'I tore it accidently on a nail sticking out, in the cart shed,' he says, noticing Emma looking at him.
'Mam said we might be able to see the baby,' Miriam states, standing there, gazing at her big sister, expectantly. She is in washed-out shorts and an old tee-shirt that used to be Jacob's. Her black fringe needs cutting and she pushes it out of her eyes. 'Dad is going to cut it when he has time,' she says. 'He is a bit busy though.' At that moment, Martha enters the kitchen with the baby in her arms.
'They want to see her,' says Emma. 'I think Miriam wants to hold your baby.' While the children are pre-occupied, Emma opens the envelope and unfolds a sheet of paper, obviously torn from a note-pad. She reads it quickly. Harry is coming on Sunday to visit. She is filled with anxiety at what Tom is going to say to him. She hasn't been home since her dad told her about his decision. She doesn't feel like facing her parents at present. 'But I will have to tell Martha,' she thinks. 'I am sure they won't mind me staying here a while.'

After returning from church on Sunday with Joe, Emma helps to prepare dinner, all the while dreading what is to come. Joe and Martha are aware of the situation and although puzzled about it, are happy for her to stay with them. Around two o'clock, the door opens and Tom walks in, followed by Harry.
'You two can have a talk outside if you want,' he says to Emma, 'but Harry is leaving when I do.' Emma looks at Harry.
'Let's go,' she says and he follows her outside. Eventually Tom goes out and approaches them standing together quietly talking. 'Now say your goodbyes.' He stands watching and Emma feels highly embarrassed with Harry giving her a prolonged kiss in front of him. 'That'll do,' says Tom. Emma walks away, back into the

farmhouse and upstairs to her bedroom. She curls up on the bed and cries. She is just fed-up with everything. Later in the evening, she writes a long letter to Faith explaining what has happened. She writes another to Mrs Mackey, apologising for leaving so suddenly and thanking her for all her kindness. She explains that she will be back to pick up her belongings.

The following week, Tom makes the journey to Holmestown, but the atmosphere between father and daughter is strained. Emma says little until they arrive in the town when she directs her father to her lodgings. Mrs Mackey greets them and invites them in.
'I'll get my stuff,' says Emma, after introducing her father, before disappearing upstairs. She crams all her clothes and spare shoes into her suitcase along with other bits and pieces that she has accumulated. Tom has declined a cup of tea. He wants to get back home. He is sorting out any monies owed to Mrs Mackey when Emma re-enters and she stands there feeling deflated. The journey home is equally strained with Tom concentrating on the route and neither having much conversation. Emma opens and closes the gates into Moorbeck and after Tom comes to a stop outside Bankside farm, she gets out of the van, takes her suitcase from the back of it, politely thanks her dad and walks off in the direction of Martha's.

Three days later, Tom walks into Martha's kitchen where Martha and Emma are having a cup of tea, mid-afternoon.
'A letter for you,' he says, handing Emma the envelope.
'Thanks.'
'Well, open it then.' She does so. 'From him, is it?' She nods.
'Read it and then put it on the fire.' She looks at her dad but says nothing. She lowers her eyes. He waits. She opens the letter, with Tom standing, watching. She reads it quickly as it is quite lengthy. The last page ends with Harry declaring his love and adding lots of kisses. Emma looks at her father before walking to the open fire and placing the letter on the coals, stands watching while the flames lick the paper before the edges begin to singe and curl. Soon all that is left is black ash. 'I must get back,' their father says, walking out. 'I have things to do.' He is not happy. He mulls things over, trying to reassure himself that he is not being too harsh. 'It's best for her,' he tells himself, troubled at how miserable and distant Emma is, towards him.

Over the next two weeks, two more letters arrive and the same procedure is followed. Mary is very distressed over it all and Tom chides Emma for digging her heels in, thus upsetting her mam. Emma doesn't care.

'I can't help it if mam is upset,' she thinks.' It is all so unfair being told what to do.' She doesn't write back to Harry. She doesn't know what to say to him and wants the whole situation to evaporate. 'I am going to tell Father about this, after Mass,' she says to her mother as they walk into church. 'I don't think it is right how I am being treated.' She hangs around at the end of Mass until most of the parishioners have left, before speaking to the priest, but she receives no sympathy.

'You go home and listen to your parents. They are doing what they think is best for you,' he states.

'Well?' asks Mary, waiting at the end of the path for Emma to join her.

'He says I should listen to you and dad.' Mary is relieved but wishes Emma was happier. Later in the day when Tom calls to see Martha and to discuss something with Joe, he also speaks to Emma.

'Can't you see what you are doing to your mam?' Emma doesn't see that it is her fault. She feels that she has her own life to live. The following day she receives a letter from Faith, who, although upset about Emma moving out, expresses her sympathy and promises that she will keep in touch. *Don't worry about me. I'm very happy here and I have Rory. Let me know how it goes...*

'How will it go?' wonders Emma. 'All our plans and dreams have disintegrated. What of my future now?'

Summer 1958 / Winter 1958

In her bed at Bankside farm, Emma glances at her alarm clock, realising that she seems to have been reminiscing for some time. 'It is still too early to get up. I don't want to be sitting around in my wedding-dress for ages,' she thinks. Worrying that her tossing about is disturbing Amy, she settles down and lets her thoughts drift back over the move from Holmestown. 'Being transferred to the tax office in Middlesburn was a turning point,' she decides, thinking back to that unhappy period in her life. She remembers those weeks dragging on at Martha and Joe's and filling in her time by going for long walks, longing to have a life back. Harry's letters cease coming and Emma makes no communication with him. She is desperate to get back to work and one beautifully sunny day in early June, she walks the two miles into Windrush to make a phone call from the public telephone box. She wants to ring the tax office in Holmestown to find out if her starting date has come through and she is delighted to learn that she can begin work the following Monday in Middlesburn. The letter is in the post. Emma returns to Martha's with the good news.

'I'll walk over to mam's tomorrow and tell them. You and Joe have been great having me these few weeks. I am so grateful to you.'

'You have been a good help. Come and stay any time,' her sister replies. 'I am glad your life is going to get back on track.'

Emma saunters along the rough track, the next morning, in good spirits.

'What a beautiful day,' she thinks. The valley is quiet with hardly a breath of wind. The cows are away over the pasture. The air is already warm and the birds are singing.

'Good news,' she says to her parents, as she walks into the kitchen. 'I start work again next Monday.'

'That is good news,' says Mary, smiling at her daughter. 'When did you find out?'

'I phoned them yesterday from Windrush.'

'You walked?'

'Yes.' Her mother is glad to see her daughter more cheerful. Mary has been stressing about her and the whole situation.

'Have you thought about where you will stay in Middlesburn?' her dad asks, trying to be supportive. He is sitting at the kitchen table pouring tea into his pint mug. 'I have a suggestion to make, as I

38

have been giving this some thought.'
'I was going to take the bus to Middlesburn and visit the tax office
and ask the manager about lodgings,' explains Emma.
'Why not stay with aunty Marjorie?' Tom suggests. 'The van is off
the road but we can go by bus tomorrow and I'll introduce you, if
you like. You never did meet her, did you?' Emma shakes her
head.
'I was at boarding-school, the times she visited. That sounds a
good idea, Dad. Thanks.' Even though she can't forget what has
happened over the last weeks, she pushes it to the back of her
mind. She knows her dad is trying to build bridges and she wants
to be on better terms with him.
'Tomorrow, then; we'll catch the early bus. Is that okay, lass?' His
daughter nods.

Emma knows of this aunty, only a few years older than herself
because aunty Marjorie has visited Bankside farm, a number of
times. Martha, when writing to Emma at boarding-school, told
many stories of the fun she had with her. It was all a bit of a shock
to Emma's parents at first, especially for Mary, when her own dad
turned up one day to introduce his second wife, some years
younger than himself, along with their teenage daughter. Although
he'd been in contact with Mary by letter and had visited a couple
of times, he hadn't told her about re-marrying until he finally
arrived one day with his wife and their daughter. All this was
second-hand news to Emma, away at school.
'Maybe dad will explain more when we are on the bus and it will
be something to talk about,' she thinks, still worrying that things
might be a bit strained between them.

'What's the story then about aunty Marjorie, Dad?' Emma
immediately questions, when they are both settled in their seats on
the red bus, having walked the mile over the moors. 'I remember
mam telling me how surprised she was when she found out.'
Emma feels this is a safe topic to talk about as she doesn't want
her dad bringing up any of the recent past. She knows, deep down
that she is still raw over what has taken place. She doesn't want to
end up in tears on the bus.
'Your grandad's first wife died,' her dad begins. 'He moved to
Whitby with your mam, when she was fourteen, in connection
with his work for British Rail. The elder daughter, aunty Maureen,
was already working in Scotland and he occasionally went back to

see her. He eventually gave up his job with British rail and took over managing the pub at Aislaby. That's where I first noticed your mam, as she used to help out behind the bar. She also had a day job in Whitby in a sweet shop. He gave up the pub and we just thought he's gone back to live with his daughter. Your mam didn't want to return with him as she was eighteen, settled in her work and enjoying nights out with her friends. When I married her, her dad came down alone, for the wedding. There was only him and my mate as we got married in a Registry Office. Later, we saw a Catholic priest and our marriage was put right in the eyes of the Church, as they say. I think your mam told you about that, didn't she?' Emma nods.

'She did, Dad.'

'Your grandad kept in touch with the odd letter,' continues Tom, 'but never mentioned that they had a little girl. It was only after moving back to England that he visited us and introduced his wife and daughter.' Apparently, he met her on his travels and the friendship blossomed and eventually they'd quietly married, in the early nineteen-thirties, I think.'

'No wonder mam was surprised. What is she like, aunty Marjorie?'

'You'll like her. She is full of fun with a bubbly, outgoing personality. She is a bonny lass. Your mam and I went to her wedding. She married a Polish chap, a few years older than her. He seemed a pleasant enough fellow. They have a couple of little kids, I believe.'

'I vaguely remember you going to a wedding in Middlesburn and it was a really bad weather forecast but you still went.'

'I believe you are right. It was February and there was a lot of snow around but we didn't want to let her down.'

'Here we are,' Emma says, as the bus pulls into the station. 'Do you know where aunty Marjorie lives, Dad?'

'No, but I have their address. We will just keep asking. All I know is that it's a new council estate and they live on a fairly main road in a row of terraced housing. They used to live with some of his family in Middlesburn until they had enough points to be allocated a council house.'

'What do you mean by points?'

'From what I gather, points are given as to how crowded it is where you live and how many children you have and suchlike. There is always a shortage of housing in towns. Marjorie will tell you more if you ask her.' Emma thinks about this as they walk along the streets. She decides that she doesn't want to live in a property allocated by the Council when she gets married. She concludes that she will have to save money and buy her own house if she wants to choose where to live. They seem to walk miles and Emma is sure there must be a local bus to the new estate but Tom is adamant that they walk. They are heading further out of the town along a winding road.

'Looks like a mixture of housing and businesses,' Emma thinks, glancing at either side of the road. 'Are they gardens, Dad?' she asks, pointing to a number of enclosed plots. 'Look, over there. They are all close together.'

'I think they will be what you call allotments. Some folks, who haven't a garden, rent a piece of land from the Council and grow vegetables. That's my understanding but again, ask your aunty. She'll know.' Emma's legs ache. She soldiers on not wanting to complain, even though they have been advised by one passer-by from whom they asked directions, to catch a bus, but Tom was having none of that. When they reach the estate, they seem to take a long way around, road after road. Emma vows to make enquiries about buses if she comes to live here.

'Hello, Tom. Come in. Come in,' the rather robust-looking lady says, on opening the door. 'What a lovely surprise. You must be Emma as I've met Martha. You look just like her. Come and say hello to Cathy. Look who's here, Abe.' Marjorie is holding a little boy in her arms, with skin not as pale as his mother's and a mop of dark hair and a moon-beam face. 'I'm trying to get Andy to sleep,' she explains, 'but he's a little rascal at settling down.'

'Dad is right,' thinks Emma. 'She is a bonny lady with her light-brown, curly hair, framing her face and with clear-blue eyes. She's so friendly and chatty, too.' They follow her into the large living-room with its flowered wall-paper and white, painted woodwork. A darker-skinned stocky man with jet-black hair is seated on the settee with a small child standing near to him staring at the visitors.

'This is your uncle Abraham,' Marjorie continues, introducing her husband, 'but he gets Abe for short.' He stands up and shakes Emma's hand. When he speaks, his broken accent is quite noticeable and she remembers that he is Polish. 'Cathy,' his wife calls to the little girl standing next to her daddy's chair, her long, fair-haired ringlets hanging down past her shoulders. 'Say hello to

41

aunty Emma.' Turning to Emma, she adds, 'I know you are really her cousin but you're more my age than Cathy's and I think it is easier to let her call you, aunty.'

'You'll wear yourself out, lass,' Tom says to Marjorie, watching her pacing up and down while gently rocking her toddler in her arms.

'He's just about off. I'll make you a sandwich and a cup of tea. I am sure you are ready for one,' she replies. The sandwich turns out to be a spread, including buttered scones and biscuits, which Marjorie insists they eat. Her hospitality is outstanding. Over the meal, Tom explains why they have come but with no reference to the reason for the transfer and Marjorie immediately says that it will be fine for Emma to lodge with them. 'I stayed with you plenty of times,' she responds, 'and we will have a built-in babysitter,' she jokes.

'We can't stay long,' says Tom. 'We have to get the bus back and I have milking to do, although Martha did say she'll go over and start for me.' After the meal, Tom and Emma get ready to leave.

'I will see you next Sunday, Emma,' are Marjorie's parting words. She is standing at the door with Cathy, both waving goodbyes. Later in the day, when on the bus, Tom and his daughter chat about their visit.

'What do think?' he asks.

'It will be great, Dad. I'm sure I will be fine there and if not, I can get to know the area and find somewhere else to live.' Although there have been one or two uncomfortable silences between them as the day progressed, Emma feels that, generally, things have gone well.

The following Sunday afternoon, Emma, once more, says goodbye to her family and journeys on the bus to Middlesburn. Her uncle Abe was most helpful when they'd visited and had given Emma a bus timetable and a road map to help her find her way around. Arriving in the town, she gets off the bus and taking the map from her pocket, studies it before making her way to another stand to catch a bus to the estate. There are many stops and starts before she realises that she is in the road where her aunty lives, as the house is almost opposite the bus stop.

'Come in. You don't have to knock. Treat this like your home,' Marjorie says, after opening the door. 'Abe has a front door key for you,' she continues, as Emma follows her into the living-room. 'Take off your coat and bring your case and I'll show you upstairs.' The two little ones are on the settee with their dad but as Marjorie leaves the living-room, Cathy climbs down and follows her.

'Shall I take your hand?' Emma asks, but Cathy shakes her head.

'She is a bit shy but she will soon get used to you,' Marjorie says, climbing the stairs. 'Now here is where you will sleep and there is a small wardrobe for your clothes. You'll be sleeping with Cathy for the time being. I will be getting a bedroom suite for the other bedroom when we can afford. I will get it on hire purchase as soon as I have finished the current payments in a couple of months. I only buy one thing at a time as I don't want to get into debt.'

Emma hasn't realised until this moment that she is going to be sharing a single bed with Cathy.

'I don't mind,' she voices to her aunty. 'I've been sharing beds for years at home. I am so grateful that you are taking me in.'

The first morning, Emma finds it strange exploring the kitchen to get herself breakfast and making a sandwich for her dinner-break. Abe has already left for work, being on an early shift. Marjorie is still in bed but explained to her last night that sometimes, if she's been disturbed in the night by Andy, she will not be up, but for Emma to help herself. Leaving quietly, Emma walks along the road and crosses it to await the bus. Making sure she is in time for it, means she is early and she waits ten minutes before it finally arrives. On reaching the bus station in town, she checks her map before quickly making her way to Larch Road, thinking that there is probably a stop where she could have got off, nearer to her place of work. She walks along the pavement checking door numbers, but struggles to find them as many shops don't seem to have them. Eventually, she comes to a tall, old building with the correct number. She hunts for the Inland Revenue offices and finds a side door with the name on. The offices are on the first floor. She walks upstairs and tentatively pushes open a door denoting *Staff*, hoping that she is in the right place. She is. The room is filled with people at their desks, working. On enquiring, she is directed to the manager who is tucked away in his office in the far corner of the room.

Emma feels a little apprehensive as she knocks on the glass-panelled door. Waving her in, the manager stands to shake her hand. He is very lean and not much taller than Emma. His dark hair, smattered with grey, is sleeked back and she notices that his metal-framed glasses have very thick lenses.

'I'm Emma Holmes.'

'Take a seat,' he says, in a rather high-pitched voice. 'I have been expecting you. I'm Mr Wiles. You didn't visit last week. I take it that you have found your own lodgings?' Emma nods and smiles. 'I'll just take a few details and then take you upstairs to the PAYE office and introduce you to Miss Markey, who is in charge.' He returns to his seat and writes down her address and next of kin.

'Follow me,' he says, as he leaves his chair.

'He's pleasant enough, but a man of few words,' Emma decides.

They walk upstairs and into a large open-plan room. There are many desks. Some people are on their telephones, the cords hanging down. 'It's noisy,' she thinks, 'but no doubt I will get used to it.' Crossing over to the far side, Mr Wiles speaks to the lady at a desk, and then introduces Emma.

'Miss Markey will help if you have any problems,' he advises, before disappearing back across the room.

The telephone rings just as Miss Markey is standing up to speak to her.

'Excuse me. I'll take this call,' she says. 'I won't be a moment.' The lady at the next desk, smiles.

'I'm Sylvia,' she whispers.' She is stunning, with black hair, red lips, a beautiful complexion and looks like a movie star. Emma smiles at Sylvia, before turning her gaze back to Miss Markey, who is still on the telephone, speaking in a sharp voice. She is a tall, slim lady, with cropped, grey hair, pointed chin and also wearing glasses not unlike Mr Wiles' metal-framed ones.

'She looks stern as if she is very strict,' thinks Emma, but when Miss Markey puts down the phone and smiles, apologetically, she re-thinks that maybe she won't be as strict as she appears.

'Come with me,' Miss Markey says, walking across the room to a desk with an empty chair. 'Have you done counter duty before?'

'I did some at the Holmestown tax office.'

'Good. You will be on the Rota. We have quite a number of the public coming in with enquiries or wanting a claims form. This is your desk and there is little outstanding paperwork as members of staff have been dealing with most of it since Rosemary left. Dorothy will help you, if you have problems,' she continues, indicating the lady at a nearby desk. 'We have a ten-minute tea-break, mid-morning. If you intend staying in over the dinner-break, you may use the kitchen facilities to make a drink.' Her

introduction completed, Miss Markey gives Emma a brief smile
and returns to her work. Emma looks at Dorothy, who is a little
over-weight but a pretty girl with dark, wavy hair almost to
shoulder length. They acknowledge each other with smiles before
Emma sits at her desk and begins her first day's work in this new
environment.

The daily post is sitting in the in-tray. Emma quickly becomes
engrossed in dealing with the forms and letters, some from other
tax offices and others from the public. She is familiar with the
layout of the desk: in-trays and out-trays; large drawers at each
side filled with folders labelled with taxpayers' names; and a
variety of forms in small pigeon-holes on the desk top, that are
used when answering queries. There is a telephone on the right-
hand side of the desk, its wires curling around over the edge.
Everyone uses a telephone, as calls are put through from their
other offices or from members of the public, or tax offices further
afield. Emma is busily working, her head down, when she hears
movements of chairs scraping the floor. It is break-time. A tall and
broad young man is ambling across to her.
'Hello, I'm Matthew,' he says, in a deep, guttural voice, 'but I get
Matt for short.' Emma looks up, smiles and introduces herself. 'If
you need any help, I'm just at the next desk along from Dorothy.
Come with me and we'll get a drink.' Even when she stands, she
still has to look up to Matt.
'He must be over six feet,' she thinks, studying him and taking in
his broad forehead, large nose, thick lips and a shock of dark-
brown wavy hair. They go together to the small kitchenette and he
makes two cups of coffee and they wander back to her desk, with
Matt acknowledging other colleagues along the way. Back at her
desk, they chat, not noticing the time until Miss Markey walks up.
'Don't be keeping Matt from his work. The break is only ten
minutes,' she states sternly to Emma, before disappearing. Emma
blushes but smiles as she catches Matt winking at her behind Miss
Markey's back. A little later, when walking past, he bends his head
towards her.
'Don't worry about her,' he whispers. 'She's not really a battle-
axe.' The rest of the day is uneventful and Emma leaves the
building relieved that her first day is over without any mishaps.

Later, when in bed, she is conscious of little Cathy lying stiffly
beside her and Emma realises that she must not rush things. She is

used to siblings and giving hugs and kisses but she is a stranger to this one. The little girl is usually asleep each night when Emma goes to bed and still asleep when Emma crawls out early in the morning to get her breakfast and make it to work on time. For the first few nights in bed with Emma, if Cathy is awake, she doesn't speak or move. It is after about a week, when, one night, crawling quietly into bed so as not to disturb her, Emma feels a movement. Two little arms curl around her neck and hug her tightly. From then on, at some point each night, Emma wakes up to find a warm, little limpet, clinging tightly to her.

Days flow into weeks and Emma soon adapts to her new colleagues and lodging with her aunty. Matt is attentive and helpful, showing his obvious interest in her. She finds him to be a friendly, kind and supportive colleague and also pleasant company. She soon realises that he is hoping for more than just a friendship, but she also is aware that she has no inclinations that way with him. She doesn't feel ready to move on. She thinks of Harry sometimes and the unhappiness and is content to be at work and spend time at her aunty's. Living at Scarborough, Matt lodges during the week in Middlesburn and returns home some weekends, his transport being his beloved motor-bike.
'I can give you a lift and drop you off on the way,' he offers to Emma, on finding out that she goes back to Bankside. 'I don't go every weekend, but when I do, you are welcome to a ride. The only request I have is that you wear a crash-helmet. I know they are not legally required, but I will be happier if you wear one.'
'That will be great. I'll love that. I will get one before Friday. I'll help with petrol money, too,' Emma enthuses.
'No thanks. I'm going anyway. Keep your money,' he says, kindly. Emma is happy with this arrangement. Not only will this save her fare, but it will be much more enjoyable on the bike than the bus journey.

On her dinner-break, Emma goes shopping and buys a red crash-helmet and a red, suede jacket to match.
'They will look great with my black trousers,' she decides, when walking back to work. She is delighting in shopping and buying her own clothes, but only if necessary as she doesn't believe in wasting money. Matt is equally pleased that Emma accepted his offer as he is quite enamoured with her friendly and chatty personality. He knows he isn't as good-looking as some, but he

tries to make up for it with his generous and happy-go-lucky attitude.

One Friday tea-time, as Emma dresses in her red jacket and takes her crash-helmet out of the bag that she brought to work, Sylvia walks by, one of the last to leave the office.

'My, you look good,' she comments, gazing at Emma, who is secretly quite chuffed. She politely thanks her for the compliment. Later in the evening, Emma is telling her mam how she has come with Matt, on his motor-bike.

'He's not handsome, you know, but he is really pleasant and enjoyable company.' She knows Matt is aware of her lack of interest in him as a boyfriend because he told her on one occasion to hang on to him when sitting as pillion.

'Even though you don't want to, you need to put your arms around me to cling on to stop any blast of air between us. I like to know you are there behind me.'

'I feel a bit bad about it, but I'm not interested in him that way,' she tells her mam. 'If he is happy to be a friend, then I'm fine with that.'

On one of her weekend visits to Moorbeck, in late July, Tom discusses with her about accompanying Mary on a short break.

'She's been under the weather and I can't take time off from the farm. There's really no-one available but you. We've thought about somewhere outside Carlisle. There's a village called Brampton and apparently her mother was buried there. She wants to find her gravestone. Are you able to get time off?'

'I'll ask. I may be able to book a few days holiday.' Emma isn't that bothered about going but feels she ought to. She makes enquiries and tells her dad that she can go and to book a place. In late August, Tom takes Mary and Emma to Brampton to a little B & B which has optional evening meals. It is a long drive for him but he feels his wife will benefit from a short break. The whole episode about Emma has affected Mary and he thinks this will be good for them both.

'Look after her, lass,' he says to his daughter, on leaving them.

Mother and daughter are sharing a small twin-bedded room and Emma finds it strange to be sleeping in the same bedroom as her mam.

'Can you go and ask if they have any aspirins?' Mary asks, late one evening, when they have settled in for the night. My headache is bad.' Emma is reluctant to go. 'You are meant to be looking after me,' reminds her mam, cajoling her. Emma disappears downstairs to find the owner, who is very obliging and gives her a couple of tablets.

'I hope she feels better soon,' the lady says, as she hands them over.

Mary and Emma spend their days out walking and having a coffee in one of the little tea-rooms in the village. They enjoy a meal out each day in a quiet café and one sunny afternoon, ask directions to the cemetery. It is on the outskirts of the village, down a long, winding lane, almost two miles. Pushing open the old wooden gate at the entrance, they venture through and systematically start walking up and down the paths running between the gravestones. The writing on some is easy to read but on others, eroded and worn and barely decipherable. In the two far corners of the large plot, the pathways are overgrown and headstones crumbling. The sun is twinkling through the leaves of the tall trees along one side. 'We're never going to find it,' says Mary, dejectedly, after over an hour of searching. She sits on a well-worn wooden bench that has a couple of slats missing. She pulls out her packet of Woodbines from her black handbag and lights up.

'I'll keep looking,' says her daughter, knowing how much it means to her mam, who lost her mother when she was only a child. 'After she died, I used to pray and pray for her to come back just once, but she never did,' Mary had told her.

'Mam,' Emma calls. 'Over here.' Mary stubs out her cigarette with her shoe and quickly walks down the uneven footpath and across the grass to where Emma is standing. She reads the inscription on the headstone to which her daughter is pointing and drags her finger across the words *beloved mother*. Mary sheds a few tears. Emma draws closer and puts her arm around her mam and they stand there in silence with not a breath of wind in the warm afternoon. No-one else is around. There is stillness and quietness. Emma says a prayer for the grandmother that she has never known. Mary dries her eyes.

'Thanks,' she says, smiling and hugging her daughter. 'You found it.' They wander quietly back down the stone pathway to the wooden gate, each immersed in their own thoughts.

Back at work and mid-week, Matt asks if she would like to babysit with him on the Friday evening, for a colleague. Bill has three small children and he and his wife rarely go out, but they have been invited to a friend's birthday party and mention to Matt that they will probably not go with having no family close by to mind the children.

'I'll ask Emma if she will come,' Matt suggests. Then we can babysit for you. She is good with children as she is used to them.' Bill is delighted.

'I don't mind,' says Emma. 'It will be something different to do as I'm free most evenings.' At this, Matt looks at her quizzically. He cannot understand how a young lady like her is not having a busy social life. He makes reference to this and Emma changes the conversation but inwardly thinks that he is right and maybe she should do something about it. The babysitting goes well. Emma sees that the baby has his last bottle before settling him down. Matt makes small talk before switching on the television and they both enjoy a light supper that they find already prepared in the kitchen. There is little furniture in the lounge and they share the same settee. Emma surmises that the family struggle on Bill's salary. She is glad that she decided to help. It is almost midnight when Matt drops her off outside her aunty's house.

The next week passes quickly.

'Isn't Matt going with you?' Marjorie asks Emma, watching her touching up her lipstick before going out on the Saturday evening. Emma shakes her head.

'He told me he doesn't dance.'

'He likes you a lot, you know,' replies her aunty. Emma grins. Matt has called once or twice to see Emma in the evenings and Marjorie, as is her nature, encourages him to stay for a cup of tea and biscuits.

'I know, but I don't egg him on. I think he knows I'm not interested in him that way. He is just a good friend.' Cathy is listening, dressed in her pink pyjamas, ready for bed.

'Will you dance with us next time?' she asked, sweetly. This is because on the previous Saturday morning, Abe and Emma, on the settee, had been watching Marjorie and her little ones enjoying themselves. Cathy and Marjorie, with Andy in her arms, were dancing around in front of the black and white television screen to the music of the pop group, The Beatles. The Fab Four, as Marjorie calls them, were smartly dressed in their navy-coloured suits and each with a mop of dark, thick hair, cut in the shape of an upside-down basin. Emma thinks that they are amazingly talented with their singing and playing their instruments. She is used to hearing their range of songs at the dances.

'I will,' she promises. 'Your mammy loves The Beatles, doesn't she?' Cathy nods and smiles. 'I do, too,' Emma replies, bending down and kissing her. 'We will have fun on Saturday and dance around the room, as I'm not going home and you are so sweet.' Not wanting to leave Andy out, she kisses him on his little, moon-beam face, his dark eyes gazing out at her as he snuggles into his mam. 'You are very cuddly,' she says. 'They are lovely children,' she adds, to Marjorie.

'Are you sure you don't want Abe to walk you to the dance-hall?' her aunty asks. 'I'm not happy about you being on your own.'

'I'll be absolutely fine. It's not far and I will be careful.'

It is the usual set-up in the dance-hall. The girls are sitting down one side and the lads along the other. Emma finds a seat and looks around. The music is good. A disc jockey (DJ) is playing the records and introducing each dance. Emma is asked to dance by different lads and enjoys herself. Realising how much she has been missing it, she vows to come again. Over the next week or two, she finds that the only downfall is the undue attention from some of the lads when she leaves the building. They can be become quite a nuisance when they spot a young lady leaving the dance-hall unaccompanied. She decides that it will be better in future to leave slightly earlier so as to avoid any amorous young lad asking to walk her home. One particular young man who regularly asks her to dance, is a little older than most of the lads. He is an excellent dancer and Emma thinks that his movements are so polished and smooth. He is average height but slim with short brown hair and intense blue eyes. She discovers that he is called Vince and that he works in the council offices.

A month or so later on one particular evening just before the last dance, Vince walks over to Emma and after asking her to join him on the floor, also offers to walk her home afterwards.

'I don't like to see a young lady unescorted at this time of night,' he tells her. 'I have noticed you leaving early to avoid others hanging around after the evening is over.' Emma is secretly pleased. It is around four months since she's seen Harry and thoughts of him no longer bother her. She considers him part of the past. Vince has been dancing with her regularly now and she looks forward to him asking her to partner him each week. 'Do you live far?' Vince questions, as they leave the venue together. She tells him her address and they chat amicably along the road. 'I must tell you that I'm married,' he says, 'but my wife doesn't like dancing. She has no problem with me going as she knows how much I love it. We have two little girls and I wouldn't like to think of them walking home alone.' Emma is dumbounded. She doesn't know how to reply. Her hopes are dashed just when she is feeling that she has moved on and ready for something new. They part company when she points out where she lives. She thanks him for seeing her safely home. Letting herself in with her key, she takes off her coat and goes into the kitchen to make a drink. Everyone is in bed. Emma sits on the settee and mulls over the evening, feeling frustrated and annoyed.

'I think it is totally deceiving, frequently asking someone to dance just because they want a good dancing partner. It spoils my chance of meeting up with a lad I might want to get serious with,' she thinks. 'It reminds me of that conductor chatting me up on the bus, when I go home to Bankside when Matt stays in Middlesburn.' She'd talked to Inga at work about him.

'His name rings a bell,' Inga had said. 'I think he goes to football matches with my dad and others.'

'The cheek of it,' Emma had thought, on finding out from Inga that that he is married with two kids. 'Now I find this bloke is married. I'll have to find somewhere else to go dancing, because of him.'

Emma finds her work colleagues friendly and helpful. The union representative, George, a slightly built, middle-aged man, approaches one dinner-break while she is talking with Inga, a tall, vivacious and chatty young lady. They are having a giggle over Inga's latest story about her social activities and a boyfriend saga. 'I wonder,' George begins, 'if you two will join me at a union meeting next Wednesday after work. It won't last long but I'm struggling to get anyone to go and I'm supposed to drum up people to attend. I will be able to take you, one on the back of my motor-bike and the other in the side-car.' The girls looked at each other and grin.

'I'm free,' voices Emma.

'So am I,' states Inga. 'Let's do it. The ride will be fun.' It is. They decide that Emma will ride pillion as she had a crash-helmet and

Inga can go in the side-car. They find the ride hilarious, quite making up for the meeting which they found boring. Emma isn't that interested in union matters but thoroughly enjoys her early evening excursion, especially as George treats them to a drink in a local pub as his thanks for going.

'Was it good, then?' Marjorie asks her, when putting her evening meal out, that she has duly kept warm in the oven.

'Not the meeting,' Emma replies, 'but the ride was great and we had a little drink afterwards.'

The nights are pulling in and the weather deteriorating. Emma babysits occasionally for her aunty and uncle so that they can have an evening out and unfortunately let slip about it when talking to Matt, one tea-break.

'I'll join you if you like,' he volunteers. 'Let me know the next time and I will come round and keep you company.'

'Okay, but I'll check with my aunty that she doesn't mind.'

'She'll be all right about it, I'm sure. She is so welcoming whenever I visit.' Emma thinks about this.

'I'm sure you are right,' she replies, 'but I'll mention it anyway next time she asks.' Emma enjoys his company but doesn't want to raise his hopes. She knows that he is still hoping for a relationship with her. The last time that he'd given her a ride on the Friday, he'd insisted on taking her to the farmhouse instead of dropping her off at the end of the minor road into Moorbeck. He'd followed her in and introduced himself to her mam.

'He's a very pleasant guy,' her mother said, afterwards, 'but you're still not interested, are you?'

'No, I'm not and I don't ask him for rides. Anyway, I'll be staying in Middlesburn more often, with the weather turning, but I am taking a few days off at Christmas to spend with you all.'

Matt is persistent in his attention towards Emma. He offers another invitation to her that sounds extremely exciting. He walks across to her in his usual ambling gait when she is putting on her coat at the end of a busy day.

'There's a new romantic musical released and it's showing at Newcastle cinema all next week. I think you'll enjoy it. We can go on the train on Saturday if you fancy going,' he proposes to her. Emma hesitates.

'Should I accept,' she wonders, thinking that it sounds too good to miss. 'Thanks, Matt. I love the pictures and a musical too.'

'You'll really enjoy this one, then,' he replies, pleased that she has agreed to go. Emma meets him at the dingy, run-down railway station at the bottom end of the town. Matt finds her in the draughty waiting-room. There is barely any heat in the place.

'I hope it's warmer on the train,' she says, as they wander towards the platform area. Matt joins the queue to purchase a return ticket and offers to buy Emma's but she explains that she bought hers, on arrival.

'Well, let me pay you into the cinema, then,' he insists. 'After all, it's me who's invited you out.'

'Okay,' she replies. 'That's really kind of you Matt, but you don't have to.' She knows he will. 'At least I paid for my own train ticket,' she thinks.

The lights in the cinema are dim as they walk down the centre aisle, following the usherette who is looking for their seat numbers. They are about half-way when she indicates the row. They shuffle along the seats, squeezing passed other people, until they find theirs.

'It's very posh,' Emma whispers, looking at the plush seats, 'but it is lovely and warm.' They remove their coats and settle down. Matt produces a box of chocolates and passes it to her. 'You know how to treat a girl,' she says, laughingly.

'Not that it will do me much good,' he replies, gazing at her, 'but I do enjoy being with you.' The music starts and the lights go out. From then on, from the moment the words *South Pacific* flashes onto the massive screen, Emma sits, riveted.

'It's widescreen,' Matt whispers. Conversation ceases as Emma is hanging on to every word and action. The fantastic scenery and amazing colours; the catchy, amusing songs and serious ones, beautifully sung; the different characters; and the intriguing romantic stories, all totally engross her. It is almost coming to an end when Matt starts to move.

'We will have to go or we'll miss the last train,' he says, but Emma hardly hears. She is mesmerised. 'Emma, come on. Get up.' She slowly gets to her feet, picking up her coat while watching every happening on the screen.

'I have to see the end,' she whispers.

'No, I'm sorry, but we need to leave. We are also blocking the view for others.' They step into the aisle and Matt takes her hand to drag her away as Emma tries to continue watching. The hero on the screen is just walking up towards the heroine, hearing his two little dark-skinned children singing to her. He joins in, gazing at the woman he loves, not yet knowing that she's realised, after he'd left to carry out dangerous work and where his brave companion died, that she wants to spend the rest of her life with him. Emma finally turns away. Leaving the picture-house together, they gallop down the streets to the railway station just in time to step onto the train before it pulls out of the station. 'You'll give me a heart attack,' Matt jokes, as they sit down, panting.

'Wasn't it just amazing? It was thrilling,' is all Emma can say. 'If it ever comes to Middlesburn, I'll go again and watch to the very end.' Turning to Matt, she says, 'Thank you. It's been wonderful.' Even when in bed, after creeping into the house very quietly, Emma can't sleep for some time, as visions of what she's seen are whirling around in her head.

In early December, Emma spends a weekend at Bankside as she hasn't been for a while. The family is just about ready to sit down to Sunday dinner when there is a knock at the door. Tim goes to open it and comes back into the kitchen followed by Harry. There is a silence for a moment.

'You said six months,' Harry states, breaking the ice.

'It's actually a week off,' replies Tom, who has been checking the dates and knows exactly when the six months runs out.

'It's near enough,' says Mary. 'Take off your coat. Would you like to eat?' Harry gratefully accepts her offer. He removes his coat and struggles to hang it behind the kitchen door as the nails, which substitute as coat hooks, are laden with a variety of coats. He is wearing a brown suit and white shirt with a dark-brown tie. He looks smart even though the suit is not of high quality. His hair is neatly cut and he is clean-shaven. Tim makes room for him at the table and Mary places a plate of dinner in front of him. Emma says nothing.

'You found work, then?' Tom enquires.

'I did. It took a while but I'm working in a warehouse, operating the machinery that load up stock that go out to the wholesalers.' He looks over at Emma but she keeps her head down. The conversation is intermittent as everyone eats. 'I can't stay long as I have to catch the bus back,' says Harry.

'Have a cup of tea before you go,' Mary insists. Eventually he gets up and puts on his coat. Emma also leaves the table and walks over to the door.

'Just wait for me outside,' she says to Harry. He thanks Mary for his meal and says goodbye and leaves. As Emma reaches the kitchen door, she turns back and says curtly, 'Don't look so worried. I'm not going with him. I'm just walking him to the bus stop.' Even though she is no longer interested in Harry, she feels the anger and hurt resurfacing as she speaks to them.

The pair set off walking across the cobbles to the track.
'You look smart,' Emma begins, not quite knowing what to say.
'How are you, really?' Harry hesitates.
'Thanks. I'm okay. I wanted to prove myself to your dad. That's why I came back. He gave me the kick up my backside that I needed. I also wanted to see you the once last time to see if you were all right. How have you been?'
'I've settled in Middlesburn and lodge with my aunty, but I'm so glad we've met up this once and I'm sorry for all the upset. I was unhappy for weeks. Once I got back to work, I started to feel better. You were my first serious boyfriend. We had some great times together, the pair of us.'
'Yes, we did. I've grown up a lot through it and learnt a lot. I've brought you that money you gave me.'
'Keep it. I'm fine. I helped you when you needed it and that's what you do for people, isn't it? I don't regret giving you the money. My dad just saw it from a different perspective. You've done well to come all this way.' She grins. 'Put it towards the bus fare.' He smiles back at her.
'I've been seeing someone else over the last couple of months,' he says, coyly.
'That's good. I've started to go to dances again but I haven't met a lad yet to go steady with but I've made new friends.' Emma asks about his parents and his singing. He asks about Faith. When they arrive at the main road, Harry stops walking and turns to Emma and they hug each other for the last time. Emma stays on her side of the road as Harry crosses over. The bus appears over the horizon and she waits until it stops and Harry gets on, before giving him one last wave. Then turning around, she slowly makes her way across the moors. She is glad that Harry is happy. 'Just a chapter in my life,' she thinks.

Back in Middlesburn, Emma continues venturing out to dances, but at another venue closer to the town centre. The mixture of young people who attend is different. There are a number of Irish lads, each living in bedsits of a large, old house in a rundown area of the town, who frequent the dances. She finds them interesting, as they mostly come from farms, like she does. She enjoys hearing about their lives in Ireland. On two or three occasions, she returns to one lad's room on his invitation. Liam shares cooking and washing facilities with others and his only private living space doubles as his bedroom. She doesn't mind until on the third visit, he begins a heavy petting session and although she knows that he is lonely and missing his family, she decides it is time to leave. In a conversation with Marjorie over dinner, the next day, she mentions where the lad lives but neglects to tell her aunty that she visited him.

'It's just as well, I didn't,' she thinks, on hearing her advice.

'I wouldn't go to his lodgings if he invites you. It's a rough area and not safe for young girls like you.'

Emma is reminded of Liam when home at Bankside on her Christmas break and her mother handing her a letter.

'This came for you yesterday, but how the Sorting Office managed to get it delivered, is quite something. Just look at that address.'

Tom and Mary await Emma's response as she opens the letter, having seen the vague attempt at her address, although Bankside farm is clearly written. She is surprised when she discovers it is from Liam and explains about him to her parents.

'I'll go through and pick him up, if you want,' her dad says, on hearing his daughter's tale. Tom will do anything to show his daughter that he cares and is willing to help. Emma declines the offer.

'I'm not that bothered, thanks. It's just that I feel sorry him and the others living so far from home. He did well to remember the name of our farm, though. I must have told him in our conversation. The GPO (General Post Office) did an amazing job tracking us down.'

'There is another letter,' says Mary. 'I almost forgot. It came a few days ago.' She takes it from behind the spill-holder on the mantle-piece and hands it to Emma.

'This one is from Faith. I recognise that handwriting. I must write to her while I'm here. I need to tell her about life in Middlesburn. I should have written sooner.' She briefly skims the letter, but it is a lengthy one. 'I'll read it properly, tonight,' she says to her mam. 'I'll do that baking for you, now.'

Later in the evening, Emma re-opens the white envelope and takes out two folded pages written on both sides. Faith is happy. Her relationship with Rory is going strong. She has visited his family many times. Mrs Mackey has taken in another lodger, an Irish girl, whom Faith describes as quiet and shy but very pleasant and easy to get on with. Mabel is thinking of leaving work and going to college in order to take up teaching. Faith describes her trips to the shops and to the picture-house and is still going dancing.

'A lovely, newsy letter,' thinks Emma, feeling happy because her friend is content and enjoying life. The next day, she finds time to write a long letter to Faith, mostly sharing her thoughts on the different boys that she has met. 'Can you give it to the postman when he turns up, please, Mam,' she says to Mary, knowing that that is how letters are posted when living on an isolated farm.

When in bed and thinking over Faith's letter, Emma starts wondering when she will find a steady boyfriend. 'Martha is happily married;' she thinks, 'and Faith and Rory are getting serious. After such a turbulent year, maybe the New Year will bring promise. I wonder, will it will be my turn next?'

Winter 58 / Summer 59

The New Year begins with a change around of staff at the tax office. Emma is a diligent and hard worker who finds the work easy and the small amount of paperwork and enquiries that arrive on her desk each day are barely sufficient to keep her occupied. This hasn't gone unnoticed.

'You are being moved to Schedule E. We like our staff to have experience on all Sections, if possible,' Miss Markey informs her on her arrival at work. 'It's downstairs. Mr Turnbull is in charge.' Emma knows who Mr Turnbull is as he usually stays in the office for his midday meal. He has a very bent back and can't hold his head up properly but she doesn't like to ask him about it, even though she is curious about his condition. He is always courteous and friendly with her and she often washes his pots for him, after his midday meal. Emma makes her way back downstairs and soon spies him in the far corner of the room. She walks across and says hello.

'So, you've come to join us, have you,' he states, with a twinkle in his blue eyes. 'I'm delighted. I have had good reports about your progress. Meet Tony. You and he and I make up this Section. It is only small but just as important as the others. We cover income that's not earned, such as from rented properties. You'll learn as you go along.' Tony stands up to greet her. He is a young, slim man, with dark, sleeked-back hair and narrow features. He is not much taller than Emma. During the tea-break, he tells her that he is married and the father of two little girls.

'You might find me nodding off at my desk at dinner-time,' he says. 'We had a very disturbed night with Emily who is teething.' Emma grins. She knows all about babies and toddlers with having four younger siblings.

A few days later, at dinner-time, Mr Turnbull comes across to her as she is finishing her sandwich.

'I wonder if I can ask you a favour.' he says. 'I need my library books changing. The library is near the town hall, not far from here. Would you mind?'

'No. I don't mind at all. A walk out will do me good. Do I just hand them in?'

'Thank you. I'm very grateful. There are four in this bag. Take them to the counter. The lady at the desk knows me and she will choose four more for me. She knows the sort I like. I read a lot of

books, you see, as I'm limited in what I can do.'
'Ask me anytime,' Emma says, 'or if there's any other shopping that you need.'
'My wife sees to most things but this will save her an extra trip,' Mr Turnbull explains. Emma is pleased to have a wander out and look in shop-windows as she makes her way across to the library. 'Maybe I should join. Then I can borrow books to read,' she thinks. Mr Turnbull is delighted with the books, when she returns. 'Just the sort, I like. She has chosen well.' Emma finds him good to work with and Tony is helpful when she has a problem. She is enjoying life.

The weekend seems to arrive very quickly.
'Where are you going tonight?' Marjorie asks, on Saturday afternoon. She is pacing up and down, rocking Andy to sleep while Cathy is pushing her baby dolly to sleep in a little pram. Before answering her aunty's question, Emma bends down and peeps into the pram.
'She is so cute, isn't she,' she says to Cathy. Looking at Marjorie, she continues. 'I always wanted a doll's pram but my parents couldn't afford one although dad did make me and Martha a cot each, in which to put our dollies. At that time, my idea of heaven was a very large cave where I walked around and around pushing a pram. Maybe I will get my heaven on earth,' she jokes. 'The girls at school predicted that I will have lots of children. To answer your question, I am going to try St Paul's parish hall opposite the Catholic church in Larch Road. I was talking to someone at St Anne's church last Sunday and they told me that it is a decent-sized hall and that the dances are well-organised.' When Emma stays for the weekend, she regularly attends St Anne's church on the next estate which is not too far a walk.
'Just be careful,' her aunty advises. 'There should be a bus you can catch, to get home safely.'
'There will probably be a bus stop near to the hall,' Emma says, trying to reassure her aunty. 'I'll find out where it is. Don't worry.'

The venue is easy to find and Emma ventures inside, leaving her coat in the cloakroom. The band is playing. The hall is already filling up with couples dancing to a quickstep. She wanders down the right-hand side wondering where to sit, feeling rather overdressed as she is wearing a brightly-coloured, floral dress, with puff sleeves, that looks something like a ball gown. I should have worn my black taffeta skirt and white top,' she thinks, feeling a little out of place. About halfway down, she stops.

'Do you mind if I sit with you?' she asks of a young lady. 'I don't know anyone here.'

'No, I don't mind. I'm Angela,' she says, pleasantly. 'I've come with some other girls but they are dancing.'

'Thank you.' Emma replies, sitting down on a small, wooden, brown chair. Angela, with her short, brown, wavy hair framing her round face, is a bonny girl. Her eyes are pale-blue, Emma notices. Her only makeup is a touch of pale-pink lipstick. She is wearing a flared, brown skirt and beige top with short sleeves. As they chat, after Emma introduces herself, she decides that Angela seems a quiet, gentle sort of person and easy to converse with. 'I feel overdressed,' she confides in her. 'I wasn't sure what to wear.' Angela is comforting in her reply.

'You look all right. I wouldn't worry about it. You aren't the only one in a dress. There are others.'

'Do you smoke?' Emma asks. Angela shakes her head.

'I only tried once, but I nearly choked and it tasted horrible.'

'Do you mind if I do?'

'Not at all. Plenty of people smoke.'

'I have a cigarette when I'm feeling a bit nervous. I don't smoke many.' Emma takes her cigarette packet from her small handbag and lights a cigarette. She also carries a tiny metal container in which to drop the ash.

'I wouldn't have taken you to be nervous, walking in here alone. I don't think I could have done that,' Angela says.

In the course of their conversation, Emma discovers that Angela works in administration for a Finance Company. She comes from another council estate, bordering the one where Abe and Marjorie live. The girls are in the throes of discussing office work when a tall, slim, handsome guy, smartly dressed in a grey suit with white shirt and a flamboyantly coloured tie, approaches them and asks Angela for a dance. When she stands up, Emma realises that she is quite petite, compared with her. The evening progresses and Emma is invited to dance a number of times. She enjoys the music and at the tea-break, chats to her new friend.

About half-an-hour before the end, Ralph, the tall young man who has given Angela a number of dances and who is obviously interested in her, comes over yet again to ask her to partner him.

The lad, who has been sitting with him all evening, is walking beside him. As this other lad is walking across the hall, Emma can see that he isn't much taller than her. She senses that he is coming to her. She is right.

'Would you like a dancing partner for the rest of the evening?' he asks, coyly. Emma grins.

'An unusual question or his sense of humour,' she thinks, 'but so what! He seems pleasant enough.' She has been studying him when sitting out and been fascinated watching him trying to light his pipe as it never lasted more than a minute. 'I bet he has only just bought it,' she thinks. He is a good-looking guy, quite broad and his thick thatch of brown hair is combed back, apart from a quiff at the front. He is wearing a smart, dark-blue suit and white shirt with his tie a deeper shade of blue, patterned with small black squiggles.

'What's your name, then?' he asks, as they step in among the dancers. 'I'm Ron and a mate of Ralph's.'

'Emma. I thought you must be friends. You've been sitting with him all night. You like your pipe, don't you? I've been watching you trying to light it.' She notices how blue his eyes are.

'I've only just got it,' he answers, rather embarrassed by her comment. 'My older brother Clive and my dad smoke pipes. I thought I'd try one. You seem very confident, sitting smoking.'

'Not really. It's when I'm nervous that I light up. It's all an act. I've even bought one of those cigarette holders, you know, the long ones you sometimes see film stars use. I haven't brought it tonight, though.' Emma pauses, knowing she is doing what she always does when nervous; she is talking too much.

'That's not the impression you give,' Ron replies, feeling much better knowing that he isn't the only one lacking in confidence.

The couple dance together a little nervously and at the finish, he walks her towards Ralph and Angela. It is typical, at this time of the evening, for girls and boys to be mixing. After another couple of dances, the four of them stand together awaiting the announcement of the last dance.

'There's a good picture on at The Gaumont,' Ralph says. 'Us two are going tomorrow night,' he adds, looking at Angela. 'You'll enjoy it, Ron. It's a swashbuckling affair starring Edmund Purdom and David Niven.' Ron hesitates for a moment, while Emma waits, expectantly.

'Would you like to go?' he asks her.

'Yes. I'd love to.'

'We'll see you both tomorrow, then,' Ralph states, 'say around seven-thirty, outside the picture-house.'

The band strikes up and the four youngsters join the others on the dance floor for the final dance. Ron is a smooth dancer and easy to follow. Emma breaks the silence after glancing at the large clock on the far wall.

'I have to catch the last bus. I need to leave now.'

'I'll walk you to the bus stop,' he responds. They glide towards the door and Emma goes to collect her coat. She loves her new coat. It is a delicate grass-green colour, in a straight-backed style, with small pockets and V-neck collar and fastens with large buttons. She bought it in Middlesburn, finally discarding the Flash Harry one from her school days. Her plain scarf and gloves are in the contrasting colour of beige and Emma feels very pleased with her new rig-out. Ron reappears from the Gents cloakroom wearing a dark-navy, belted overcoat. They make their way across the road and a little way along the pavement to the bus stop. Emma is intrigued by him deliberately placing himself between her and the road.

'I'll see you tomorrow night,' she states, stepping onto the platform, after the bus slows to a stop.

'You're going out again?' Marjorie asks, the following evening, watching Emma putting on her coat. 'Where are you going this time?' Her aunty takes a great interest in Emma's social life.

'I'm meeting with a lad I met last night and he is taking me to the pictures. His mate is coming too, bringing the girl I chatted with. She is really nice.'

A little later, Emma arrives at The Gaumont picture-house on Larch Road where Ralph and Angela are standing outside the large doors. They hang around talking until Ralph looks at his watch.

'I think we'll go in,' he says to Angela. 'He will turn up,' he reassures Emma. 'He will just be late, knowing him.' They disappear inside and Emma keeps glancing up and down the road, wondering if she has been stood up. She is feeling disappointed as she has been looking forward to seeing Ron again and going to the pictures. She is studying the poster advertising *The King's Thief*, before spotting him, walking very quickly from the direction of the town centre.

'Sorry, I'm late,' he offers, on approaching her and looking a little sheepish. 'I went to The Odeon by mistake.' Emma is just grateful that he has finally arrived. They go inside just as the lights dim. Emma is soon engrossed in the film. The lights come on at the interval and she turns to Ron.

'Isn't the eye a wonderful thing,' she exclaims. Ron laughs. 'Whatever makes you say that?' he questions, not knowing how else to reply.

'I've been thinking about all that I've been seeing. It is amazing that these two little eyes convey all that to me. Don't you think that is incredible.' He doesn't comment but wonders about her, finding the conversation a little unusual. He sees her to the bus stop again and suggests they meet up at the dance at St Paul's, the following Saturday. He rather likes her even though he can't forget her strange comment.

Emma lay in bed that night mulling over her meetings with Ron. She has discovered that he works in a shipyard drawing office. He is an apprentice draughtsman with a company at Southtees on the outskirts of Middlesburn. She has also found out that he seems fascinated by aeroplanes as he makes models of them. She is looking forward to Saturday night.

'He must be taking an interest in you,' Emma's uncle Abe says to her a few weeks later, after asking her how things are. 'You are seeing him quite a lot.'

'Yes. I like his company. We are going to visit one of his friends tonight. They meet up to together to play their guitars. I think they have bought them recently.'

'You can invite him here, one evening, if you like,' Marjorie adds. 'We want to meet him, don't we,' she says to her little girl. Cathy nods, smiling at Emma. She loves her aunty.

'I'll tell him. He knows about you. He is quite shy, I think. Don't expect a great conversation, but he will talk about his job. He is in the Air Training Corps (ATC). He told me that he wanted to join the Royal Air Force (RAF) but failed his medical test on account of having no hearing in one ear. His dad is the same, apparently. Ron regularly goes to the ATC, two nights a week and a Sunday morning.'

'You've learnt a lot about him in a short time,' says Abe. 'You bring him here and I'll sound him out,' he adds, jokingly.

On her way to meet with Ron, Emma mulls over this conversation.

Ron in ATC

'I suppose we are seeing each other quite a lot,' she surmises, 'but he's a decent lad. I like him. He is interesting.' On arriving at Ron's friend's house, she is introduced to Dan and his girlfriend Barbara. They are quite a contrast as he is slight, to almost being skinny, whereas Barbara is on the heavy side and taller than him. She is friendly and easy to talk to. The lads strum on their guitars. Neither can play much but guitars are all the rage after the phenomenal rise to stardom of The Beatles. When on the bus together, at the end of the evening, Emma mentions to Ron, the invitation from her aunty and uncle.

'My uncle is Polish with an accent, but you can understand him. You'll be fine. I think they feel responsible for me.'

The following Sunday afternoon, Ron arrives to meet Emma's aunty and uncle. Marjorie fusses over him trying to make him feel welcome and insists he stay for tea. No-one escapes her hospitality. Ron chats to Abe about aircraft and what the air cadets do and tells him that they have an annual week away staying at an RAF station. He then listens to Abe reminiscing about his war-time experiences and how he and his brother escaped and made their way to England. It is a fascinating tale. Emma is quite content to sit beside them and learn about such things. She knows little about the war because her father was exempt from call-up, as some farmers were needed at home to work the land, but he was in the Home Guard as part of his war effort. The conversation ceases when Andy crawls onto his daddy's knee for a cuddle and Marjorie announces that tea is ready. While they are eating, she makes a suggestion.

'We can go to the pictures, Abe. I haven't been for ages. Will you two babysit for us? You haven't anything planned, have you?' The two young adults look at each other.

'I haven't,' Emma replies. 'Are you okay to stay, Ron?'

'It's fine by me,' he answers, graciously. The evening is planned. After the two little children are tucked up in bed, Abe and Marjorie put on their coats and make for the door.

'Be good,' her aunty says, as she is leaving. Emma blushes.

'She is so cheeky sometimes but she doesn't mean anything by it,' she says to Ron.

They settle down to watch *Sunday Night at the London Palladium* but not before Emma has switched off the living-room light, as it is cosier sitting close together in the dark watching the black and white television screen; like being in the pictures, she thinks. Bruce Forsyth is a confident, entertaining compere. The Tiller Girls, a troupe of young ladies with amazing dancing skills, are in full swing when Emma thinks she hears a knock at the door.

'Who can be calling on us?' she wonders, getting up and making her way to the front door. She opens it and comes face to face with the parish priest. She invites him in and turns on the light, flustered at what he might think. Ron stands up. 'This is Ron, my boyfriend,' she explains. 'We are babysitting for my aunty.' She goes over to the television to turn the sound down, trying to hide her feelings of embarrassment. Father Brent looks at Ron.

'Good evening,' he says, before turning back to Emma. 'I've found a lady, Miss Watson, she's called, who is happy to give you

lodgings. You asked me a week ago. You are still interested?'
Emma nods. 'I've written her name and address down. Go along
and see her. Let me know if you find her suitable.' He passes her a
piece of paper.
'I will, Father,' Emma replies, showing him to the door. 'Thank
you for your help.'
'Enjoy your evening,' are his parting words.
'Are you moving?' Ron asks.
'That was a surprise,' Emma begins, in reply. 'I don't know what
he thought of us having the light out, but yes, I've been thinking
about it for a while before I approached the priest. I've been here
almost nine months. Cathy is moving into the back bedroom
shortly and I think Andy is more than ready to move from his dad
and mam's room. I feel, although they're good to me, that it is
time I moved out. We can still visit and offer to babysit. I'll tell
them after I've been to see this lady.'

Emma turns off the light and they settle back down to return to
Bruce Forsyth.
'Can you ride a bike?' Ron asks her, when the advertisements are
on the screen. Emma nods.
'I can but I'm not very good at it as I only learnt when I was
seventeen, on an old bike I found at home. I used to practice on the
mud tracks. Why do you want to know?'
'I was thinking with warmer days ahead of us that we can go bike
riding.' Emma ponders for a moment. 'Maybe I can buy one. I can
put down a good deposit and pay in instalments.'
'There is a good bicycle shop on Broad Road,' Ron tells her. 'You
can't miss it as it is really big and you can see the bikes through
the large glass fronts. I'll meet you there on Saturday and look at
them with you, if you like. My bike is second-hand but in good
nick as I cycle to work, occasionally.'
'This is exciting. I haven't bought anything like this,' Emma
enthuses. A fun game, *Beat the Clock*, is just beginning and they
both take an interest in the competitive side of it.

The remainder of the evening is uninterrupted except when she
thinks that she hears Andy cry out. On dashing upstairs to see to
him, she realises he is dreaming. She strokes his cheek for a little
while and gently kisses him before quietly returning to the living-
room. As Ron is leaving to catch a bus back to Thorntees, they
arrange a time to meet the following Saturday afternoon at the

bicycle shop. Emma goes to bed wondering how she will explain to Marjorie, that she is leaving.

'So many different bikes to look at,' Emma thinks, on entering the shop. It is huge inside with rows of bikes in an array of colours and sizes. She doesn't know where to start.

'Can I help?' A short, stocky, middle-aged man is approaching her as she is studying the line-up of bikes. 'If you're after a lady's one, these are the ones you need to look at,' he explains, pointing to a row down one side of the shop. Have a look and come and ask me if you need advice.'

'Thank you,' she replies, not having realised that there are different bikes for men and women.

'Have you found one you like?' Ron asks, coming towards her and still breathless from running to the shop from the bus stop.

'Not really. I don't know much about them.' They finally settle on one with red trimmings and after sorting out the payments, walk out together with Emma's bike.

'I'll walk to Marjorie's. It is quite a way, but I've done it before with my dad,' Emma says to Ron. 'You are coming with me, aren't you? I can practise a bit on the way, if you don't mind.'

The couple set off and Emma has a few turns on the bike on quieter roads. It seems a heavy one and she isn't sure if it is a good buy, but too late now, she thinks.

'I'm not sure where I'll keep it,' Emma says to Ron, when they finally arrive. 'Maybe in their wash-house at the back, if it will fit, but I don't know how to get there other than taking the bike through the house. You wait here. I'll go in and ask.' She leaves Ron standing outside while she goes inside. Abe is in the living-room minding the children as Marjorie is at the shops. She explains her predicament to him.

'Bring it in,' he says. Abe inspects the bike. 'I wish you'd told me that you were buying one. I would have helped you to pick a lighter one. It's a bit heavy, this one.' He is disappointed for her. At that moment, Marjorie walks in with her bags of shopping and Abe explains about the bike. They both discuss putting it in the wash-house.

'Will it be safe in there? I wouldn't like it to get stolen,' Marjorie says, concern showing on her face, 'but I suppose there isn't anywhere else.' Still looking worried, she takes her bags into the kitchen and puts her shopping away.

'There is a road around the back which you can use to reach our garden gate and then inside our small garden is the wash-house,' Abe tells Emma, 'but we'll take it through the kitchen, this time.' He wheels the bike passed Marjorie and out to the back to put it away. Emma feels uncomfortable and doesn't know what to say. She realises she should have discussed it with them, before rushing to buy one.

Marjorie bustles about in the kitchen, preparing tea.
'Ron's leaving,' Emma calls to her. 'I'll just walk to the bus stop with him.' Marjorie comes into the living-room.
'No. Stay for tea, please. I've already made sandwiches for us all and the kettle is almost boiling. There are later buses. I can't let you go home hungry,' she adds, smiling at him. 'You're not in a hurry, are you?' she says, directing her question to Ron. He shakes his head. He isn't sure what to say about the whole situation. 'Abe, can you open up the table, please?' She is referring to a dark-brown drop-leaf which stands in the corner of the living-room. Abe carries Andy to his high chair and puts him in, before fetching the table. After raising the side leaves, he placed around it five dining chairs that have padded seats and are covered in a maroon-patterned floral material.

Over the meal, Emma breaks the news about moving, thinking that this maybe is a good time to tell them as it means the bike won't be stored for long and Marjorie needn't worry.
'I've decided to move out,' she says. 'I know you have the furniture arriving anytime for your back bedroom and that Cathy will be moving in. Andy is ready for his own room instead of being in yours. I asked the parish priest at St Anne's if he knew anyone who takes in lodgers and he has given me a name. I called in after work on Thursday. She lives in Ida Road which is convenient for the buses. She seems okay. She asked me to give her a couple of weeks to prepare for me going. It's not that far from here. I explained about getting a bike and she has a small garage that I can keep it in. I'll still be able to come and see you all.' Emma pauses, catching her breath after her lengthy statement. She realises that she is doing it again, talking too much when she is nervous. Looking at Cathy, she adds, 'I'll still be your aunty Emma. I can babysit too.' There is a short silence while the news registers. Emma continues. 'I have loved being here. Just like a

family. It won't be the same but I think it's for the best. I'm very grateful that you've given me a home all this time.'

There is a lengthy pause before Abe voices his thoughts.

'We've enjoyed having you. If it doesn't work out, you can always come back, can't she?' he asks, turning to his wife. Marjorie nods, still thinking about this turn of events and realising her little family will be on their own again. The thought quite pleases her. 'I'm still waiting for that cardigan, you promised you'd knit for me,' Abe continues, but he is smiling as he speaks.

'He is such a nice man,' Emma thinks. 'I will knit you one when I've finished the jumper I'm doing. You want maroon colour, don't you?' she asks him.

'Yes. That's his favourite colour,' Marjorie chips in. 'I'll just refill your cups,' she adds, leaving the table to get the teapot. Trying to console Cathy who is becoming teary over Emma moving out, Marjorie tells her about her new bedroom and having her own dressing-table and that she will be able to take her two dollies to bed to sleep with her. There is no further mention of the bike.

The move to her new lodgings goes very smoothly as Emma has only a few possessions. She walks her bike along the pavements and carries her case and bag. Abe is unable to help her as he is at work on a late shift. It is a bit awkward wheeling the bike with one hand but she finally arrives and rings the doorbell. The door opens to reveal a tall, thin lady with a narrow face and pointed nose and chin. She wears a calf-length, pleated, navy-blue skirt and white blouse. Her short, grey hair is tightly permed, no doubt to give it some pretence of thickness, Emma thinks.

'You are very prompt,' she says, on greeting Emma. 'I like that. I'll get the garage key. It is kept on a hook here behind the door. You can then put your bike away.' Emma places her case and bag inside and takes the key. On returning to the house, she remembers to hang the key back on the allotted hook. The lady is standing, waiting, with another key in her hand. 'I will give you this front door key so that you are free to come and go. In case you're wondering how to address me, you may call me Mabel,' she says, handing over a small silver-coloured Yale key. 'Bring your bags and I will show you upstairs.'

The bedroom is sparsely furnished, but adequate, with a large, dark-brown, old wardrobe and chest of drawers plus a small wicker chair. The wall-paper is cream with tiny yellow flowers and

with pale-yellow curtains to match. Back downstairs, Mabel shows
Emma the kitchen and living-room. The furniture is rather dingy as
if having been there for many years, especially the two settees. The
cushion seats are well-worn and faded compared with the backs
that display a brightly-coloured floral pattern. Everywhere is neat
and tidy.

'This is the parlour, not often used, but you mentioned when you
first came to see me that you have a boyfriend. He may visit if you
wish and you can chat in here,' Mabel states, on opening another
door for Emma to enter. Inside the small room are two easy chairs
with loose grey covers and matching cushions. There is an old-
fashioned china cabinet full of glassware and ornaments. A writing
bureau stands in a corner. 'You might want to unpack now and I'll
make us a cup of tea,' Mabel concludes.

'She is very prim and proper, but thoughtful,' Emma decides,
making her way back to her bedroom.

It doesn't take her long to empty her case, following which, she
returns to the living-room. A silver tray is sitting on a plain brown,
small table. An identical but smaller table is beside Emma's chair
and another, even smaller, next to where Mabel is sitting. The tray
displays delicate china teacups decorated with bluebirds and with
gold-trimmed edges. The dainty milk jug and sugar basin match
them. There is a selection of biscuits on a slighter larger, plain
white plate.

'I don't take sugar, thank you,' says Emma, as Mabel indicates the
sugar pot. Emma takes a custard-cream biscuit offered to her and
places it on a fragile-looking small plate with the same design as
the teacups. She thinks about the cups at her home on the farm,
odd ones, mostly given and sometimes stained and chipped, in
total contrast to these. She isn't surprised to find out that Mabel is
a retired teacher. She speaks very correctly, asking Emma about
her work and also about Ron's occupation.

'I have lived in this house all my life. My parents were here before
me,' she explains. Changing the subject, she continues with details
of how things are to be. 'I will have your evening meal ready for
six o'clock each day. That seems reasonable and will give you
time to get home. If you intend staying out or eating elsewhere,
please let me know.' Emma agrees that that will be fine.

'I had dinner today at my aunty's and I promised Cathy I will go
back for tea, if that's okay.' She is glad to have a reason to go out.
She is finding it difficult making conversation although she

realises that Mabel is trying to be pleasant with her. 'It will probably get easier as we get used to each other,' she thinks, 'but it doesn't seem homely compared with Marjorie's or Mrs Mackey's.' Mabel isn't around when Emma goes down to breakfast, early Monday morning. The small table in the living-room is set out with crockery and cutlery, marmalade and butter. She makes herself toast and notices a packet of sandwiches by the toaster. 'She hadn't forgotten, then,' thinks Emma. The bus stop isn't far and she is early for work.

'How are you doing? I don't see much of you since you moved downstairs?' Emma looks up from her desk to see Matt standing there.

'I didn't hear you approach,' she answers, laying down her pen. 'I wonder if you would like a ride home this Friday, as I'm going back to Scarborough for the weekend.' Emma thinks about it.

'Yes, please,' she replies. 'I'll let Ron know that I won't be at the dance on Saturday?'

'Boyfriend?' queries Matt. She nods and smiles.

'Yes. We've been going out since January. I don't go home as much now, as we spend a lot of time together at weekends. I moved at the weekend too, which reminds me, I must give Mr Wiles my new address. I will still visit my aunty and babysit for them sometimes.' She stands up.

'You kept that quiet. But you'd still like a ride on Friday?' Matt asks, looking downcast.

'Yes, if you don't mind. I'd like to. The little ones miss me.'

'See you on Friday, then,' he says, before making his way back upstairs. Emma begins walking over to the Manager's office. On her way, she passes by Mr Turnbull, busy at his desk. He looks up at her.

'You can't by chance take my books today, to change, can you Emma?'

'Not a problem. I'll get them at dinner-time.' The changing of his library books is becoming a regular occurrence. A gentle friendship is building up between them.

Miriam is delighted to see her big sister on Friday evening. She is getting ready for bed when Emma walks in. Jacob looks up from his jigsaw and gives her his big, lopsided grin. Mary enters.

'Hello, Mam,' Emma greets her.

'It's nice to see you? You haven't been for a while. Did Matt bring you?'

'Yes, but I suspect he won't doing it much longer. I have a new boyfriend.'

'You can tell me about him later. Your dad will be ready for his supper when he comes in, shortly. He will probably want a game of cards if you want to join in.'

'I don't mind. I'll get something to eat first, though, as I came straight from work. Is it good being a weekly boarder?' Emma asks, turning to Amy. After her sister's first year at boarding-school, the arrangements have changed and boarders are allowed home at weekends.

'It is much better. I can help more at home. Being a full-time boarder wasn't much fun. I don't know how you stuck it for so long.'

'By the way,' Mary says, 'Martha has just told us today that she is expecting again.'

'Is she? I must go and see her. Another baby! It doesn't seem two minutes since Sandra was born,' Emma responds, while making her way to the pantry for food.

Over the next weeks, Ron and Emma meet regularly. When Emma isn't returning home to Moorbeck for a weekend, which is happening less and less, they book a tennis court in Albert Park on a Sunday afternoon, or early evening during the week, weather permitting. They both enjoy the competitive game.

'You must have played a lot,' Emma comments, one Sunday afternoon, after Ron beats her yet again. 'You're better than me.' He laughs. He enjoys being with her and admits that he also enjoys winning the games.

'Yes, I've played before. You're not a bad player. You might beat me one day,' he says, 'but not if I can help it,' he adds, jokingly.

'You won some of the games.' Their hour is up and they wander through the park, hand in hand, alongside the lake, watching the ducks on the water, dipping their heads in or reaching for pieces of bread thrown to them by the visitors. They hear the chimes of the ice-cream van close by. There is a long queue, but even so, Ron offers to buy two. Emma loiters by the swings waiting for him.

'You ever heard of Hadrian's Wall?' he asks, while she's licking her ice-cream. Emma shakes her head.

'Is that History because, if so, I dropped that subject and chose Geography at school? I was no good at remembering dates.'

'Yes, it is. The Romans built a wall, from East to West. It runs

roughly between Newcastle and Carlisle. I've read about it as I am
really interested in the Roman period. Maybe we will go one day.
There are ruins up there that I'd like to see.' The conversation
continues, mainly one-sided as Emma listens with interest, until
eventually it is time to leave.

'It has been a lovely day,' says Emma, as they reach the bus stop.
'We can meet next week for a bike ride,' Ron suggests. 'I am
supposed to be studying but I can fit both in.' She knows he works
in a drawing office, but he explains that he is taking the Ordinary
National Certificate (ONC) as an apprentice shipbuilding
draughtsman. Over the five years of the apprenticeship, there is the
opportunity to obtain a Higher National Certificate (HNC)
qualification but he says that getting the ONC will be fine. 'I was
deferred from joining up for my two years National Service with
doing this apprenticeship, but I may still have to go when I'm
twenty-one. Conscription is very gradually being wound down and
I'm hoping that I won't have to.' Emma hopes so, too, as she
doesn't like the idea of him going away for two years. 'I will see
you on Wednesday then,' he says and kisses her. After seeing her
onto the bus, he walks down the road to another bus stop and
Emma watches him. She likes him a lot.

The friendship continues but, by the end of July, Emma is
wondering where it is going. Ron gives no inkling of wanting a
more serious relationship. Having just passed her nineteenth
birthday, Emma decides that it is time to find out how he feels. She
thinks that a good six months is long enough to have some idea.
She isn't quite sure how to approach him about this.

'Maybe I should bring the subject up when he comes tomorrow
night,' she thinks, one Saturday late evening, when tossing about
in bed, unable to sleep. 'Should I just be honest enough to explain
that if it isn't going to be more serious, then it is time to finish? Is
that what I want?' She knows that it isn't. 'What shall I do?' she
asks herself.

Summer 1959 / Summer 1960

The sun is shining and bringing warmth to Emma, as she walks
along the pavement to church, the following morning. There is
little traffic and crossing the normally busy road, is easy. Emma is
deep in thought. She is tired. A restless night and many dreams
disturbed her sleep. She slides into an empty bench and kneels.
She chews over her dilemma, finding concentration difficult
during Mass. The words of the priest at the homily drift gently
over her as her own thoughts crowd her mind.
'It is so difficult. I don't want to finish with him, but we're at a
standstill.' After finally deciding that she will talk to Ron, she feels
more at peace. On leaving the church, she says good morning to
the priest who is standing near the doorway.
'You seem deep in thought. Are you settled in?' he enquires.
'Yes, thank you, Father. I'm fine.'

It is early evening when Ron arrives. Emma takes him through to
the parlour. After kissing her, he begins talking about his trip away
with the cadets to Benson camp in South Oxfordshire, in a week's
time. They are travelling by train from Darlington to Kings Cross
station in London and then crossing to Paddington station. He is
excited about it. He is looking forward to flying. They always have
at least one flying session when at the airfield, he explains. While
he talks, she listens, patiently.

'You're quiet,' he says, after a short pause. 'Are you okay?'
'Not really. I want to talk about something.'
'Is it serious? You look worried.'
'It's just difficult saying it.' Emma takes a deep breath. 'It's about
us.'
'What about us?' Ron has no inkling of any problem. He thinks
that they are happy together. Emma finally blurts out her
misgivings, becoming quite emotional, as she speaks. Ron gets up
and goes to her chair and puts his arm around her.
'I don't want to finish. I think we have a great thing going.'
'But you never say anything.'
'I thought you would realise.'
'I'm not a mind reader.' Emma is almost in tears. 'So, you want to
be serious?' she questions. He nods and kisses her. The
conversation continues.

Much later, Ron checks his watch. He looks at Emma in dismay. 'Have you seen the time? I've missed the last bus. They stop running earlier on a Sunday evening.'

'What are you going to do?' she asks. There is a silence while Ron ponders his dilemma and Emma awaits his reply. He looks at her. 'Would you mind if I borrow your bike?' he asks, hopefully. He knows that otherwise it is a long walk home. Emma laughs.

'I don't mind, if that's what you want.' She walks out and goes to get the garage key, with Ron following.

'I'll have one more hug,' he says, holding her close, before they make their way outside. He returns the key after taking her bike from the garage. She stands on the doorstep watching him, until, with a final wave, he disappears. She is tired but happy. 'Now to bed and sleep,' she decides.

A week later, Ron goes on his annual trip with the cadets and Emma takes a week's holiday and returns to the farm. After the second postcard arrives, Mary is curious.

'You must tell me more about him,' she says, looking at her daughter, quizzically. 'Sending two postcards when away with other lads, means he must be thinking about you a lot.' Emma is smiling, reading the message. 'Are you going to show me then?' She passes the card over to Mary. 'What's the nine and nine-tenths mean?' her mother asks, looking at the fraction after his name.

'It's just a code, Mam. He's having fun.' Emma is smiling secretly to herself. She knows what it means. He'd put a similar one on the first postcard. Not quite a full percent but almost. He is serious about her.

'You can bring him over one day to see us. I am sure your dad would like to meet him.'

'Yes, I'll do that, Mam.' Emma takes the postcard to her bedroom and picks up her handbag. She takes the first one out and re-reads it before placing them both inside. She wanders back into the kitchen.

'Do you want to come for a walk down the pasture?' she asks Jacob and Miriam. 'It is such a lovely day.' The children scamper outside with Emma following, their mother pensively watching them from the doorway.

September arrives. One Saturday evening, Emma and Angela are chatting together while the band is playing an Elvis Presley song. The friends meet up regularly at St Paul's, but Angela's boyfriend,

Ralph, is no longer around as Angela had explained to Emma
weeks ago that they'd finished.
'I've met someone,' she confides to her friend. 'Des is coming
tonight. I think you will like him.' Ron arrives and joins them.
'You two dance. I'll be fine,' says Angela. 'He will be here in a
minute or two.' The young couple step onto the floor.
'Before I forget,' Ron begins, 'my mam has asked me to invite you
round. She wants to meet you. She wasn't happy about Sunday,
when I was so late home with missing the last bus again. It's a
long walk. She heard me come in. You can come tomorrow and
say hello and then we can go for a bike ride, if you like.'
'I'll come straight after dinner. I'll get my bike back, too. Then
you will be able to borrow it if you miss the bus again,' she adds,
jokingly.

'Five Lamps stop,' shouts the conductor. Emma jumps up and
makes her way to the front of the bus. Stepping off, she looks for
the street she has to walk down, as explained by Ron. She is
feeling apprehensive. The weather is warm for late September and
Emma is casually dressed in a pair of black slacks and a multi-
coloured summer-flowered blouse. The cobble street is narrow
with terraced housing and shallow pavements. She stops at number
twelve and takes a deep breath. Glancing up and down, she notices
a corner shop a few yards up the street.
'That must be handy for them,' she thinks, while gently knocking
on the green door. It opens inwardly and Ron is standing there
with a big smile on his face.
'I'm glad you've made it. Come in.'

The corridor is narrow and they go single file because Ron's bike
is parked along it, taking up much of the space. Emma notices the
steep stairs opposite. They pass a brown door on the left.
'That's the parlour,' he states, 'but we hardly ever use it.' Ron
goes through the second doorway on the left with Emma close
behind. They step into the living-room. 'My mam and dad,' says
Ron.
'Hello,' greets a lady, standing up. A middle-aged bloke gets out
of his chair and shakes Emma's hand.
'They are like a pair of cottage loaves,' thinks Emma. Both are
rounded. His dad is going bald but has a ring of hair around his
head. His mam has short, wavy, brown hair, speckled with grey.
'This is Clive,' indicates Ron, as a young man, steps forward. He

is about the same height as Ron and with the same blue eyes, but
he is slimmer.

'Pleased to meet you,' he says. 'I wanted to say hello, before going
to see Nancy, my girlfriend. Hopefully we'll meet again. I'll bring
her over next time you come,' he adds, before walking out. A
short, pleasant conversation follows. Emma notices that the room
seems crowded with a table and chairs along one wall; and taking
up a lot of space is a three-seater settee and matching easy-chairs,
all of which have floral covers.

'We're going for a bike ride, Mam,' explains Ron, a little later,
getting up and edging towards the door.

'You are welcome to come back for your tea,' his mam says to
Emma.

'Thank you,' she replies, quietly, 'but after our ride, I will be
taking my bike back to my lodgings.'

'Well, come next Sunday, then,' his mam persists, trying to make
Emma feel welcome. Before following Ron through the doorway
and into the corridor, Emma graciously accepts the invitation.

'You get your bike from the parlour,' he calls. 'I will take mine
outside and you can bring yours out.'

'Can you manage?' his mam says, appearing in the doorway of the
living-room.

'We're fine, thanks. I'll see you later,' her son calls out, but his
mother helps Emma with her bike and watches them from the front
door, until they are out of sight.

The young couple cycle to Southend Park and walk their bikes in
through the large, metal, open gates.

'I'm glad that's over,' says Ron.

'Me, too,' Emma replies. 'First time is always hard, but your
parents are welcoming. My mam mentioned last time I was home,
that my dad would like to meet you. Your turn next to get the
once-over,' she jokes, but Ron doesn't reply to her comment.

'Let's get an ice-cream at the little shop,' he says. 'Did I tell you
that my mam and dad go to The British Legion club every Sunday
night? We can stay in next week and watch television if you like,
after they've gone out.' They walk together, wheeling their bikes,
enjoying each other's company and the sunshine.

'There's an empty bench over there,' she points out. 'I'll take the
bikes over while you get the ice-creams.' She minds the bikes and
Ron joins the end of the queue that is weaving its way out from the
shop. Plenty of people are milling around: some are looking at the

menagerie of animals and poultry inside their enclosures; small children are footing it along the pathways on their scooters; mothers are pushing prams; and dads are running around on the fields playing catches with their children. Ron and Emma sit and talk until late afternoon, wrapped in each other's company, before cycling back to her lodgings.

The following Saturday evening, Emma catches up with her friend. 'How was it then?' Angela asks her. Emma knows she is referring to her meeting with Ron's parents.
'It was all right. They were very welcoming. We didn't stay long but I've been invited to tea tomorrow. Is Des coming tonight?' Before Angela answers, her eyes light up. She is looking beyond Emma, who turns to see what the attraction is. Des is approaching, smartly dressed in his small-checked, brown suit; cream shirt with plain, tan-coloured tie; and wearing brown shoes. She stands up to greet him. Des is slightly taller than Angela, a little stocky and with thick, very tousled, ginger hair. He smiles at Emma, his eyes twinkling. He says hello.
'Ron not here?' he asks.
'No, but he is coming.' All four have an enjoyable evening and towards the end, Des makes a suggestion.
'Do you two fancy a game of tennis next Sunday afternoon? The courts are open until the end of October.' They agree to meet at two o'clock in Arthur Park.

The young adults meet up as planned and have a stimulating game, with Des and Angela declared the winners, before heading towards the ice-cream van. After buying four choc ice-creams, they sit on the grass and continue chatting. Des is an apprentice joiner working for his dad in the building trade and is concerned that when he finishes his apprenticeship, he may have to do his National Service. Being a few months older than Ron, he knows that this is more than likely and laughingly says that now he has met Angela, he doesn't want to leave her for two years for someone else to snap up.
'He is a gentle lad and fun to be with,' Emma thinks. 'They just seem to click as a couple.'
'It's time we make a move,' she says to Ron. 'Your mam will be waiting for us.' The two couples part company, promising to meet up at St Paul's in two weeks, as Ron is tenting the following

Saturday with his mate, Dan. They are going fishing. Emma
intends to have a weekend at home, on the farm.

When Ron and Emma arrive at his parents, the table is already laid
with an ample spread of sandwiches and cake. Clive is out again.
'His girlfriend, Nancy, isn't able to come today,' explains Ron's
mam, 'but she will be coming one Sunday to meet you. They are
getting married at the end of next March. They have lots of
planning to discuss.' Emma is asked about her lodgings and his
mam thinks she is paying a lot of money. 'I have a friend in the
next street. I'll have a word with her. She may enjoy having your
company.' She starts clearing the table.
'I can do that if you want to get ready to go out,' offers Emma.
'Ron will help, won't you?' she asks.
'Do I have a choice?' he retorts. Her answer is no, but everyone is
laughing.

Meeting Emma's parents happens sooner than Ron expects and in
unusual circumstances. On the following Saturday when Emma is
at home, she tells her mam that she is going to pay him a surprise
visit where he is fishing with his friend at Shepton, the village over
the moors.
'I'm taking a jacket because the nights are cooler now,' she says. 'I
may be late back.' Leaving the farmhouse, she walks along the
narrow lane running down by a field; then crosses the wooden
bridge and joins the lane uphill to the neighbouring farm where it
peters out. She takes the rough track at the back of the farm onto
the moor and picks up the sheep track across the heather, until
eventually meeting the tarmac road into Shepton. She wanders
down into the village and quickly spies the lads on the river edge,
with their fishing rods. She creeps up behind Ron and taps him on
the shoulder. He turns around and grins.
'This is a welcome distraction,' he says, getting to his feet. 'I'll
just tell Dan that I'm going back to the tent.'

On reaching the tent in the Blacksmith's field behind the pub, he
places his rod inside, before joining Emma to go and explore the
village. They stop at the cake shop to buy sandwiches and bottles
of coke and walk along the riverside until they come to a grassy
patch away from other visitors. There, they enjoy the view and the
chance to be alone. Evening is descending when they finally go
back to the tent.

'Come in for ten minutes,' says Ron. She knows he wants to kiss her before she leaves. They sit down and talk further before he finally says goodbye.

'You call this fishing, do you?' a voice asks. They both look up, startled at seeing a face peering in. The bloke quickly disappears, chortling, as he walks off.

'He looks like one of the locals. He may have recognised me,' Emma says, anxiously, as she stands and picks up her jacket. 'He'll tell my dad.'

'It's the bloke who owns the field,' Ron replies. He peers outside the tent. 'Do you realise how late it is? I'll walk you home. It will soon be dark.'

'It is quite a walk. What about your mate?'

'He'll be fine. He will know I have gone with you.' They set off up the tarmac road before turning onto the moor track. Walking through the heather, Ron follows closely behind Emma. 'How can you tell where we are going?' he asks.

'I'm following the sheep track. It will peter out shortly but I know where we are.' As far as Ron is concerned, they are in the middle of nowhere. Just moor all around. He can't turn back. He has no choice but to trust Emma and keep walking. Further on, he expresses more concern.

'Are you sure you know? There is no path at all, now.'

'Don't worry. We will be fine.' She thinks it is hilarious wandering over the moor in semi-darkness. Eventually they come to a stone wall and Emma knows that they will shortly see the dim light of their farmhouse, across the valley.

Finally walking up the rough stone path to the house, she pushes open the door and walks in, followed by Ron. As they enter the kitchen, six pairs of eyes look up briefly before continuing a game of cards. Emma and Ron sit down and watch as she knows that there is no point in speaking until the game is over. The six players have the usual inquest at the end of the game before turning their attention to the visitors. After introductions, ten-year old Jacob goes to bed, leaving Mark and Amy having a last game of knock-out-whist while Mary makes a pot of tea.

'You won't know your way back in t' dark,' Emma's dad says to Ron. 'You'd better sleep over.'

'I don't know where he will sleep,' his wife responds, looking at her husband.

'We can push two chairs together and he can have my army

greatcoat as a cover. It'll keep him warm enough.' Joe, Martha's husband, pulls out his pipe and begins filling it from his tobacco pouch.

'Do you smoke a pipe?' he asks Ron, noticing him eyeing the old pipes on the mantelpiece. Ron nods.

'My dad and brother smoke them and I've started, but I left mine in the tent.' Getting up from his chair, Emma's dad passes Ron a pipe. Joe gives him the pouch.

'Here. Have some,' he says. 'By the way, I'm going to Shepton early tomorrow morning. I'll give you a ride on the tractor.' Ron verbalises his thanks. The night passes with plenty of chat and banter. Much later, Ron is left downstairs on his makeshift bed, physically and mentally tired after this whirlpool introduction to Emma's family.

It is early morning when Ron awakens, stiff and cold. Mary comes in and lights the fire, but it is slow-burning.

'Have some bread and marmalade,' she says. 'I'll make us some tea.' Ten minutes later, Tom appears and makes straight for his milking cap and ragged jacket hanging from a nail behind the kitchen door.

'I need to get the cows milked before going to church. Bring me a mug of tea down, will you, lass,' he asks Mary. 'You're welcome any time, lad,' he says to Ron, before disappearing. Emma appears in the kitchen and is just starting to talk to Ron when there is a knock at the door.

'That will be Joe,' Mary says. 'You better go. He won't want to hang around. Take your sandwich with you.' Ron jumps up, thanks Mary for his stay, takes his coat and putting his half-eaten bread into a pocket, makes his way outside followed by Emma. Joe is already on his tractor, the engine running. It is a misty, drizzly, cold morning, not an ideal way of travelling, when being exposed to the elements.

'You will have to stand on the back and hang on,' Joe explains to Ron. Away they go, Ron holding tightly with one hand while waving to Emma with the other, as she stands in the doorway, watching.

'I hope he'll be all right,' she says to Mary, when back inside the house.

'You'll be going back on the bus, will you?' Emma nods.

'I think Ron is a bit shell-shocked meeting our lot. He only has one brother.'

'He'll get used to us,' her mother replies, matter-of-factly.

It is the following Saturday evening before Emma has a chance to find out how Ron feels about her family, as he has been occupied with the ATC and his studies during the week.

'Have you recovered?' she asks him, when they meet up. He grins, widely.

'It was a bit of an eye-opener and I wouldn't walk over the moors like that on my own.'

'Martha and I used to walk that way to dances. We always got a ride back, either on a motor-bike or crammed into the local taxi.'

Des and Angela join them and are fascinated to hear about the trip to Moorbeck, especially Ron's tale of wandering over the moor in the dark and his ride on the tractor.

'We have yet to meet our families,' Des says, 'but it will happen soon. I want them to know how I feel about this lovely girl.'

Angela looks at him, coyly, but says nothing.

It is while the girls are at the toilets washing their hands that Angela asks a favour of Emma.

'I want to go and see a priest because although I'm a Catholic, I don't feel I know a lot, with our dad being in the army. We were always moving around and we didn't often go to a Catholic school or even church,' she explains. 'Will you come with me to St Patrick's one evening, as you said that you've met the priests there when you sometimes go to early morning Mass. We are in that parish.'

'Of course, I will. When do you want to go?'

'I don't need you to stay, but just if you will come the first time with me. Des is a regular church-goer and knows a lot and I'd like to learn more.' Emma hasn't told anyone except Angela that, at least once during the week, she leaves for work earlier than needed so as to go to Mass. She walks to St Patrick's which is on the edge of the estate and from there, catches a bus into town. She enjoys the quiet time and the service lasts less than half-an-hour.

'Thanks,' says Angela. 'Will next Wednesday evening be okay, about seven-thirty?'

'It will be fine. I'll get a bus to town afterwards and go over to Thorntees for an hour, to see Ron.'

'Don't mention it to anyone, please,' Angela says. 'This is just between us.'

The news for Emma, on her next visit to Ron's home, is a surprise.
'I've spoken to Hannah, my friend,' Ron's mam says. 'She is
happy for you to lodge with her. There are plenty of buses into
Middlesburn for you to catch to get to work. Go and see her. I said
you would probably call around, today.'
'It will be almost like living next door to you,' Emma states, as,
within a couple of minutes, they arrive at the house. Hannah Black
invites them in. She is a big, broad, elderly lady, heavily-built and
with a prominent local accent.
'You sit there, Ron. I'll show Emma upstairs,' she says, in her
brusque fashion, after he introduces Emma. They are standing in a
small living-room. 'I spend my time in here. Cyril sits mostly in
the parlour except when he wants to eat,' she says, referring to her
husband. At this point, a scrawny-looking, elderly man walks in.
'This is the lassie I'm taking in,' she says to him. He nods at
Emma and disappears. 'You won't be paying as much, with me. I
don't want to make a profit out of you. Company will be fine.'
When back downstairs, she adds, 'Just tell Ron when you want to
move in. Bed's there for you.' She gives them a big smile as they
leave.

'What do you think?' Ron's mam asks Emma, on their return.
'I think it will be all right. Thank you for asking her.'
'I've lit the parlour fire if you two want to sit in there.'
'Your mam tries hard, doesn't she,' Emma states to Ron, as they
sit watching the flames spluttering around the coal pieces.
'She probably thinks we want to be together on our own, but there
is a film that's on the television in ten minutes that I'd like to
watch, if you don't mind. It has aeroplanes in it,' he adds, by way
of explanation. Emma knows how keen his interest is, in aircraft.
'I don't mind at all,' she says. She also understands his enjoyment
of films, after him telling her early in their courtship that he has
spent every Saturday morning for years going to the pictures.
'I guess there wasn't much else for him to do,' she thinks, 'and he
is within walking-distance of the picture-house, but it is such a
contrast from my upbringing, doing jobs inside or out, on the
farm.'

Within two weeks, Emma is moving in with Mrs Black, after
thanking Mabel and explaining to her that the reason for leaving is
that it will be more convenient to be nearer to Ron's home.
Walking along the pavements, yet again, with her case, bag and

bike, she feels happy to be moving.

'Mabel was all right but it wasn't homely,' she thinks. 'Hopefully it will be better at Hannah Black's place.' She spies Ron coming to meet her.

'I'll take that,' he says, removing the bike from her grasp.

'You always walk on the outside. Why?'

'I just think it's a gentlemanly thing to do, to protect a lady from the splashes of rain-water caused by any passing vehicles.' Emma is impressed. Arriving at the house, Ron takes the bike through to the backyard and Emma carries her belongings upstairs. The room is small and contains a single bed, a small dark-brown wardrobe, plus a chest of drawers displaying a free-standing mirror. The wall-paper is faded and the window is in need of a coat of paint, but the room is clean and smells of lavender.

'This will do me fine,' she thinks. 'I will be saving money.' Ron comes into the house and tells Mrs Black that he has managed to get the bike into the shed, much to Emma's relief, as she has been wondering about how to store it.

'You needn't hang around,' Hannah tells them. 'I've been young once. Off you go. I'll see you later.'

'She's great, isn't she,' states Emma, when they are out of earshot.

'Very matter of fact, but seems warm-hearted. I think I will like living with her.'

Christmas is the next marked event on the agenda as Mary and Tom have invited Ron to join the family over the festive season. With Christmas Day falling on a Thursday, Emma and Ron have a four-day break. Emma is pleased but a little concerned about how he will fit in. With a family their size, Christmas is noisy and there can be arguments. She will be going to midnight Mass. She tries to fore-warn Ron, but he is not worried.

'I'll come Christmas eve, but it will be late, as I'm at work all day.'

'Another thing, I must tell you,' Emma says, 'is that we only have a bucket outside in our lav that dad has to empty. We pee at the back of the buildings and only use the lav for the other. Otherwise, the bucket fills up far too quickly.' Ron doesn't comment but reassures Emma that he will be there on Christmas eve. A highlight for Emma is her plan to visit Martha on Boxing Day and introduce Ron as well as meeting the new baby. Martha gave birth to her second child, a baby boy, a few weeks ago and Emma has been busily knitting baby clothes.

'Hasn't he arrived yet?' Tom asks, after coming in from milking, on Christmas eve. 'Will he want picking up at the bus stop?'
'I don't know what time he is coming, Dad.' The evening draws on. Emma keeps glancing anxiously at the clock and is beginning to wonder if he has changed his mind. The family has long since had their tea, the customary Christmas eve giblet pie. Miriam and Jacob are in bed having a sleep before they all journey out to midnight Mass.
'You will have to sleep with Amy and Miriam,' Mary tells Emma. 'Mark will move in with Tim in the double bed and Ron can have Mark's single bed.' It is late when Ron finally appears.
'There wasn't a direct bus over the moor road,' he explains. 'I took a coast road bus to Whitby and caught the last one out. It's eerie walking down that lane at night in the dark. You can almost imagine footsteps behind you, but when I paused, I heard nothing.' Everyone relaxes.

Ten minutes before the family leave for church, Mary asks Ron a question.
'Are you coming with us?' Ron shakes his head.
'I'm not a Catholic.' He pauses and there is a silence. 'I'll just stay here, if that's all right. It's been a long day.' Ron has never been inside a Catholic church. He is quite wary about such things, but he smiles at Emma and hopes it is okay with her.
'You can look out for Father Christmas while we're at church, then,' Mary, says, smiling at him, trying to help him feel at ease, but she is secretly disappointed. She would prefer all her children to marry Catholics and was delighted when Martha married Joe, who comes from a large Catholic family.
'I did go to Sunday school at the Congregational church when I was young,' Ron tells them, sensing a little tension. 'I even won a prize.' He tapers off, not sure if he is saying the right things.
'I'll go and get the little two up,' states Mary, changing the subject. 'We need to be leaving.' Emma moves closely to Ron and whispers some reassuring words, before putting on her coat and hat.
'See you when I get back,' she says, smiling at him.

In early January, there is another unexpected move at work.
'I'm going to Schedule D?' Emma says, repeating what she has been told and trying to clarify this in her mind.
'Yes, you will be taking over from Mr White,' Mr Wiles informs

her. Emma walks back to her desk.

'I am moving,' she says to Tony. 'Someone else will be joining you. He didn't say who.'

'I hear that you are leaving us,' Mr Turnbull comments, at break time. Emma nods, as she is eating a biscuit. 'Mr White's is a heavy caseload. You will be very busy.'

'It is still in the same room and I can keep exchanging your library books,' Emma responds, before taking his cup with hers, to the kitchen.

An older bloke, almost ready for retirement she guesses, is still at his chair when she finds her new desk, the following morning.

'You're welcome to this lot,' are his opening words. 'I've been tidying it up for you. I'm a bit behind with paperwork and I've about had enough; best of luck with it all.' He gets up from his chair and moves away. Another man is approaching, tall and thin and in his early fifties, Emma thinks, noticing that he is going grey and his hair is receding.

'Hello, Emma. I'm Mr Cummins, in charge of Schedule D. I have seen you around. If you get stuck, just give me a shout.'

Emma knuckles down, day after day, trying to get on top of the constant flow of post to be dealt with. It is tea-break on Friday and she is looking forward to the weekend. She joins one or two others and taking out her knitting, unwinds the maroon jumper from around the needles. It is over a foot long. She then sees Mr Cummins walking over to them.

'Can I have a word, Emma, please?' She places her knitting on her chair. They stand a little distance away. 'I don't think you should be knitting in the office.'

'But I'm on my tea-break and I am very careful to only take the ten minutes that we are allowed.'

'I know, but it doesn't look good, sitting knitting in the middle of the office, mid-morning. I noticed you yesterday. I prefer that you don't.' Emma sighs and returns to her chair, rolls up her knitting and puts it away.

'Might take a bit longer, now, Abe,' she thinks, as the jumper is for him.

In spite of her rather brusque manner, Hannah is motherly towards Emma and they spend winter evenings chatting in the small living-room while Emma knits. Over the weeks, Emma learns that when

Hannah was pregnant with her second child during the war, she received a notification that her husband had been killed.

'Then, days later, I receive a letter from him,' she recounts, becoming teary-eyed. 'Letters from soldiers were often delayed during the war. I was broken-hearted. He was such a good, kind man and he loved me. Eventually I met Cyril and he offered me a home and we married and had a son who is now married but calls in to see me. The older two are down South.' Emma guesses it wasn't exactly a love match but Hannah seems to have made the best of it, she thinks. 'Are you going to do my hair again?' Hannah asks her, changing the subject.

'I can do it this Saturday morning if you like.' It was two weeks ago that Emma asked if she could put rollers in Hannah's hair after it was washed, to take out the frizz. After a couple of hours, she'd removed the rollers and gently combed out the snowy white hair. 'It is so beautiful and soft,' she'd told Hannah and she could tell that the old lady was emotionally moved to have someone care for her so gently. 'I don't mind doing your hair any Saturday if I'm not going home.'

As Ron is often busy weekday evenings with the ATC or studying, as his exams are approaching, Emma decides to join the Young Christian Workers (YCW). She has discovered, on the notice board in the church porch, information about a local group that meet weekly. There was little information except that it is a Movement run for, by and amongst young people. She decides to go the following Thursday evening to learn more about it. On arriving, she is approached by a lady, a few years older than the others. Mary is tall and slim, wearing tortoise-shell glasses with her brown hair hanging loosely at shoulder length. She introduces Emma and there is a short general chat before Mary explains, for Emma's benefit, a little about the Movement.

'It won't hurt for you to hear again what we are about,' she states to the other half-dozen youngsters. 'The YCW was founded in nineteen-thirty-seven by a Belgium priest with its aim to help young people live life to the full. The idea is to live an active apostolate in whatever situation you find yourself, either in work, the community or your studies. We take a situation, reflect on it in the light of the Gospel and take action to bring about a positive change in our own lives and the lives of our peers. We focus on an everyday experience and see how we can make a difference in order for everyone to live a life of dignity. In short, we see, judge, and act. Usually, we bring up situations that we are experiencing in our lives where we feel we would like to change something for the benefit of ourselves and others.' She pauses. 'I think that's enough from me. Anyone like to offer something?' A young woman brings up a situation at her place of work. Emma listens and is soon feeling at ease and confident enough to join in the discussion. She doesn't know of any Catholics at the tax office. She finds being in the company of like-minded young people when discussing Gospel values, is stimulating. Having enjoyed her evening, she decides to return each week. As she says goodnight, she is approached by one of the girls.

'I'll walk your way,' says Joan. 'I don't live far from you.' She is a robust girl with unruly, brown wavy hair and with freckles spattered across her rosy cheeks. They chat amicably for a couple of minutes while walking along the pavements.

'I might see you at church on Sunday,' Emma says, on arriving at her street. 'If not, I will see you next week.'

It is the wedding day of Clive and Nancy. Emma is wearing her green coat as it is a chilly morning. She has treated herself to a beige felt cap which perches on her head, slightly to one side.

'You'll do fine,' says Hannah. 'I might walk up to the church and have a watch. Enjoy yourself. It will be you and Ron next, I guess.' Emma smiles and wanders across to Ron's house.

'My, you look smart,' she says to Ron, as he opens the door for her, dressed in his black suit with a white carnation in the lapel. His mam is wearing a blue two-piece costume with matching hat and gloves. Sitting in church a little later, Emma, looking at Nancy in her long, scalloped-neck, white wedding-dress, with veil and tiara and white-satin high-heels, bringing her up to Clive's height, ponders over the fact that Nancy had asked her to be her chief bridesmaid and she'd declined. It had been a dilemma for her knowing that Nancy was a Catholic but for some reason had decided to marry in St Cuthbert's Church of England (C of E) church. Knowing that being a witness and signing the register is important, Emma mentioned it to a priest. He told her that it was inappropriate for her to be a chief witness to a wedding of a Catholic marrying outside her own religion. Emma regretfully told Nancy that she would just come as a guest.

'I don't think it has enamoured Ron's mam to Catholics,' she thinks. She feels a bit sad about it as Nancy has no sisters, only brothers.

Later, as best man, Ron gives his prepared speech, mentioning how he looks up to his brother and has learnt a lot from him. Emma thinks it is touchingly complimentary and glad it goes down well, knowing that Ron has spent hours chewing over it and practising his words.

'Was I okay?' he whispers to her, when mingling later with the guests.

'You were great. I think Clive was pleased with what you said about him.' After the bride and groom leave for Edinburgh where they will spend their honeymoon, a few of the younger guests make their way to a pub in Thorntees. Ron and Emma join them. Feeling much more relaxed, they all have a good banter after the formality of speeches and polite behaviour mixing with many guests that they didn't know. Some hours later, Ron and Emma leave to make their way home.

'I feel slightly drunk,' laughs Emma, linking her arm with Ron's to keep her balance. 'We should not have had that last round of drinks.'

'It's my brother's wedding day and a celebration,' he replies. She giggles. 'I will be all right with a black coffee.'

With Easter approaching and over a year since they first met, Ron and Emma begin to have serious talks about their own future together. They feel more settled now that Ron, who is nearing his twenty-first birthday, has received a letter saying that he will no longer have to do his two-year stint in the forces.

'Lucky for you,' comments Des, when discussing this at St Paul's, on a Saturday evening. 'I received my letter a few weeks ago telling me where I have to go. I'm a few months older than you. I must have caught the tail-end of the call-ups. We are getting engaged though,' he adds, putting his arm around Angela, 'before I go. Then as soon as I'm demobbed in two years' time, we will get married.'

'I am so pleased for you both,' says Emma. 'That is great news, except for the long engagement.'

'I haven't asked her dad yet, but I don't think he will mind. I have completed my apprenticeship and there is plenty of work in the building trade. Her mam will be pleased that I am from a Catholic family like Angela.' It must be the time of year, Emma thinks, on opening a letter from her friend, Faith, two days later. Faith shares her news that she is getting engaged to Rory on her twentieth birthday in May. Not only that, but they are planning on their wedding to be around Christmas time.

'Exciting times,' thinks Emma. 'I bet she will be having the wedding in Holmestown with not having parents to support her. Mrs Mackey will be good to her.'

The weeks pass and Emma enjoys the YCW meetings and chatting to Joan. Des has left for the forces but Angela keeps in contact and invites Emma, occasionally, to her home. There are three younger siblings. The mother is a gentle, quietly-spoken person, who is welcoming. On another evening, Emma visits Marjorie and Abe, taking the jumper, finally finished. Abe is delighted and tries it on. 'It's a perfect fit,' her aunty states. 'I have just put the children to bed. Go up and say goodnight to them. They will be so pleased to see you, especially Cathy.' It takes longer than a goodnight kiss as Cathy pleads for a story and Emma happily obliges. Emma is pleased to have finally delivered the jumper. She is already knitting another one, this time for Ron. The wool is bright blue but the pattern shows a different colour for a broad band across the front and she has chosen sunshine yellow.

'Do you think it is too bright?' Emma had asked Hannah one evening. Her landlady was very reassuring. 'He won't mind what colour it is. It's you knitting him one that'll please him.'

'Have you ever thought about being a nun?' Ron asks one afternoon in early July, as they're sitting close together on a park bench after a game of tennis. 'You go to church a lot.' Emma looks at him in surprise.

'I go every Sunday as many others do and not just Catholics. All sorts of people go, like Church of England people, Baptists, Methodists, Jews and others. It's not unusual. Yes, I did give it some thought about being a nun when I was in my teens, but decided it wasn't for me.' Ron jumps in.

'Well, I better ask you now in case you change your mind again,' he says, jokingly and she is beginning to realise that when he is nervous, he makes light of it by trying to be funny. Emma smiles at him. She knows what is coming. 'Will you marry me?' he asks, his clear blue eyes gazing into her hazel ones. She whispers 'yes' and they kiss in public, not caring about passers-by. 'How about we get officially engaged in July on your birthday?' he suggests, 'and we can tell our families then. Before that, I want to ask your dad for your hand in marriage, as they say. Maybe next time I go, at a weekend.'

'That's a great idea, making it official on my birthday,' Emma enthuses. 'It will be eighteen months after we met.'
'We can go shopping next Saturday and choose a ring if you like. I have been saving up.'
'It doesn't matter about spending a lot. I've been thinking about things and I think we ought to start saving together for a deposit for a house,' suggests Emma. 'I was listening to a discussion at work last week when the pros and cons of buying or renting a house were being discussed.' It is common for girls of her age to get married and she finds conversations with some of the office staff, enlightening. Tony, when buying his own house, explained to Emma his difficulty when applying for a mortgage, as he hadn't quite enough deposit. Remembering this, Emma continues. 'I don't want to rent a home. Maybe we should open a joint bank account at the Halifax because then, they will know we are good savers and it might help when we apply for a mortgage. What do you think?'
'It would be good to own our house.' Ron says, before pausing. 'I've just had a thought,' he states. 'It will be easier for you than me at a dinner break to go to the Halifax bank to place deposits. What if I give you your lodging money to pay Mrs Black and you pay the equivalent into the account as my contribution?'
'That's a great idea. If I save the same amount from my wages, the deposit will grow quite quickly. Shall we keep this between us though, as I'm not sure whether my parents will approve us having a joint account, before we are married?' She continues, excitedly. 'You know those houses in Aeron Street. They have a little garden at the front. Maybe we can buy a house like that.' The couple continue conversing, happily planning their future together.

Hours later, in bed and although initially feeling excited over her future with Ron, Emma is unable to sleep as she appreciates that there will be hurdles to cross. She has never brought up at work that she is a Catholic as she knows that some people have strange ideas about the religion. The YCW is different. They have beliefs in common. She is aware that the Church is not keen on mixed marriages and she was told recently that if you want a marriage service in the Catholic Church and one of you isn't a Catholic, you can only walk out after the service, through the side door.
'That won't happen at Windrush as they only have one door anyway,' she thinks, 'and that wouldn't bother me anyway.'
However, she suspects that both families will have misgivings about them marrying.

'I will have to explain to Ron that he will be obliged to take instructions from a priest before marrying me. We won't be able to have nuptial Mass but we can have the wedding service, but that's okay. I don't know how Ron's mam will react about her son marrying a Catholic and on the other hand, I think my mam is equally concerned because he isn't one, knowing what it was like for her and dad when they decided to marry when she didn't know anything about the Catholic Church.' Emma's dad comes from a family who kept the Faith during the Reformation. His ancestors harboured priests illegally and his close family ancestors lost their farm through having to pay tithes because they wouldn't follow the official Church of England. 'I think my parents will be okay about it, though, but will Ron, when I tell him about the Catholic stuff? Am I making the right decision?' she wonders, the questions mulling around her tired brain while she falls slowly into a troubled sleep.

Summer 1960 / Spring 1961

Ron and Emma go ahead with their plans to save together and Ron
furtively gives Emma her weekly lodging money. She tentatively
brings up Church and he admits to being a bit scared about going
into a Catholic church.

'I have never been inside one and you do hear things about
Catholics.'

'I'll take you into St John's when it is empty and we can walk
around it. You'll see that there's nothing strange about it.' One
evening, as planned, Ron meets her at Mrs Black's and they
wander, hand in hand, to St John's church. The large wooden door
is slightly ajar and she pushes it open. They enter the porch and
Ron watches her dip her fingers into the holy water stoup and
cross herself. Through into the main part of the totally empty
building, Emma genuflects, before walking down the centre aisle.
Ron doesn't ask questions but gazes around as Emma points out
the fourteen Stations of the Cross, the confessional boxes, the
statues and candle stands, the altar with its tabernacle and the
small, red light that is always glowing. After half an hour, they
leave. 'It's quite ordinary, really, nothing to worry about,' she
says. 'Shall we go and have a cup of tea at your mam's?'

It is later in July when they return to the farm with Ron's intention
of approaching her father.

'Don't worry,' she says, trying to reassure him. 'Dad will be fine.
He might not be pleased but he won't stop us getting engaged.'
Ron disappears after tea on the Saturday evening to seek out
Emma's dad who is in the cowshed, milking. Emma waits
patiently in the farmhouse kitchen, hoping everything goes well. In
a little while, the door opens and Ron walks in with a big smile on
his face.

'It's fine,' he says. 'We can.' She takes a deep breath with relief.
'I'm glad that's over,' Ron adds.

'You have a big mouth, haven't you,' a little voice says.

'Miriam!' says Emma, sharply.

'It's all right,' Ron interrupts, a little bashful at her comment. 'It's
my big smile, isn't it?' Miriam nods.

After Sunday dinner, Ron and Emma walk out across the pasture
with Miriam and Jacob.

'I didn't know you had a camera?' Emma says, watching him

remove it from the bag he is carrying.

'I have had it awhile but haven't used it much. A nineteenth birthday present, before I met you. I think I'll take a few photos. How about taking one with you and a cow?' he suggests, jokingly, looking around at the cattle, resting in the warm sunshine.

The Pasture: Emma and cows

'You think I won't?' Emma says. 'Watch this.' She walks over to the nearest cow and kneeling down beside it, places her arm across its large body. Looking back at Ron, she smiles, while he takes the shot. The docile animal doesn't even flinch.

'I can't wait to have that one developed,' Ron says. 'I'll take one or two more, maybe with Trigger and Miriam,' he adds, on seeing Amy approaching them with the dog at her heels. Trigger, the black and white sheepdog, looks up, expectantly, on hearing his name.

On their way back on the bus to Middlesburn, later in the evening, Ron and Emma chat about their future.

'I'll go and tell the local priest, later in the year,' says Emma.

'Why go to him?' Ron asks. 'We're not getting married where I live. We have agreed that we are getting married at Windrush.'

'I know but it is my place of residence at present and where I go to church. So, banns must be announced there as well as at my church at home. He will ask about you and I will have to tell him

that you are not a Catholic. He will then say that you will need to have some instructions from a priest.' Ron looks puzzled.
'What do you mean? What instructions?'
'He will tell you about the Catholic Faith. It's to help you understand what you are taking on, marrying a Catholic. There will probably be only a handful of sessions. It gives you a chance to pull out if you're not happy about it,' she adds, grinning at him. 'I won't do that,' he says, putting his arm around her. 'I take my time making a decision, but then, it's definite.'
'It isn't as if you don't know anything,' Emma reassures him. 'You can tell him you went to Sunday school and about that book *The Jewish War* that you've been reading. It amazes me that it was originally written in the first century by … what was his name?'
'Josephus.'
'Yes, that's right. You have talked about it a lot, educating me about Roman Emperors.' Emma laughs. 'Not that I mind. You said that it mentions brief details about the life of Jesus.' Ron's parents bought the English translation of the book for his twentieth birthday in June and Ron was full of it when telling Emma.

They meet on the evening of Emma's birthday and Ron gives Emma the ring, a slim one with a tiny, single diamond in a small setting. After celebrating together with a visit to a café, they return to his home to show the ring to his parents who congratulate them. The next day after work, Ron tells Emma that when she'd left their house, his mother commented on her being a Catholic and asked what he was going to do about having children.
'What did you say?'
'I just shrugged my shoulders and didn't reply. She is just worried, I guess and she cares. She is friendly with a Catholic family in the house opposite and knows how they struggle as they have lots of children.' Emma ponders for a moment.
'We could have four kids by the time you're twenty-eight.' Ron smiles at her. He thinks she is joking.

Marjorie and Abe are delighted when Emma and Ron visit them on Sunday afternoon to show them the ring.
'Look at it, Cathy. Isn't it pretty?' says her mother. Cathy nods as she listens to Emma explaining how Ron gave her the ring on her birthday and that means that they are getting married.
'And, you, we want as a bridesmaid,' she says to Cathy. 'You are similar in age to my youngest sister, Miriam. You two will look so

sweet together.' Marjorie is delighted at the thought of her little girl being a bridesmaid.

'Have you fixed a date?' she asks.

'No, not yet, but it will be sometime next year.'

'Let's go for a walk in the park,' Marjorie says. 'It's a lovely day. Abe has a camera and he will take a photo of you. You can stay for tea.'

Engagement: Emma and Ron

Another exciting event to look forward to, Emma thinks, on receiving a wedding invitation in September from Faith. Her friend is planning a December wedding. Emma writes a long letter to Faith, accepting the invitation and telling her of her own good news. The following evening, she meets up with Angela who tells her about a marriage preparation course taking place later in the year, advertised at St Paul's church.

'There are number of sessions. You don't get told what to do. I think it is to encourage engaged couples to think about some important aspects of married life that will crop up that they may not have thought about. It covers things such as whose church are you happy to marry in; how to budget and who pays the bills; which family will you be spending Christmas with; are you both agreed on whether you're having children; and suchlike. Mostly it will be engaged couples there. I am thinking of going, but with

Des being away, I will be on my own. Would you like to come with me? I know our weddings are a way off, but it will be something to do over the winter months.'

'Yes, I'll be happy to join you,' says Emma, obligingly. 'Sounds like it will be interesting. I don't think Ron will want to go but I will be able to discuss it with him, afterwards. I went to tell the parish priest that we intend getting married next year. He told me I was too young but took down the details and asked me to let him know, as soon as we have fixed a date.'

'But you're not getting married there, are you?'

'No. We will marry at St Peter's at Windrush, where my family goes to church, but because I live in St John's parish at present, banns have to be displayed there, too. Ron has arranged to meet with the curate for instructions. He hasn't told his mam and dad about those, but that is up to him.'

In early October, Ron arrives for his third meeting with the curate, only to be told that it will not be taking place. The housekeeper is very apologetic, but gives no reason. Ron goes to Mrs Black's, as he has arranged to meet Emma afterwards. He is earlier than expected and explains why.

'How strange. Did she give you another time?' He shakes his head. 'She seemed very flustered. I didn't like to ask.'

'How about when we go to the farm next time, I ask our priest if he will see you. After all, we are getting married there. It won't be every week but that doesn't matter. If Father mentions it to me here, I will tell him that you are continuing with the instructions at Windrush.'

Emma hears more about the curate at the next YCW meeting when Mary doesn't turn up and Joan explains quietly that there is a rumour going around that Mary and the young priest have gone off together.

'No wonder the poor housekeeper was in a state,' thinks Emma. 'I didn't think priests did that.' It is the first time that she has heard of this happening and she is quite shocked. After recovering from this news, the young women settle down, with another member offering to take over the meeting, temporarily. On the way home, Joan surprises Emma with some good news.

'I will make your wedding-dress for you, if you like. It will be my wedding present. You buy a pattern and the material and cotton.'

'Are you sure you want to? It's a big undertaking.'

'I'd love to. I've not made one before but I use the sewing-machine a lot and my mam won't mind me using our front room.'

Within two weeks, Ron goes to see the priest at Windrush.
'What is he like?' Emma asks, after his first visit.
'He is great. He gave me tobacco for my pipe and we just smoked and chatted. It was very informal.'
'Well, I'm going to test you,' a little voice pipes up. They are in the sitting-room and Miriam is very interested in hearing about why Ron is going to see a priest on Saturday afternoons.
'Go on then,' Ron encourages her.
'Who made you?' she asks, in her bossy manner. Ron looks bemused.
'My mam and dad made me.'
'No. That's wrong. God made you,' she insists, giving the pat answer from the catechism that she is learning at school. Ron smiles and Emma laughs. 'But that's the right answer,' Miriam states, adamantly.
'It is. You're just a clever little six-year-old, aren't you?' Emma concedes. Miriam gives a serious nod.

Ron has another visit to Windrush and is very relaxed about it all. The priest gives him more tobacco. Emma wonders what he is learning and Ron reassures her that they do talk about aspects of religion. On the way back to Middlesburn, on the bus, he drops a bombshell.
'I've seen a job advertised in Cheshire. I am thinking of applying for it now that I am a qualified draughtsman.' He pulls a paper-cutting from his pocket to show her the advertisement. She sees that the firm is based at the airfield at Woodford aerodrome. 'I will be able to see the planes taking off while I am working,' he says, excitedly. 'What do you think?' Emma ponders, while reading the details.
'If you get the job, we'll be living down there, won't we. I don't mind, though. We can live in a flat for a while. I can ask my manager if I can be transferred to a tax office in the area. If that is what you want, go for it.' He puts his arm around her and hugs her. 'Have you told your parents?'
'Not yet. I'll apply and if I get an interview, then I will tell them. We need to fix a wedding date. I know we suggested September, but if I'm in Cheshire, we could bring it forward, maybe at Easter.

That way, we won't be separated for very long.'
'Let's see first if you get it and then we will make our plans.'

In November, Ron is offered an interview.
'Good luck,' Emma says, as the train pulls in at Thorntees station. After Ron gets on the train, she watches until it is out of sight and walks back to her lodgings.
'It'll be good for him, you know,' says Hannah, looking at Emma's downcast face. 'You two will do all right together. He's a good lad.' It isn't until the following evening that they meet up, after he returns from his overnight stay in a Bed and Breakfast (B & B).
'How did it go?' Emma asks.
'Great. I got the job. Woodford is a beautiful place, but quite posh. We won't be buying a house there. I have to give a month's notice where I am. I start in January. They gave me the address of lodgings and I checked them out this morning, before leaving. The landlady was pleasant and I've arranged a starting date.' They hug each other tightly.
'It's so exciting but I have butterflies in my stomach,' says Emma. 'It's like an adventure. While you have been away, I have been thinking about what you said about no point in waiting until September if you get this job. I'm not sure if the Church allows marriages to take place during Lent, but this year, Easter Monday falls on April the third. That works out very well for us because getting married just before the end of the income tax year, the fifth of April, means that you will get a tax rebate by claiming the marriage allowance. It will be extra money towards our savings.' Emma's knowledge concerning income tax is considerable, having worked over three years in tax offices.
'That sounds a great idea,' Ron says. 'Will your parents be okay about it though?'
'My parents won't say anything as they know that I can get married without permission three months later when I will be twenty-one, but I suspect they will worry about it a bit. We'll go through next weekend and tell them. I want to ask my sisters to be bridesmaids. You can tell Father Jo that you won't be going anymore after Christmas.'
'Speaking of Christmas, I'll spend it at home as I was at yours last year and we will be in Cheshire next time.' Ron tells her.
'I'll still go home this year as it might be my last with my family,' Emma replies. 'I wonder if Des will be home for Christmas. It will

be lovely to meet up with him and Angela for a night out. I'll ask her next time I see her.'

The couple realise that they have a lot to do before Ron leaves in January for his new job. The following evening, Ron tells her that his parents are pleased for him getting the new job as they know how much he loves aeroplanes, but saddened to think that he is moving away. They are quite surprised about them marrying in a few months. The two of them spend the evening in Mrs Black's kitchen, making a preparation list for their forthcoming wedding. Days later, Emma goes shopping in her dinner-break.

'So much going on,' she thinks, as she ploughs through the wedding-dress patterns. She chooses a plain, V-neck, full length and slightly flared at the bottom, with fitted waist and long sleeves. 'It's very stylish and unfussy. I like it.' Choosing material is much harder but with advice from the shop assistant, she chooses white brocade. 'I also need white netting for a veil as I can make that myself,' she says, 'plus a reel of white thread suitable for a sewing-machine. I will look at bridesmaid patterns and buy the material for those, in January.' With her purchases paid for, she hurries back to work, carrying the heavy shopping. Her mam has told her that a lady in the village will make the three dresses for her sisters and Marjorie will see to Cathy's. As Martha's third baby is due in January, she wants to wait as late as possible before having her dress made because she wants to lose some excess weight after her baby is born.

'There's a letter for you,' says Hannah, as Emma is taking off her coat. 'I've put it on the table and your dinner is in the oven.'
'Thank you. I'll do your hair tomorrow if you like.' The elderly lady and young woman are very fond of each other, without being demonstrative. 'You are a lovely landlady,' Emma suddenly blurts out, feeling a little overwhelmed with the kindness. Hannah's face light's up.
'I've never had a daughter, lass, but one like you would have been a joy.' She wipes a little tear that's sliding from her eye. 'Now look what you've done,' she says, hiding her emotions. 'Go and get your dinner.' Emma smiles at her before going into the living-room where she sees the letter and recognises the hand-writing. She is surprised as she doesn't see how Faith would have found time to write, with it being two weeks before Christmas and her wedding taking place in a few days. She opens the letter. It is

short. The wedding is cancelled. There is an apology for such short
notice, but no further details. Emma is gutted for her friend.
'What can have happened? How awful. She must feel terrible. I
wonder if she will stay in Holmestown, but how courageous to call
a wedding off at this late stage. There must be a good reason.' She
picks at her dinner and although no longer feeling hungry, slowly
finishes it as she appreciates Hannah's effort with the cooking.
Later in the evening, she writes to Faith, not knowing what to say
and not wanting to go on about her own wedding.
'At least it's a letter,' she thinks, walking to a post-box, two streets
away.

Ron and Emma make a last journey to Whitby on the Saturday
before Christmas. Walking along the sea-front, hand in hand,
watching the waves pound the harbour, they chat excitedly. The air
is fresh, but chilly.
'There's a photographer shop. Let's go in and see if they do
weddings. We will need one, won't we,' says Emma. They wander
across the road and enter the shop. Half an hour later, they walk
out with smiles on their faces.
'Well, that's sorted,' says Ron. 'What else have we to do?'
'We need to find a florist to order the bouquets and button holes.'
The flowers are expensive and Emma decides two small posies
will be fine for the little girls and a small spray of carnations for
each of the older sisters. They stand in the shop and the assistant
waits patiently while they count up how many carnations they
need for buttonholes.
'Just my flowers, now,' she says. Eventually all is sorted and they
wander outside.
'Let's get fish and chips before we catch the bus. There's plenty of
time and I'm starving,' says Ron.

'I wasn't expecting you this weekend,' Mary says, as they wander
through into the farmhouse kitchen. 'We've been to Whitby. We
have had a great day. We have ordered a photographer and the
flowers,' says Emma, brimming with excitement. Tom has just
come in from milking and is pulling off his wellingtons.
'Which shops did you go to?' he asks. Emma explains. 'They'll be
too expensive. I'll order your flowers. We can go together another
Saturday. I have a mate I know and he'll give me a good deal. I
have a photographer in mind, too. You should have spoken to me.
They'll have to be cancelled.' He is annoyed at this impulsive

daughter who goes her own way at times. Emma looks crestfallen. Ron keeps quiet. Mary puts the kettle on.

'You're not seeing Father Jo this weekend, then?' she asks Ron.

'No. I told him last time that I probably wouldn't be going again. He says I can always continue when I get settled in Cheshire, but he is happy for us to marry, if I don't. He said he thinks that Emma and I will be fine.' There is tension in the air. Amy, witnessing all this, asks if anyone wants a game of cards.

'I will just make us a sandwich first. Then I'll play,' says Emma, glad to have a change of conversation. The evening passes without further reference to the wedding plans.

January has arrived. It is cold and bleak at the small railway station where Ron and Emma are making their final goodbyes.

'I'll write tonight and send you the full address,' Ron says, as he picks up his suitcase. The train is approaching. They have one last hug and Emma waves until she can no longer see him. She takes a handkerchief from her pocket and wipes her eyes. Suddenly she feels alone. No more chats in his mother's parlour or late-night hugs as he leaves her at Hannah's. She feels the tears well up.

'Be sensible,' she tells herself. 'You can do this.'

The marriage course begins and Emma and Angela meet up at St Paul's. There are a number of couples plus, Emma notices, a young woman on her own. They listen, make notes and whisper quietly. Some of the participants ask questions.

'That has been an interesting evening', says Angela. 'I'll see you in two weeks for the next one. Have you heard from Ron?'

'Yes, I've had a letter. He is enjoying working there. His digs are comfortable. He has met up with a lad called Ben who has a motor-bike and has offered to take Ron flat-hunting, as we will need somewhere to live after we are married.'

The following Monday, Emma is back at the shop where she bought the wedding-dress material and the assistant remembers her. It takes her a while to go through patterns but she finally decides on a knee-length dress with long sleeves, a sailor collar and broad ribbon around the waist to tie at the back that she thinks is ideal for the two little girls.

'Can I have enough for two dresses please, in this pink material,' she asks the assistant, quoting the size from the pattern.

'It is very delicate and pretty,' says the friendly lady, measuring and cutting the lengths needed and folding them into a neat pile. 'I'll just leave that on the counter and choose for the older bridesmaids,' Emma tells her. She decides on a slightly flared dress, knee-length again and with a large collar. She picks a pale turquoise colour. 'Can I buy head-dresses here?' The assistant shows her an array of shapes and colours. 'Two pink ones, the Alice band ones with stand-up petals, please and two to match the turquoise dresses.'

'You want machine-thread too?'

'Yes, please, one turquoise and two of the pink as different people are making the smaller two.' Emma gives a sigh of relief. That's another job done. 'I'll go Marjorie's tonight and take Cathy's. Then I will go home on Friday and take the rest.' She just wants to get things organised. The pressure is building.

'I need you to come and try on the dress,' Joan insists, as they are walking home from the YCW meeting, later in the week. I've not sewn it yet but I have pinned all the panels. I know I took your measurements but I think you have lost some weight.' Emma pulls a face.

'It's all the worry. I was nine stone, six, but now I am only nine stone. I weighed myself at my aunty's when I took the material for Cathy's bridesmaid dress. They are very happy with it, which is a relief. I will walk to yours tomorrow evening after I have eaten. I have just remembered that I meant to discuss with my manager about my transfer. I intended doing it today but was too busy.' Emma goes to bed early and writes to Faith after re-reading her last letter. Faith has moved to Royston and is staying with her sister's family. She explains in her letter that the tax offices in the London area are having difficulty finding staff and are offering jobs with a guarantee that you can be posted back to your original office after three years, if you want to return. This suited Faith as she was able to take up a position in a tax office at Hitchin in Herefordshire, not too far from her sister's family and thus fitting in well with her move from Holmestown after the wedding cancellation.

'Maybe I will get to see her again,' thinks Emma. 'I hope so.'

'So, you are getting married,' Mr Wiles says, peering at her over his steel-rimmed glasses.

'Yes, on Easter Monday. I'd like to go back to work afterwards. Is there a possibility of me being transferred to a tax office near

Stockport, please?' Emma knows that Woodford isn't far from Stockport and Ron's lodgings at Heatonfield are around that area. 'I'll look into that for you. You will be taking a week's holiday after your wedding?'

'Yes. I can return to work on the tenth.'

'I will let you know.'

'Thank you.'

The bag is heavy as Emma trudges along the lane and down into Moorbeck valley. It is almost dark and the night air is frosty. Finally walking into the farmhouse, she places her bag on the kitchen table.

'That's all the material for the dresses, Mam,' she says, wearily.

'You look tired,' comments her mother. 'We need to have a talk about your wedding. I want to discuss numbers of people coming. Your dad is taking you to Whitby tomorrow to order the flowers.' Emma sighs.

'I've come straight from work, Mam. I am tired. I'll just get a sandwich and have an early night. We can talk tomorrow.'

Next morning Emma and her mam decide to chat in the sitting-room as it is noisy in the farmhouse kitchen.

'No Miriam, stay out. We need to talk,' Mary says, sternly. 'Amy, come and take Miriam, please,' she shouts. Amy, coming up fifteen, is a bonny, dark-haired, slim teenager. She appears and grabs Miriam's hand.

'Come on, you,' she says, dragging her little sister out of the room. The door closes behind them.

'Now, let's get down to business,' Mary says, holding a notepad in her hand and with pencil poised. 'We are having the reception in the canteen at the village hall. It only holds about thirty. How many guests do Ron's parents have?' Emma thinks about this.

'Ron's parents, of course; Ron's brother, Clive and his wife, Nancy; his mam's elderly sister Mary; and his dad's brother, wife and twelve-year-old daughter. His dad has a sister and grown-up daughter but I don't know if they are asking the daughter. It depends on numbers. That makes a definite nine, possibly ten. Then there's me and Ron. I'd like Hannah and her husband to be invited, plus Marjorie, Abe, Cathy and Andy, if that's possible, please. Ron wants his fishing mate, Dan and fiancée, Barbara. Dan does photography and has offered to take some pictures for us.'

'That's nice of him,' says Mary, 'but I think your dad has asked a bloke at Whitby. Ron's friend can still take some.' Mary ponders over the numbers. 'If I add on your dad and me, your brothers and sisters and Joe; uncle Jack; and maybe aunty Maureen from Scotland, it makes thirty. I was thinking of asking Veronica who is making the dresses and isn't charging me. Also Eddy, from the village, whom we've asked if he will put ribbons on his car and pick you up and bring you back to get changed and also to be there for anyone else who might need transport. Your dad is good friends with his dad. The village ladies are doing the food but they won't expect to be asked.'

'Full house, then,' comments Emma.

'Are you happy with the list?'

'I don't really care anymore. Whatever you think, Mam. Just ask who you and dad want. I'll explain to Joan, who is making my dress, that we haven't room for more guests. She'll understand.' Mary looks at her daughter, after this outburst.

'Ask Ron's mam to make sure she is happy with the names you have given me, will you?' Emma nods as she stands up and walks out. She has had enough of all this planning. It doesn't seem like her wedding.

A little later, Tom puts his head around the door.

'Are you ready, lass? We need to be leaving.'

'Just coming, Dad,' says Emma, standing up and reaching for her coat that is hanging from the nail behind the door. She walks out and gets into the passenger seat of the van. Conversation is brief as they travel to Whitby. She goes through the ordering of flowers as before. The man is very helpful and explains that prices vary, depending on the choice of flower and the time of year.

'I don't need a large bouquet and neither do the two older bridesmaids. Let's keep the price down,' she says. Her dad nods. 'Two little poises with a mix of small, spring flowers will be fine for the two young bridesmaids. You count the buttonholes, Dad. Ron's mam will want one.'

'Aye, lass; I did all this for your sister.'

Afterwards, Tom wants his couple of pints in The Wellington. He is greeted as he goes in, as it is his local when he goes to Whitby. Emma has a glass of lemonade and sits quietly, listening, while the farmers discuss their livestock and weather conditions. She thinks about Ron and wishes she was with him.

Later in the day, Emma walks to Martha's place.

'You look like you are ready to have that baby,' she says, on greeting her sister.

'I am. I'm weary. Let's have a cuppa. I can do with a sit down.' Sandra looks up from playing with her dollies.

'She is such a bonny little girl. Her hair is almost ginger, isn't it?' Emma states. Sandra has a chubby face with thick, wavy hair and bright blue eyes. Martha nods.

'It is. Brian is darker. He is a freckle-faced little charmer.' They look at the little boy busily playing with his cars, putting them into a small, wooden, home-made garage. 'He is nearly walking,' continues Martha. 'I'll be glad when he does. He is a hefty lump to carry. Did you clear with your manager about coming to stay a week when I have the baby?'

'Yes, he is fine about it. Get someone to write as soon as you go into labour. I'll be here in a day or so. Something else I want to mention. You said you'd make our wedding cake. Are you still okay about that? How are you going to fit it in with your busy life?'

'I've already made the cakes for the three tiers. They will be better for eating, being kept a while. I will ice them much nearer the time. Don't be worrying about that. Also, I did mention that you can borrow my tiara if you like. It will save you buying one.'

'Thanks, Martha. I'll do that. It's a relief about the wedding cake, too. All this organising is hard work. I have given mam the material for the bridesmaids' dresses and asked her to have your dress done last.' The two sisters talk until teatime when Emma makes her goodbyes and wanders back home.

The week off looking after Martha and the little ones is hectic, after which Emma is ready to return to work. Ron has written to say he's coming home early in February as he wants to take his bike back in order to use it to cycle to work. She meets him at the railway station on the Saturday and receives a big hug and kiss. They spend the day in town looking at wedding rings.

'Just a plain, thin, gold one will be fine,' Emma says. 'I'd rather keep the money towards a house deposit.' The weekend passes all too quickly and in a very short time, it seems to Emma, they are back at the station.

'Won't be long, now,' Ron says, trying to console her. 'I need to put the bike in the guards van,' he explains, as the train pulls in. 'I will let you know as soon as I've found a flat and you can come and stay somewhere and we'll look at it together.' Emma fights the tears as she waves goodbye.

The wedding preparation talks are continuing, giving Emma the chance to catch up with Angela.
'Has Ron found a Catholic church where he is staying?' asks Angela.
'No. He doesn't feel that he needs to, as Father Jo says he can get married. He has been looking at one or two flats though, but hasn't found anything suitable yet. I've been thinking. I will have to go shopping for something to wear to go away in. I'll be glad when it's all over and it is just me and Ron together. Changing the subject, how about coming to the farm next Sunday? I'll be home.'
'I'd like that. It will be something different to do while Des is away.'

Emma arranges for her brother Mark, who has the use of Tom's van, to pick up Angela at the road end where she gets off the bus. She arrives late Sunday morning and the family all sit down to a Sunday dinner.
'Have you been to church? Tom asks her.
'No. I caught the bus here instead.'
'Well, you can go into Whitby after tea, with Mark, if you like and go to Mass there with him and catch a bus back to Middlesburn from Whitby.' Angela is surprised at this but feels she has to accept the offer and utters her thanks. Later when walking along the pasture with Emma and her younger siblings, Angela mentions it.
'I was going to travel back with you but feel I will have to go with your brother now.'
'Yes. I'm sorry about that. That's my dad, thinking he is doing the best for you as he wouldn't want you missing church, just to visit us.'

During the next week, another dinner-time is taken up shopping.
'That is a smart two-piece,' Emma thinks, as she watches the shop assistant wrapping it up; a knee-length skirt and box jacket, mottled light-green and white. 'It is just perfect for springtime. I hope Ron likes it.' She has something else on her mind and coming out of the shop, she glances at the town hall clock. 'It is too late today, but I'll go tomorrow unless Mr Turnbull wants his books changing,' she thinks. Emma asks him the next morning, but

he doesn't.

'I'll miss you,' he says. 'I will have to find someone else. It has been great for me having you change my library books and do other odd pieces of shopping, sometimes. I hope you and Ron are very happy as I'm sure you will be. I wish you both the best of luck.' Dinner-time arrives and Emma puts her plan into action. She makes her way to the Cathedral at the bottom end of the town. It is a very old building, dark and gloomy inside, often with flickering candles that have been lit at morning Mass by a few regulars who attend. Emma finds sitting quietly alone, in church, very comforting. She doesn't tell anyone that she is doing this but has been a number of times and finds it helps her when pondering about whether or not she is making the right decision, marrying Ron, a non-Catholic and moving away from family and friends. 'Maybe I'll get an answer,' she thinks. She knows the answer she wants. She takes out her rosary beads and prays.

That night, sitting on her bed, she writes a long letter to Ron. One of her tears falls onto the paper and she rings it with her pen and tells Ron what it is. She'd been earlier to see Joan for another fitting of her dress.

'You've lost more weight,' Joan says to her, almost accusingly.

'I know. I'm down to eight and a half stone. I think it is all the stress. I can't eat properly.'

'Well, don't lose any more,' admonishes Joan.

'I'll try not to,' Emma replies. She doesn't tell Ron in her letter about this as he is worried enough over where they are going to live. She tells him about giving an advert to the lady in the corner shop, to sell her bike. The advert was placed in the window for all to see. Within days, a buyer makes enquiries and offers Emma a little less than the asking price and Emma agrees; and glad to see it go, as it is one less worry for her.

Another week passes before Ron's letter arrives. *If you can come down next Saturday, we can view two flats, either of which will be all right, I think. I'll book you into a B & B, nearby. I can't wait to see you...* Emma hasn't done much train travelling but remembers to take a book to read on the journey to Manchester Piccadilly station. On arriving, she walks along the platform amidst many others scurrying along. She heads towards the centre of the station to study the very large display board denoting all the train times, as she wants the platform number of the Heaton Chapel service, the station quite close to where Ron is living. After a short journey, she arrives and spies Ron at the end of the small platform. She is so happy that she almost cries. He hugs her and takes her small overnight case and they walk together hand-in-hand out of the station and along the pavement.

'Have you eaten?' he asks.

'I ate my packed sandwiches on the train.'

'That's good. We'll go to your boarding-house to leave your case and then walk to the flat that I have found at Heatonburn. It's not far. Is that all right?'

'It's fine. I'm just so happy to be with you.'

Soon, they are ringing the doorbell of a large, old, red brick, very tall, terraced house. A small, middle-aged lady opens the door. She pushes a strand of hair away from her face. Her hair is shoulder-length and a mixture of grey and brown.

'This must be your fiancée,' she says to Ron. 'I'm pleased to meet you. It's Emma, isn't it,' she states, looking at her. I'm Mrs Maughan. Just follow me.' After climbing three flights of stairs, they walk into an attic living-room. 'There are two bedrooms but the second bedroom is quite small. You share the toilet on the next floor down. The bath is in the kitchen, covered by a sheet of wood which can act as a table, but you'll see that there is a table at the far end of this living-room where you will probably want to eat. You can use the twin-tub downstairs in the scullery for your washing and you will find a bag of pegs there if you wish to hang the clothes out in the garden. I'm sorry that there is no television in here but there is a wireless. In the small bedroom are spare sheets, pillowcases and blankets in case you have visitors. I'll leave you to have a look around.' She disappears and Emma walks into the kitchen.

'It's very small but it will do for us two. Come and look at this, Ron,' she calls. He squeezes into the kitchen and together they examine what looks like a small cupboard the size of a bedside cabinet but the front has a door of very fine mesh. There are two shelves inside. 'I think it is a meat safe,' says Emma. 'It's to keep the flies from getting at the meat and other such products.' They re-enter the living-room that is long and narrow, with two fireside chairs and a well-worn, brown, three-seater settee. 'It is very clean and fresh, isn't it,' she comments to Ron. 'It is reasonably priced too. I think it will be all right. It's not far from the station which is good, as I will have to catch a train into Manchester for work. I

have been given a transfer to Salford tax office. I'll have to have a dummy run after our honeymoon, to find it, before I actually start.'
'Speaking of honeymoons, is it okay if I book a place in Chester?' Ron asks. Emma looks at him.
'Any reason in particular?'
'It's an old Roman town and I went once, a few years ago, with the ATC, but I'd love to go back and explore it more.' She laughs.
'Is this going to be married life, with you and the Romans?' He grins.
'Not all the time. Let's go. My landlady says you can come for the evening meal, before you go to your B & B.'

The next morning, Emma is up early and goes to church, having found out where it is, from the owner of the boarding-house. St Winifred's looks modern and is light and spacious. She walks halfway down the centre aisle and genuflects, before sliding into a bench. It is all so familiar, with the candles, the Stations of the Cross, the confessional boxes and the little red light permanently glowing. The Mass is in Latin and she doesn't have her prayer book with her but she follows it with ease. She knows a lot of the Latin responses by heart, having had plenty of practise with almost daily Mass at boarding-school. Feeling happier, she makes her way back to the B & B for breakfast and checks out, as she is going back home today. Ron is walking out of his lodgings as she arrives. He gives her another hug and kiss, before he takes her case.
'It's what I have been missing,' she says, smiling at him. They catch a train to Cheadle Hulme to view the second flat, but it is smaller than the first one and more expensive.
'I'll go back to Heatonburn after you leave and tell the owner that we will take the flat,' says Ron, 'now that we are both agreed on it. You don't have to go back to Manchester for the train home, you know. You can catch it at Whaley Bridge. I'll go with you that far.'
'Isn't that a chew for you?'
'No. I've nothing else to do. Come on. Let's find a nice pub and have a meal together before you go.'

Moments later, they walk into The Huntsman, well-named as there are lots of framed pictures of fox-hunting on the walls, signed by a local author.
'I love scampi and chips,' Emma tells Ron. 'It is such a treat to eat

out. I found the church, by the way. It will be a walk from our flat but you won't mind me going, will you?'

'Not at all. I might even come with you. Who knows,' Ron replies. 'Changing the subject, I made enquiries and I've been to an ATC meeting. I am joining as a civilian instructor. I also went to Manchester one Saturday to have a look around and found the Young Men's Christian Association (YMCA) up a little side street. I joined and have taken up sword-fencing. It's great fun.' The couple, wrapped up in each other, continue talking until it is time to leave for the train station. Ron buys two tickets and within minutes, the train pulls up. On arriving at Whaley Bridge, they leave that train to await the one from Manchester. 'I'll see you in a few days,' Ron says, passing Emma her case. He watches on the platform and waves until the train disappears.

Goodbyes at the office are short as Emma doesn't want a fuss. It is Maundy Thursday and the tax office is closed on Good Friday. Emma has decided to return to the farm on the Saturday. She walks around to Joan's, after the three o'clock service on Good Friday, to pick up her wedding-dress. It is very heavy.

'When you come back to visit, get in touch,' says Joan. 'YCW won't be the same without you.'

'Thanks again for this. You have done a great job. Please thank your mam for the use of her front room.'

'I will. I think she is very relieved that it is finally finished and she will get her room back. I hope all goes well on Monday,' she says, as Emma leaves.

Emma feels despondent, saying goodbye to everyone. She'd visited Angela a couple of nights ago and they promised each other that they'd keep in touch. On returning to her lodgings, she packs her home-made short veil; her dress; and her small-heeled, white satin shoes. She needs to pick up her tiara from Martha, when she goes home.

'Here you are,' Hannah says, coming into her bedroom and giving her a beautifully embossed white table-cloth. 'And no daft tears,' she adds, but they are both teary. 'You've been like a daughter to me. If you ever come back up, come and see me. I won't be coming to your wedding, though. Cyril wouldn't have come, anyway.' Emma is disappointed on receiving the news even though she understands.

'It's not Hannah's scene, either,' she thinks, 'having to socialise with people she doesn't know.'

'You can always write, you know,' Hannah says. Emma gives her a gentle hug, not something she usually does with Hannah, who becomes emotional and fishes for a hankie to wipe her eyes.

'I'm just going to visit my aunty,' says Emma. 'I promised Cathy that I would call in tonight to look at her bridesmaid dress, but I won't be long.'

It is later in the evening when she arrives at Marjorie's. Abe opens the door.

'Come in,' he says, but he doesn't look happy.

'Is something the matter?' questions Emma.

'Marjorie will tell you.' Marjorie gets up from the settee. She looks upset.

'What's wrong?' Emma asks, with a sinking feeling in her stomach.

'I am so, so sorry but we can't come to your wedding. Cathy has the measles and Andy is sickening too.' Emma's face drops.

'But she's my bridesmaid,' she states, as if somehow that will make a difference. The news is sinking in. Emma sits down. It is the final straw. She wants to cry.

'Take the dress and maybe your dad will find a little girl in the village to wear it. You can always have it returned to us later so that we can take a photo of Cathy and Andy in their wedding outfits, when they are better.'

'I'll go then as I don't want to miss the last bus back to Thorntees,' she says, rising to her feet. Marjorie hands the package to her and wrapping her arms around her niece, hugs her tightly and kisses her.

'Don't forget to visit us when you come back up.' Emma nods. She is too upset to speak. Even Abe, who is not usually demonstrative with her, places his arm around her. She stumbles out of the door and makes her way to the bus stop.

Later that evening, tossing about in bed and unable to sleep, Emma wonders if it is all worthwhile. Should she just give up? She feels drained and despondent. Maybe it is a big mistake.

'Don't think like that,' she tells herself. 'You didn't get a negative feeling when you prayed.' She curls herself into a ball and hugs her pillow, her salty tears soaking in.

Spring 1961

'Emma. Emma.' The voice is coming from downstairs. 'You really need to get up.' Emma slowly opens her eyes at the sound of her mother's voice.

'It is today,' she realises. 'It is finally here.' She recalls how, on arriving home on Saturday, laden with bags and her case, she'd blurted out her disappointment.

'I'll go down to Blue Hill farm, in t' village,' her dad immediately said. 'They have a couple of little lasses around Miriam's age. One of them can be a bridesmaid for you. Their mam and dad will be only too pleased to help.' On the Sunday, after church, she'd gone with Tom and he'd explained her dilemma. Two fair-haired little girls sat listening with eyes aglow.

'I'll tell you what,' their mam said. 'You two go on home for your dinner. I'll try the dress on them and I'll turn up tomorrow at church with one of these two. They both have white sandals from last year. Don't worry, Emma. It'll be all right. You can stop worrying.'

'Bring the two of them and come into the canteen afterwards. There will be spare places now. We can fit you in,' Tom replied.

'Come on, lass. Let's go.' On the way home, there was more good news. 'One of my sheep has just given birth to twins,' Tom explained and Emma remembered wondering about where the conversation was going. 'As a wedding present, I'll give you and Ron a lamb each but I'll rear them and in t' autumn when I sell them, you can have money. You can put it towards your savings you were telling me about, for a deposit on a house. I'll get money from mother's fleece.' Emma remembers thanking her dad for such generosity and for sorting out the bridesmaid problem.

'But that was yesterday,' thinks Emma, crawling out of bed and putting an old, worn, grey cardigan around her shoulders. Today she is feeling nervous again. Mary appears in the bedroom.

'Emma, it is time you were getting ready. I know it is traditional for a bride to be late but you need to get a move-on.' Emma follows Mary downstairs. Her five siblings are busy eating.

'I don't think I can eat anything, Mam. I will just have a cup of tea.'

'You must eat a little, even if it is only half a slice of bread.' Tom walks in, from milking.

'Hurry up, you bairns,' he says. 'You need to be getting ready.'

Miriam is now prancing around, having finished her breakfast. Amy stands up.

'You come with me and I'll help you into your bridesmaid dress,' she says to her little sister.

With all her packing done the night before, Emma takes down her wedding-dress from behind the door and puts it on. She feels sick but knows it will soon be over and she will be on the train to Chester with Ron. They'd seen each other last night.

'Not what the couple are supposed to do on the night before their wedding', she'd said to him, 'but I don't really care.' Ron had kissed her goodnight before making his way to Martha's where he was staying.

'Aren't you putting any make-up on?' her mother asks, seeing her daughter walk into the farmhouse kitchen in her white, full-length wedding-dress.

'I don't wear it. Ron likes me as I am.'

'Well, maybe a touch of lipstick, then. It is a special day, after all. A bit of blusher, too. You look very pale this morning.' Emma obliges, before putting on her short veil and tiara.

'That's better,' states her mother, before shooing Miriam and Jacob outside to their dad, who is revving up his van.

Barely minutes after the family leave, there is the noise of a car pulling up and then Eddy knocking at the door. Emma has known him since her childhood as he's not much older than her. He grins sheepishly, conscious that he's dressed in a suit which is most unlike him and with his brown, wavy hair, neatly combed back. He is a quiet lad. Two long, white ribbons decorate his small, black car. She steps out, gingerly, holding her wedding-dress off the ground so as not to get it dirty.

'Thanks for this,' she says, as he is pulling away. It is a two-mile ride but Eddy puts on the brake at each of the four gates out of Moorbeck, gets out of the car, opens the gate, drives through and afterwards, closes it, adding many minutes to the journey.

'Wouldn't want you to get your dress dirty,' he says. Parking on the roadside outside the wooden gate that leads down the path to the church, Emma climbs carefully out of the car and sees her dad waiting.

'This is it,' she thinks. Her stomach lurches. 'Just take deep breaths,' she tells herself.

The next hour or so passes in a blur for Emma. She whispers her vows. Father Jo looks at her in the sacristy when they sign the register and when realising how nervous she is, decides to keep quiet for fearing of upsetting her. She manages the smiles outside in the slightly chilly air. It seems to her that she has a fixed, artificial smile on her face.

Wedding: Ron and Emma

'Isn't the bride saying few words?' Ron's aunty Bridget asks, after the speeches are given, but Emma shakes her head. After the meal, Eddy drives her back to the farm to change out of her wedding-dress, but Ron stays with the guests as he is travelling in his smart, black suit. The guests have all congregated at The Hunters Lodge where Emma joins them and finds herself a corner, next to Mary and Amy. Joe has taken Martha home with her three little ones as the baby needed feeding, but he is returning. The guests are scattered across two adjoining rooms, with a walk-through open door and each with access to the bar.

'Where is the bride hiding then?' an aunty asks, walking towards Emma. Mary whispers to her daughter.

'You should really be circulating with everyone. Your suit is very smart by the way, but don't be losing any more weight.' Emma stands up and graciously eases her way out of the corner and chats to this aunt of Ron's. She glances at the large, black clock on the wall above the bar.

'Not much longer,' she thinks. Joe, Martha's husband, is taking them to Darlington to catch their train.

'Come outside, everyone. It is time to wave them off,' Clive calls. Emma retrieves her case from the boot of Eddy's car and transfers it to Joe's. Rainbow-coloured confetti is being tossed over them. Miriam loves throwing it and Jacob grins as he pours a boxful over Emma.

'You little scamp', she says, brushing it out of her hair. Just before getting into the car, she spies her dad looking at her, rather seriously. She walks over and hugs him and is almost in tears when returning to Joe's car.

'Are you okay?' Ron asks, as she slips in beside him. She nods, rubs her eyes and waves as the car moves.

'I'll be all right now,' she says, smiling at him.

In the Ladies toilet at the railway station, Emma combs her hair and is amused to see a circle of confetti on the floor. She is excitedly happy, bubbling inside. She joins Ron on the platform and they hear the train in the distance.

'I'll leave you now,' says Joe, who has been talking to Ron while awaiting Emma's return. 'You are welcome anytime if you want to come and stay a few days. Martha will love to see you.' With that, he saunters down the platform to the exit.

'Finally, alone,' says Ron, smiling at his wife. 'Come along, Mrs Harding.' He picks up her case as well as his and they wait for the train to stop and the doors opening, before mounting the steps.

After he puts the heavy cases into the luggage rack, they move down the aisles looking for two seats together, the train being quite full.

'Here,' says Emma. They slide in and snuggle up, content to be alone at last. It seems minutes later when the train pulls into York station.

'We change here for the Leeds train,' explains Ron, as they shuffle along the aisle to the luggage rack. Their next train is already waiting on a different platform. 'It's a longer stretch this time,' he says, 'before our next change.' After Leeds, they have another change at Manchester Piccadilly before they finally arrive in Chester. 'We will have to get a taxi now,' Ron says.

The weather is deteriorating with light rain already falling as they leave the station and approach the taxi rank.

'Is it far?' Emma asks.

'No, not too far, as I thought it best to be within walking distance of the town centre. I hope the weather improves.' Emma can't remember ever being in a taxi, apart from back home where a local bloke ran one that a gang of them would pile into, occasionally, when returning from a dance. She finds this one quite a novelty. She is hungry and tired after such a strenuous day. The taxi pulls up about half-way down a street that displays many B & B signs. Ron pays the driver who is putting their luggage on the pavement. They pick it up and approach the green door at number sixty-six. The landlady, who is young and pretty with long, blonde, wavy hair and sparkling blue eyes, shows them to a large bedroom on the first floor.

'We give this bedroom to our special guests. You are just married, aren't you?' They nod. 'You look very young. I hope you enjoy your stay with us. Dinner is at seven.'

'Did you book the dinner?' Emma asks. 'I thought this was just for sleeping and breakfast.'

'I did. She said we can do that for any evening and pay the extra. I only booked the one for tonight.'

Much later, after an excellent meal, Ron and Emma decide to join others in the sitting-room watching a film on television, but before doing so, they look at the leaflets arranged in the rack near the entrance. Ron takes one that gives directions to places of interest. On entering the room, they choose a comfy two-seater and sit close together, Ron slides his hand into Emma's. He is very tired. He studies the leaflet while waiting for the film to start. The film is one that he has seen before and a few minutes before the end, he whispers to Emma.

'I'm going up.'

'I just want to watch the end. I won't be long.' She is enthralled by it. One other guest is still sitting and looks at her in surprise when she doesn't follow Ron.

'It's a great film, but my husband has seen it before,' she feels obliged to say.

When Emma joins Ron, he is unpacking his clothes.

'I'll just have a wash and clean my teeth,' she says, picking up her toiletry bag. Ron arrives at the bathroom as she is leaving. She undresses and putting on her short, cotton, pink nighty with lacy trimmings, slowly climbs into bed and slides her feet down, but they will only go half-way. 'What's happened here?' she exclaims, just as Ron is re-entering the room. 'My feet won't go down.' She climbs out of bed and examines the sheets. 'They have made an apple-pie bed. I know about these from books I've read, where the bottom sheet is turned back up half-way to make the top sheet.' Investigating further, she finds another sheet underneath and she remakes the bed.' Climbing back in, she notices Ron on his hands and knees, looking under the bed. 'What are you doing?'

'I thought as much,' he says, grinning at her. 'They have tied three, old, large, empty tins to the underside. I've read about things like this.'

'Whatever for?' asks Emma, naively.

'So that when the bed is disturbed, they rattle.' Emma blushes at this revelation.

'Shall I give them a good shake, for fun?' he asks.

'No. I'll be so embarrassed tomorrow morning if you do that.'

'Okay. Have you any scissors, please?' Emma gets out of bed and picking up her toiletry bag, takes out her nail scissors and hands them to him.

'Will these do?'

'Probably. I'll give them a go, cutting the string.'

'Interesting start to our married life,' Emma thinks, climbing back into bed.

'I hope you didn't mind our little joke?' the landlady greets them, the following morning, as they enter the dining-room. They smile.

'No, we didn't. We thought it was funny,' Ron says. Emma sheepishly lowers her head. A gentleman with bushy, brown hair and a big moustache, smiles at them from the next table.

'You look about seventeen,' he says to Ron, 'and far too young to be married.'

'I'm actually nearly twenty-two,' Ron replies, 'and Emma is twenty-one later this year.' She is gazing at the window, watching the raindrops running down the panes.

'Not the best of weather,' she says to Ron. 'We don't have umbrellas either.' The owner is passing and overhears her.

'There are plenty in the lobby. Just help yourselves and please return them afterwards.'

'Thank you,' says Ron. 'That's good, isn't it,' he says to Emma. 'We can walk out to a museum today. There are a number in Chester. When I came here with the ATC, we never visited the museums. I've been looking them up in that leaflet. Have you been to one, before?' Emma shakes her head.

Two hours of their first day on honeymoon are spent wandering around inside a museum. It is very large and on two floors. Ron loves the Roman period and is soon absorbed looking at pieces of stone and other small items, all neatly catalogued. Emma mooches around. History was not her favourite subject at school but she finds some items of interest. She is just happy to be with Ron. She knows he is enjoying their time together as well as pursuing his interest in the Roman period. Every so often, Ron seeks Emma out.

'Are you oaky with this?' he asks, worried that she might have had enough, but she smiles at him and nods her head.

'It is amazing all the different things in here,' she replies. Towards one o'clock, she suggests looking for a café for tea and sandwiches. Luckily, after only a short walk, they stumble across one.

'I haven't finished at the museum,' Ron tells her, over their sandwiches. 'We might as well go back as it is still raining. Is that all right with you?'

'I don't mind. It's not much fun walking about outside. I haven't been up to the first floor yet. The weather might improve tomorrow.'

'We'll find a café later and have a cooked meal,' Ron replies. 'It's fun eating out together.'

The rain clears in the afternoon and after their early evening meal, they saunter along the streets of Chester, quite content in each other's company. The walk leads them to a park and they wander inside, eventually coming across a bench in a secluded area. The seat is still a little damp at one end but the other end is dry and they sit down. Soon Ron has his arm around Emma and begins kissing her. She responds and snuggles up to him. Oblivious of the time, they are only disturbed when hearing the loud voice of a park-keeper shouting at them. He is broad and beefy and looks quite threatening as he approaches them.

'Come on. Out you go. This part isn't for that sort of thing. Can't you read? It's closing time, too. Young folks today have no respect,' he adds, as he turns away. On standing up and smoothing down their coats, they watch him wandering further across the park, before making their way to the exit. Only then does Emma see the notice.

'It's a special area for people who are bereaved, to have some quiet time,' she says, reading the notice. 'No wonder he was annoyed. That'll be why it is secluded. I didn't realise the park closed so early, either.'

'It's not that early, actually,' says Ron. 'We'll go back now, I think.' They hold hands and smile at each other. Although they feel slightly abashed, the keeper's angry words have not quenched their joy.

As the rain continues each day, the pattern is set. They explore museums, or walk the streets finding places of interest when the rain eases. On Wednesday evening, after their meal in the café, which has become a familiar venue, they go to the pictures.

'You'll enjoy it,' says Ron, enthusiastically. 'Elvis Presley in *G I Blues*. You like musicals, I know.' Emma is thrilled. On the Thursday when the rain subsides, they venture out on a boat on the river Dee. Emma, wearing her smart, green coat, prefers to be on solid ground, but happy to go as Ron enthuses about it. He has his camera with him and takes photos of her, and she likewise, takes a couple of Ron. Such a great week she is having with no work and being with Ron. She loves eating at the little café, a novelty for her.

'I'll get the photos developed at Boots when we go back to our flat,' he says.

'Our flat,' Emma thinks. 'That sounds impressive. Who would have thought it?' She is forever being amazed at the turn of her life.

On Saturday morning, after walking many streets, they find a fifth museum. It is very small and little of interest catches Ron's attention. 'Let's go,' says Emma, 'if you have seen all you want.'

They wander out, back to the boarding-house, to collect their bags and cases, the owner having told them that they could leave them there while having their last walk around Chester. The sun is shining. 'Just when we're leaving,' she says to Ron, 'but never

Honeymoon: Emma on the Dee

mind; I'm looking forward to getting to our flat. Let's have a cooked meal at the café. We have plenty of time before we catch our train. The little café has been their haunt all week, with sandwiches at midday and cheap, cooked meals at tea-time. 'I'm going to miss you two,' the waitress says, as they leave. 'I wish you both, good luck.'

After changing at Crewe, Ron and Emma finally arrive at Heaton Chapel station. They collect their luggage and wander down the short platform to the exit.

'I'm glad it's not far,' Emma says, as they saunter along the pavements. 'This case seems to get heavier by the minute.' Finally arriving at the flat in Heatonburn, they ring the doorbell.

'Hello again,' Mrs Maughan greets them. 'A happily married couple now, I take it.' They step inside and she gives them two keys. 'I thought you might want one each, with both of you working. If you have any problems, let me know.'

'When did you bring your bike? Emma asks, noticing it further along the corridor.

'Before I left my lodgings; Mrs Maughan was very good about it.' Arriving at the top floor, they open the living-room door and walk in.

'Look at that,' says Emma. 'She has set our tea out. What a welcome.' She is very touched at this kind gesture seeing the table laden with sandwiches and cake. 'She has even left us some milk,' she adds, on inspecting the small kitchen. 'Maybe we should walk out and buy a few items of food to keep us going, before the shops shut. There will be time before tea.'

The next day being Sunday, Emma is up early as she wants to go to church.

'I think I'll come with you,' Ron says, over breakfast.

'Will you really?' Emma responds, her eyes lightening up. 'That will be lovely.'

'I've never been to a Catholic service. You'll have to keep me straight.'

'You'll be fine. Don't worry. Just sit, stand and kneel, when I do. No-one will bother you.' On arriving at the church, Ron watches as, just inside the church door, Emma dips her hand into the holy water stoup and crosses herself. This time, Ron decides to ask questions; unlike his first visit to a Catholic church when taking in the surroundings was sufficient for him.

'What are you doing?' he asks.

'I'll explain afterwards,' she whispers. She doesn't want to go into a lengthy explanation with people milling around her. 'A new experience,' she thinks, 'being with Ron at church, making me think about the things I take for granted, having been doing them all my life.' She walks half-way down the centre aisle before genuflecting, while Ron hovers beside her.

'Why do you go down on one knee?' he questions. 'There is no priest on the altar.'

'We don't do it to the priest,' she replies, pondering over what to say next, with Ron waiting expectantly for an answer. A bell rings and the priest, his golden robes flowing, as it is the period of Easter in the Catholic calendar and the colour of priests' vestments help to identify this joyous season, walks onto the altar. He is followed by a retinue of altar-boys wearing their white surpluses over long, black cassocks. 'I'll tell you later,' she says, softly, taking her Sunday missal from her handbag.

During Mass, which is said in Latin, Emma keeps pointing out to Ron, where they are up to, as her book gives both the English and the Latin, enabling anyone to follow easily. Ron is mesmerised by it all, the standing, the kneeling, the sitting, the quiet periods except for the priest intoning in Latin and also bells ringing at certain times. Then there are responses in Latin by the congregation with Emma joining in and towards the end, people crowding down the aisles to kneel at the altar-rails for Communion, with an altar-boy holding a paten under each recipient's chin.

'Why does he do that?' Ron whispers.

'To catch the Host, in case it's dropped, I think,' Emma replies. As she hasn't fasted for three hours as the rules require and therefore not allowed to receive Communion, she stays in her bench. People squeeze past them to go to the altar rails. 'I'm just going to light a candle,' she says to Ron, after the priest and altar-boys have filed off the altar.

'Why?' he asks.

'I light one for a special intention. I pray and it's like my prayer goes up to heaven as the smoke spirals upwards and as long as the candle is burning, my prayer is being heard.' Emma pauses. She is not sure if that is the correct explanation but she thinks it sounds about right.

On the way back to the flat, Ron has many questions and Emma tries valiantly to answer them.

'It's mind-blowing,' he says at one point, actually being there, but very interesting. 'I want to understand more so that I can feel closer to you and I know it means a lot to you.' She is very touched at this and hugs him.

'Will you be going again?' she asks.

'I will probably come each week unless I have an ATC meeting on a Sunday. I have found out where the nearest one is and I am going to one this week. Meanwhile, we'd better have our dinner now,' he adds, on arriving at the flat, 'as we are going to find your tax office this afternoon, like we planned.'

It is mid-afternoon when they catch the train from Heaton Chapel station. The journey is only about ten minutes before arriving at Piccadilly station in Manchester.

'I bought a street map when I was shopping yesterday. We have to walk through Manchester to the Salford area,' Emma explains to Ron. 'It's this way.' She finds it an interesting walk peering into shop-windows, as she hasn't been to Manchester before. They follow the map until a road takes them to a rundown area of terraced housing with some houses boarded up and others with blinds drawn. The paint work is flaking on many and Emma notices a couple of broken window-panes. On the corner, at the end of the long road, is a small shop and they go inside and buy polo mints and fruit gums. After a little further, wandering, they find what they are looking for: The Offices of the Inland Revenue. The building is old and looks rather dilapidated. 'It's good that we have found it. At least I know how to get here. It is a decent walk. Twenty minutes to half-an-hour,' Emma says.

'Look over there,' Ron says, pointing his finger, 'at that old-looking building. It's Strangeways prison. It is on your map.' They both gaze at the large building in the distance. 'Let's hope they don't have any escapees. You might get invaded,' he adds. Emma laughs.

'Come on. Let's get back,' she says. 'We've had a very interesting day. I can do with a quiet listen to the wireless or a read.'

It is mid-week, when Ron leaves after their evening meal, to go to his ATC meeting. Emma decides to write some letters, firstly to Ron's parents to reassure them that everything is fine, that they've settled in nicely and that she has started work at the tax office; and then to her parents with similar news, adding that Ron went to church with her. She knows that will please them. After having written those letters, she enjoys penning a long one to Faith, asking how she is and telling her about the tax office in Salford. *We even have prison wardens from Strangeways, coming into our canteen, with bunches of keys hanging from their waists. We can see the prison from our office...,* she writes. She scrawls a letter to Martha, thanking her and Joe for all their support over the wedding and telling them about the flat.

'Who else should I write to?' she thinks, before remembering that Angela might like a letter with Des being away. 'That will do,' she decides, on finishing Angela's. She glances at the clock. Ron is late. 'I hope he's all right.' She makes herself a cup of tea and switches on the wireless, twiddling with the knobs to find a chat programme with popular songs to enjoy. Another hour passes and Emma is worried. 'Where can he be?' She turns the wireless off and tries to read, but cannot concentrate. 'What if something has happened? What will I do? I don't know anyone to turn to.' It is half-past eleven when Ron walks into the living-room. 'Where have you been? I have been so worried.' Emma is on the verge of tears, even though relieved.

'I stayed back to talk and the instructor took me for a drink, before dropping me off. I should have thought on. Sorry.' He hugs her. 'I won't do it again.'

'I don't mind if I know. Just tell me next time.' The mini-upset is soon over but Emma dwells on it for a while and she realises how alone she'd felt away from family and friends when things go wrong. 'When we have our own house, I will get to know the neighbours and I will be fine,' she reassures herself.

A couple of weeks later, the postman delivers a parcel and inside it, a letter from Mary thanking Emma for her letter. *I've enclosed the wedding photo proofs and a price list in case you want to order any,* she writes. *I posted the bridesmaid dress, head-dress and flower posy to Marjorie as you requested. I know she wanted to take a picture of Cathy in her bridesmaid outfit. Miriam and Jacob are missing you and Amy was very upset. I found her upstairs crying the day after your wedding and she kept saying, 'She's gone. She's gone.' Maybe you can write to her...* After discussing the wedding photos with Ron, Emma writes to her mother, thanking her for sending the little booklet of proofs and explaining that Ron's friend Dan has sent some slightly larger ones, a wedding present from him and Barbara. The proofs are small, only four and a half inches by three and a half, but there are twenty-one and Emma and Ron agree that they are very clear and are all that they need. *We've decided that we don't want to order any photos,* she writes. *The proofs are fine for us to keep. We can't afford an album or to get enlargements. We're happy with these and the ones Dan took, but thanks again for sending them. I've enclosed a letter to Amy. I'll pick up my wedding-dress next time we come, unless, of course, you and dad decide to visit us and then you can bring it. There is a spare bedroom...* She signs off, *with love.*

Ron and Emma settle into a routine of weekday work, with shopping and church at weekends. After receiving a reply from her previous letter to his parents, Emma writes again. His mam writes back within a few days and mentions that she'd appreciate a few lines from Ron. Emma has just finished reading the letter when he walks into the living-room, having had a sleep-in as it is a Saturday morning.

'You really need to add something at the bottom of my letter, next time I write to your mother. I've just been reading her latest one that arrived this morning. Here,' she says, passing it to her husband. He reads through the letter, before responding.

'You are right. I will. I just think you are better at writing than me. Your letters are probably more interesting.'

'It will please her, though. You know, I feel queasy,' Emma says. 'I have felt like this for a few days. I feel unwell and I'm tired, too. I don't know what's wrong with me. I must have picked up a bug or something.' She feels better as the day goes on and sees to the washing, hanging it in the garden as it is a lovely sunny morning and quite warm, being late in May. The flowers are everywhere and bushes of pink peonies and lilac add colour to the greenery.

After tea, they leave for a live show at a theatre on the outskirts of Manchester. Ron had gone into the city to have a look around, one Saturday, a week or so before they were married. He'd spotted the tickets on sale for *As You Like It* and never having been to a live show, bought a couple.

'A surprise for Emma,' he'd thought at the time, knowing that she'd studied the play at school but told him that she has never been to a theatre to see a Shakespearean play. It is a night out that they have both been looking forward to. The theatre is small but very smart with plush, brown velvet curtains hanging across the stage. The chairs are comfy and the dim lights from four corners of the theatre give sufficient glow, to enable them to find their seats halfway down the aisle on the left-hand side towards the centre. 'It is very different to seeing a film,' whispers Ron, as the play gets under way. *How, now, Orlando*, a voice calls from centre stage and on walks a guy dressed in a brightly-coloured top and black tights. For a moment, Emma stares at the actor in his skinny outfit

as she has never seen male dancers on stage. The play continues.
'I wouldn't wear a costume like that,' comments Ron, at the end of the show.
'Orlando?' she questions.
'Yes. There were others too, although they were very good actors.'
'I don't think that I will ever forget my first visit to a theatre,' says Emma. 'It has been quite an experience. I guess I'm not very cultured.'

On Sunday morning, Emma again feels sick and lethargic. They go to church and Ron buys a missal from the selection at the back of church as he wants his own, so as to follow the Mass without trying to read Emma's prayer book. Father Rodger, standing in the porch, comes across and introduces himself. He is tall and slim with thick, brown hair, neatly cut, but with beetling eyebrows that look like they need a trim. He says that he is delighted to meet them and welcomes them to the parish. He asks where they live and Ron explains about moving to Cheshire and working at Woodford.
'I see that you are buying a missal,' he says to Ron.
'I'm not a Catholic, but I like to come with Emma,' Ron explains. 'I'm trying to learn more about it.' Father Rodger is impressed. Emma keeps quiet as she is feeling unwell.
'I hope I feel better tomorrow,' she says to Ron, as they move away to allow other parishioners to speak to the priest. 'It is so unlike me to feel like this.'

As she is still nauseous next morning, she decides to go to the doctor's after work. She arrives and is given a disc with a number on. The waiting-room is full and she stands to one side, waiting her turn. She is anxious and her stomach is churning. She has no-one to talk to and feels quite alone as she waits, watching the clock ticking. 'What if there is something seriously wrong?' she thinks.

Spring 1961 / Autumn 1961

'I guess you are pregnant,' the doctor says, after listening to Emma's account of her feelings of nausea and asking a few questions. He is middle-aged, quite stocky in build and has receding light-brown hair. He peers at her over his spectacles. 'You've been married six weeks. That didn't take long. Pretty much straight away, I guess. Didn't you suspect this?' Emma blushes and shakes her head. She is stunned. His eyes roll but he keeps silent.

'I know I am late, but I thought it was to do with the stress of the wedding. I'm not regular, anyway,' she says, feeling very emotional and worried that she might cry in front of him.

'Call in next week with a urine sample and we will confirm it. Morning sickness in early pregnancy is very common and nothing to worry about. If it gets worse, come back and see me as I can prescribe something to help quell it. Otherwise, you need to come back when you are three months and we will get you booked in with a midwife.' Emma makes her way out of the surgery, overwhelmed on hearing this news. She didn't expect to fall pregnant so soon. Her emotions are spinning around. She doesn't know what Ron will say. Walking along the streets to the flat, she spies some cooking apples in a fruit and vegetable shop, but the shop keeper is just shutting down.

'I really fancy one of those. I'll call tomorrow if the shop is open after work,' she decides.

Arriving at the flat and removing her jacket, she makes for the kitchen. She wants to cook a good meal for Ron.

'That was delicious,' he says, a little later, when taking his empty plate to the kitchen. He makes a pot of tea and walks back into the living-room, carrying the tray with two mugs, the teapot and milk jug. 'How was your day?' he asks, placing the tray on the table and pouring out the tea.

'I have something to tell you.' He looks up at her.

'You look serious. Is something wrong?'

'I went to the doctor's, after work. I'm pregnant.' Ron stops pouring the tea and gazes at her.

'Are you sure?'

'That's what he said. It is morning sickness I have, quite common in early pregnancy, apparently.' There is a silence. Emma gazes at Ron, waiting for his reaction. He gets out of his seat and gives her a hug. His first thoughts are to comfort his young wife.

'It is a surprise, but we'll be fine. Don't look so anxious.' Emma has a drink of her tea and Ron returns to his seat, fills his cup and then smiles. 'We will have to get a house now,' he says. 'The landlady told me that she doesn't take couples with children. We can start hunting for one this weekend, if you like.'

'I was thinking on the way home, about our money,' Emma says, relieved that Ron seems happy about it. 'I can keep working for some time. We will have to look at our finances and decide how much we can afford on a house. I am not telling anyone yet about the baby. I'll wait until I'm three months.' At the mention of the word, *baby*, Ron looks at her again. The news is slowly sinking in.

Although he tries to be practical, Ron is quite stunned. When cycling to work the next morning, he ponders over the idea of being a father.

'It will take a bit of getting used to,' he thinks. 'I never thought I'd be a dad at twenty-two.' He is also recalling a conversation with Emma, about children, months after he asked her to marry him, when she said that they could have four children by the time he was twenty-eight. They both laughed and he thought, at the time, that she was joking. Now he is wondering if she meant it. He switches his thoughts to his evening sessions of sword-fencing, in Manchester. He hasn't been for a while and is considering not going anymore. 'It was great while I was on my own in lodgings but it is different now. It is like the ATC meetings. I don't seem to have quite the same urge to go. Must be married life,' he thinks.

Their next adventure begins. On Saturday, they first visit the Halifax Building Society in Stockport to discuss mortgages.

'I can give you a rough idea, but you will need to make an appointment to see our financial advisor. Only the husband's wages are considered to determine the amount you can borrow,' explains the lady, a rather buxom, middle-aged woman, with short, brown, wavy hair framing her chubby face. She seems very knowledgeable about mortgages and Emma guesses that she has been working there for some time. She makes a note of Ron's annual salary and advises that the maximum amount that one can borrow is a quarter of one's net salary. 'I'll book you in for an appointment. We've had a cancellation for next Saturday morning at 10am. Would you like that one?' Ron looks at Emma, who nods. 'That will be fine,' he replies. They leave to go next door to the

Halifax property department, but firstly, they window-shop looking at the properties for sale, before going inside to ask about houses to buy.

'I'd like a three-bedroomed, if possible,' Emma says to her husband. 'We will probably have family visiting overnight and the baby will need a room after a few months.' Emma pauses, after mentioning the baby. 'It's incredible,' she thinks.

'It will be handy if we get a house nearer to Woodford than where we are at present,' Ron suggests, 'making it a shorter bike-ride for me.' They leave the shop, armed with details of several possible properties around Cheadle Hulme, Hazeltrees and Stockport. Within the excitement of looking for a house, they both try and reassure each other that this is a good step forward, while each is overawed at the enormity of what they are taking on. The remainder of the weekend is spent looking through the details and discussing the pros and cons while taking into account the suggested maximum mortgage they might get, according to the Halifax assistant.

'I'll ring from work on Monday and book appointments for viewing next weekend,' says Emma, after they have whittled down the list to a possible three.

Early Monday morning, Emma is retching over the kitchen sink and feeling fragile.

'When will it stop,' she wonders. She struggles to eat a digestive biscuit. She packs some in her handbag to nibble, when in the office. Leaving Ron asleep in bed, she closes the living-room door and makes her way down the flights of stairs to catch the train into Piccadilly station. It is very crowded. She stands and holds on to a hand-rail for the short distance. On her way to the tax office, she visits the little corner shop in Salford. It is always open when she passes by and she calls in, every weekday morning.

'A tube of polo mints and a packet of Rowntrees fruit gums, please,' she says to the well-built, elderly, swarthy-looking man, behind the counter.

'You must like these a lot,' he comments, handing them over and taking her money, looking at her expectantly for an explanation. She smiles and leaves the shop. She doesn't want to explain to him about her pregnancy and how she sucks on the sweets alternatively, throughout the morning, to help her cope with feeling so physically sick.

The week passes quickly. Emma drops off her urine sample and the pregnancy is confirmed. She has a craving for green, cooking apples and has one each evening. Every morning, before eating, she retches and sometimes is physically sick. By the end of the week, she feels so rough that she decides to visit the doctor again. After work and on leaving the station at Heaton Chapel, she walks to the doctor's, knowing that there is a late surgery on Fridays. She waits three-quarters of an hour in the waiting-room, before her number is called.

'It's every morning. Can you give me something, please?' she asks. He opens a book and has a quick read of a page before prescribing medicine.

'It should help but stop taking it as soon as you feel able.'

On Saturday, Ron and Emma have early breakfast and leave to keep the appointment with the Halifax Building Society, before spending the day house-viewing. They have a break at dinner-time in Cheadle Hulme, visiting a café for a light bite after viewing a property in the vicinity; then to Hazeltrees for the second house; and finally, the last booking, a terraced house just off the main road at Stockport. After the strenuous morning and climbing up the stairs to their attic flat, they are both tired but feel exhilarated with their adventurous day.

'What do you think?' questions Ron, as they have a cup of tea, after their cooked meal of mince and mash.

'I wasn't keen on the terraced one in Stockport,' replies Emma. 'Although it was a good size and well within our budget, it was quite a busy road for traffic. I think the Hazeltrees one is best. That narrow extension on the side is big enough to take a bed, should we need a third bedroom. The present owners have a bed in it, not a double but bigger than a single. The garden is lovely with open fields at the back. No garage, but we don't have a car and Hazeltrees is closer to your workplace than Cheadle Hulme. The Cheadle Hulme property was lovely, a proper three-bedroomed one, but the most expensive and I think it's more than we can afford. Even to buy the one at Hazeltrees will be a struggle, but I can budget well.' Ron takes a moment to think about it, before commenting.

'You could catch the train from any of them, but I agree with you about the Hazeltrees property. Do you want a second viewing on it, or shall we put an offer in and see what happens? Can you do that at work?' Emma isn't bothered about a second viewing and after further deliberation about how much to offer, agrees to make the phone call on Monday. She knows that she shouldn't be making private telephone calls from the office unless it is really necessary, but feels that she doesn't have an alternative.

Emma battles through the next few weeks with medicine and sweets. She is very tired but on reading a book, borrowed from the library, she learns that tiredness in the early weeks of pregnancy is common.

'It's a wonder anyone has a second baby if this is what it is like,' she thinks. By the end of June, she is feeling much better and although the craving for sour apples hasn't subsided, she no longer takes medication. It is Ron's twenty-second birthday and they enjoy the chocolate cake that she has made. He surprises her by telling her that he has decided to become a Catholic. Emma is delighted.

'We will have to tell Father Rodger,' she says, but after informing the priest on the Sunday, she is disheartened when he explains that Ron will need further instructions. 'But he had some before we were married,' she insists.

'You should know that I can't just receive him into the Church without serious talks. You said he only had half-a dozen, was it?' Father Rodger replies, looking at her downcast face. Emma nods. She thought Ron could just be received immediately, but obviously not. The priest takes his black, slim diary from his pocket and books Ron in for Wednesday evening at seven-thirty.

'Unless something serious crops up, we will meet weekly at that time,' he says to Ron, 'if you are happy with that.'

'Thank you, Father. That's fine,' Ron replies.

'I look forward to seeing you then.' Emma resigns herself to accepting the situation.

There is good news next day when they find out that their offer is accepted on the house. It is now a waiting game not only because of all the research and paperwork to be completed but also because they are in a chain of people buying and selling. Emma also receives a letter from Faith, full of news about a young man she has met. She is pleased for her friend and spends an hour in the evening, writing to her.

On the first Saturday in July, Emma is woken early by a knock on the flat door. Ron is sound asleep. She grabs her pink dressing gown and creeps out quietly and closes the bedroom door before putting it on. She walks across to the living-room door and gently opens it, expecting to see the landlady. She gasps.

'What are you doing here?' she asks, in amazement. 'Such a silly question,' she thinks, looking at Tom and Mary. 'Come in.'

'We thought we'd surprise you,' says her mam, taking off her jacket and putting it with her handbag, on the settee. 'We wanted to see how you are. What a spacious room. I thought it would be cramped,' she adds, looking around and spying the table and chairs at one end.

Are you staying over?' their daughter asks, knowing that Ron's parents are expected tomorrow, according to their last letter.

'Yes,' answers her dad, 'if that's okay, but we will be leaving at the crack of dawn. I need to get back for milking time. Martha is seeing to things today with Mark's help, but she has plenty on at home with her little ones. I can't expect her to do it tomorrow.'

'Of course, you can stay, Dad. It's lovely you are here, driving all this way to see us,' Emma gushes, so happy to see them. 'I'll tell you now, although I was waiting until I was three months, but I am pregnant and we are going to buy a house,' she says, not able to contain the news any longer. She goes into the kitchen and puts the kettle on. 'We have eggs and bacon. Would you like a cooked breakfast or is it too early?'

'Fine for me, lass,' answers Tom.

'I'll just have bacon, please,' says her mam.

'I haven't told work, yet, but I will, about the baby, that is. I can still catch a train into Manchester, after we move, but the journey will be longer, about twenty minutes but for Ron, the journey will be shorter.' She is full of news for them, so delighted to have an audience interested in her life. Ron comes through and is equally surprised.

'I wondered who you were talking to.'

After breakfast, Tom goes downstairs to his van as they have brought wedding presents with them and Ron goes to help carry them up. Emma sits on the carpet and begins opening the boxes. 'Here is a list of presents and names beside them as I know that you will want to write thankyou letters,' says Mary, passing her daughter a piece of paper. One by one, Emma places the contents out for all to see. 'This is great. There is a dinner-set; a tea-set; knives, forks and spoons; and a kettle. These are from Ron's relatives,' she says, looking at the list. 'I guess they put their heads together so as not to duplicate things.'

'The set of pans come from Martha and Joe,' says Mary. 'The sheets and pillow-cases are from Marjorie and Abe. Your dad went through to pick them up. I also put some more of your clothes in a bag, the ones you'd left at home. We've brought those, too, plus a couple of towels and two tea-towels that were from folks in Windrush.'

'Thanks,' says Emma, her face beaming. She packs the presents back into the boxes. 'All ready for our new home. It is so exciting.' They spend the morning chatting and Ron shows them the details of the house that they hope to buy.

After dinner, they stroll around the few shops in Heatonburn and Tom spots a local pub.

'We could come out tonight and have a drink,' he suggests.

'That'll be great, Dad. We don't go out much,' replies Emma.

'We've been to the Ritz once in Manchester. It is very posh, but we loved the dancing, didn't we, Ron?' she says, turning to her husband.

'Yes, it was a good night.'

'I'll just pop in here,' says Mary, eyeing some potted plants on sale. Five minutes later, she comes out holding a red-flowered plant. 'For you both,' she says. 'It will look lovely in your living-room and you can think of us when you water it.'

'Thanks, Mam. That's really nice. I'm on the lookout for a second-hand pram,' Emma says, changing the subject with the forthcoming baby forever on her mind. 'The landlady says that if I find one, I can leave it downstairs until we move. The landlady originally told Ron that she doesn't take tenants with children but when I told her why we will be leaving, she said we could stay as she realises that we are a sensible couple and would take a baby out for fresh air. I think that's because I hang out the washing every week, in her garden, but we want to move to a house of our own, with the baby coming.' Emma is full of chat about being pregnant and the new home. Her parents look at each other, realising all their misgivings about their daughter marrying and disappearing down the country, have been unnecessary. They can see that she is happy and managing well.

Later in the evening, they have a couple of drinks in a local pub before going back to the flat for an early night. Over a cup of tea, Mary sees something.

'Emma, it doesn't bother me but there is a layer of dust on the wooden ledge underneath the fireside chair. You may want to remove it before Ron's parents arrive.'
'Oh dear; I thought I'd done everything.'
'The rest of your flat is fine. Don't worry.'
'Time for bed I think,' Tom says, having finished his tea.
'We'll say goodbye now,' says Mary, 'as we will be long gone when you two get up.'
'It has been so lovely having you both,' their daughter whispers, giving each of them a hug.
'Let us know when you get moved in and we'll be down again, but I'll be busy hay-timing, the next few weeks,' her dad explains.
'I think it will be September before we get moved,' says Ron.

When Emma gets up for breakfast, she peeps into their bedroom, only to see the bed made, but no occupants. She feels a little flat. 'Never mind,' she consoles herself. 'Ron's parents will be arriving this afternoon, but it won't be quite the same' she thinks. She is worried about cooking for them and entertaining them, although with her and Ron both at work, it will only be the evenings. She needn't have worried. His parents love the flat and treat Ron and Emma to a couple of evening meals, before they make their departure. His mam says she will be knitting baby clothes for their first grandchild. They seemed quite thrilled on receiving the news. 'It's been so good having company,' Emma thinks, on returning home on the Wednesday to find them gone. 'I do miss my family and friends. I'll write some letters tonight, one to Martha and one to Faith.'

Five days later, Emma walks into the flat after work, tired and ready to eat. She puts her jacket on the settee along with her handbag. Ron, who arrives home before her, is making a cup of tea.
'There is a letter for you,' he calls. 'I've put it on the table.' Emma walks over, picks up the letter and scrutinises the envelope.
'It looks like my mam's writing.' She opens it and quickly reads through it. 'Guess what? It's actually from my brother Mark, although my mam has addressed it. He wants to know if he can visit with three mates as they are planning a few days away for a holiday. Dad has offered to lend him his van.' Carrying the tray with tea and cups and milk, Ron walks to the table and puts it down.

'Where will they sleep?'

'Two of his mates are brothers. They can sleep in the spare bedroom. The other two will have to sleep on the settee and the floor in here. There are enough blankets as it is warm at this time of year. I'll write and tell him that they are welcome and explain about the sleeping arrangements. It will be up to them, then. They will have to fend for themselves too, with us being at work. Is that all right?' Ron nods.

'I don't know what they will do down here, though,' he states.

'Maybe we could have a night out at the Ritz,' says Emma. 'That would be something different. They are not coming until early August, after hay-timing.' She goes to cook a meal. Mince and mash. 'Always an easy one,' she thinks.

Meanwhile, Ron is reading a magazine that he purchased on Saturday but hasn't had time to fully read. He has decided he will make a dining-room suite so as to save buying one. He tells Emma, while they are eating.

'Are you serious?' Emma asks. He looks at her.

'Of course. I like woodwork and the instructions for making chairs are in this,' he says, waving the magazine at her.

'Okay, if you think you can.'

'What do you mean, if I can? Ye of little faith,' he says, with a smile. Over the next days, the living-room becomes a workshop.

'If you keep all the mess to one side, it will help,' Emma states, looking at pieces of wood, wood shavings and nails, plus a variety of tools, all cluttering the floor. Night after night, Ron whittles away on his first chair, but he is very meticulous and takes his time, especially as he likes to rest a while after their evening meal, before starting. She wonders whether he'll actually get a set of chairs made as it seems to her to be very slow progress.

At the weekend, Emma goes out early to look at advertisements in shop-windows. She is delighted to see a second-hand pram for sale. It is a black Silver Cross, well-used but in reasonable condition. The address is in Heatonfield and after asking for directions, on route, she finds the street.

'Come in,' says a tall, blonde, young woman, after Emma knocks on the door. A pre-school little girl is hiding behind the lady, wearing a pink cotton dress and with her fair hair tied back in a pony-tail. 'This is Maisie, my daughter. We are going to buy a treat for you, aren't we,' her mother says to her, 'with money from the sale.' Emma follows them and is taken into their front room. 'It is a good make and the leather patches on each corner look smart, don't you think?' the lady questions, brushing her fringe from her blue eyes. 'I had them done properly when I bought the pram, second-hand.'

'I'll take it,' Emma states, taking her purse from her shopping bag.

Half-an-hour later, she wheels it through the main front door where they live. The landlady is just coming out of her living-room. She gazes at the pram.

'You can put it in our front room seeing as you will soon be moving. I will show you. Have you a date yet?' Emma shakes her head.

'It takes so long but hopefully we will hear soon. My brother is coming for a couple of nights in early August, with friends. I hope that's all right. They won't be any trouble.'

'As long as you are happy with them, that's fine. You haven't caused me any problems. Was it your parents staying overnight?' Emma nods.

'First mine and then Ron's but they all liked the flat. Thank you for this,' she adds, placing the pram in the room.

'When is your baby due?'

'They've given me a date in January.'

'You will have plenty of time then, to settle into your new home.' Emma walks up the three flights of stairs and enters the flat, to find Ron chiselling a chair leg.

'It's more complicated than I thought,' he says, grimacing at Emma. 'Did you get a pram?'

'Yes. I'm so happy about it. It is downstairs in the landlady's front room.'

The four friends arrive one Tuesday evening after tea. Mark, now nineteen and wanting his own farm one day, works on a neighbouring farm, back home.

'You look well,' Emma says to him. He is a handsome lad with his short dark hair and brown eyes. He introduces his friends to Ron, as Emma remembers them all from primary school in Windrush and from the local dances when in her teens. Barney is tall with black, curly hair and twinkling blue eyes and very charming. His younger brother, Jed, is not as dark or as tall and has a pleasant baby-face, but is much quieter. Keith, the other friend, is stockier with brown hair. They are all wearing short-sleeved shirts in a

variety of colours and smart, dark trousers. 'You can decide who
sleeps on the settee or floor in here and you might want to swap
around,' Emma says to Mark and Keith, after the introductions.
'There are spare blankets in the bedroom but it is very warm at
night. I doubt you'll need much cover. I will give you my key,
Mark, as Ron gets in before me.' Within half-an-hour, the lads
make their leave, with the intention of exploring the local pubs.

'Is everything all right? Emma asks, the next evening.
'It's been great. We've been mooching around Manchester today,'
Mark replies. 'We've bought you both a meal, as a thank you
present.'
'Oh, Mark. That is so thoughtful.'
'We all chipped in,' he adds, smiling at her.
'Well, thanks, lads,' she says. 'We thought we could go to the Ritz
tomorrow night. It can be a celebration for my twenty-first which
was last week. Do you fancy that?' The lads think it is a great idea.
They spend the evening playing cards and having a few beers.
'Ron and I were chatting last night,' says Emma. 'We have been
thinking.' The guys stop playing and listen. 'Would it be possible
to come back with you on Saturday? We thought we could have a
flying visit back home. Could we squeeze in the back of the van
with two of you?'
'If you don't mind sitting on the floor,' answers Mark. 'It should
be all right, lads, shouldn't it?' They agree. Ron and Emma get
clearance from their bosses as they want to stay over the weekend
and maybe another day or two.

Early on Saturday morning, the six young people pile into the van.
The lads are very grateful for their short stay and have thoroughly
enjoyed the visit. The traffic builds up around Leeds causing
delays to their journey. Emma feels the need for a toilet but
doesn't like to say anything.
'Maybe one of the lads will suggest stopping,' she thinks,
hopefully. The sun is hot and inside the van, it is sweltering. She
shuffles to change her position. The van finally pulls up at a garage
and everyone gets out. Barney and Keith make a bee-line for the
toilets followed by Jed. Mark disappears into the shop and emerges
with drinks for all. Emma finds the Ladies.
'What a relief,' she says to herself, washing her hands at a tiny
sink and drying them on a grubby-looking, small towel. Finally,
after three hours, they pull up in Windrush village to let Barney

and Jed get out. It is a drive to Keith's farm, before turning into Moorbeck.

'How have you got here?' is Tom's question, looking at Emma and Ron.

'We came with Mark. He's just seeing to the van,' his daughter replies.

'There were six of you in my van? Not sure that'll do t' springs any good.' Emma looks crestfallen. She hadn't thought about the weight problem.

'We thought we'd take the opportunity to come up.'

'Maybe Martha will put you up,' says Mary, not having planned for anyone staying over. 'She has more room than us and I am sure she will make you a cooked meal tonight, but stay and have a cup of tea and a sandwich.' The family chat a short while but Emma can see that her parents have things to do.

'Is Amy not here, Mam?'

'No. She's shopping in Whitby. She will be sorry to have missed you.'

'We'll walk to Martha's now. It has been lovely seeing you all. Tell Amy we will see her tomorrow.'

'Can me and Jacob come with you?' Miriam asks. Emma looks at her mam.

'Yes, you can,' Mary says, 'but come home before tea. Martha will have enough to feed.' Tom has already gone back to his work, after saying goodbye.

Martha greets them with a smile. The two little ones are standing with her.

'What a lovely surprise. Let's go and sit at the back of the house on some grass. It is too nice to stay in.' There is a long row of nappies hanging from the washing line, across the grassy area, wafting in the slight breeze.

'It's a lovely day for drying,' says Emma.

'Yes, I wash most days, with having so many nappies in use. I'm trying to get Brian potty-trained.' The sisters have a good chat while baby Alan sleeps in his pram and the little ones play together. Joe joins them and offers Ron a pipe and tobacco and they have a short natter while having a smoke. Martha takes her cigarettes from her pinny pocket and offers Emma one, but she declines.

'I haven't smoked since I got married. Maybe I'll start again at some point.' Emma is a social smoker but isn't hooked on them and with not going out much, doesn't have the urge to have one. She thinks they will need every penny when they start paying a mortgage.

'I'll come down in January if you like and look after you. You've done it for me. Joe can take me to Darlington and hopefully I'll get a through train to Manchester. Ron will meet me, won't he?' Emma nods. She is delighted. No worries now about how she will manage, with Martha around.

The couple return home on Tuesday and on the Saturday, Emma goes shopping into Manchester, having noticed that her skirts are getting tighter around her waist. She chooses a beige-coloured, cotton skirt for work and a pair of dark-blue, cotton trousers with an elasticated waistband, for leisure wear.

'With loose blouses, I'll not show as I get bigger,' she thinks. While in the shop, she looks at some warmer skirts in the maternity department and finds a heavy-worsted one in autumn shades with an expanding waist band. 'Brilliant,' she thinks, seeing the reduced price on the label. 'It will do nicely with jumpers for work later in the year until I leave in November.' She has decided to have the last few weeks at home before her baby arrives. On returning to the flat, she shows Ron her purchases. 'It's a lovely summer day. I hope tomorrow is as nice,' she says to him. 'You haven't forgotten about Josie and Basil coming, have you?' She watches him shaping a chair leg for the chair that he is making. He is very meticulous in his handiwork.

'No, I haven't. What is he like?' he questions, referring to Basil. 'I haven't met him. All I know is that he is a student at Manchester University and has an old ramshackle Ford car that he uses to get around. Hopefully it is safe enough. Josie wants a run-out to a fairground.'

The following afternoon at two o'clock, Josie and Basil arrive. Josie works alongside Emma in the tax office and they have become quite friendly, enjoying each other's company at tea-breaks. Introductions are made. Josie is a bubbly, outgoing young lady, a little taller than Emma, with fair, wavy hair, light-blue eyes and high cheek-bones. Basil has unkempt, long, dark hair reaching his shoulders. He is tall and angular and has a cheeky grin. They are a fun couple, always having banter with each other.

'It is a bit on the small size,' Basil says, apologetically, as they squeeze into his car. He loves his car and although it is noisy and struggles up hills, they finally reach a parking lot within walking distance of the fairground at Blackpool. The sun is blazing down and their first port of call is to buy drinks and sit outside on a grassy patch, enjoying being in the open without a care in the world. Emma isn't keen to try the rides and prefers to watch as Basil and Josie go on the Helter Skelter and the Big Dipper. Ron isn't bothered either and makes the excuse that he will keep his wife company. Josie has kindly brought a picnic tea which, later on, they all devour.

'Time to be off, then,' says Basil, as he gets to his feet, followed by the others. The girls pack away the picnic paraphernalia and then wait, as Basil is having trouble starting the car. He eventually gets out of the car and taking the crank handle from the boot, lifts up the bonnet and using the handle, starts the car after a couple of attempts.

'Let's hope it gets us home,' whispers Emma to Ron.

'Don't worry,' says Josie, reassuringly. 'This happens sometimes, but he always gets back home safely.'

The prospect of a moving date is looming. On a Saturday in late August, Emma and Ron take a train into Stockport to keep an appointment with their solicitor to explain that their landlady has asked for a month's notice. He confirms that he is in the process of writing to them to aim for the twenty-ninth of September as the day when they can pick up the keys.

'That's ideal,' says Emma. 'We can now give notice about leaving the flat and it means our landlady can look for new tenants.' On leaving the solicitors office, they go shopping, looking for bedroom furniture. 'Maybe we can buy a small table and chairs and a couple of fireside chairs also, for the living-room,' Emma suggests to Ron, 'as we will need something to sit on. The lady said that she was leaving the carpet in the living-room and the one on the stairs. They were well worn and the one on the stairs was threadbare in parts, but they will do to start with. The front room will have to stay empty for now.'

The furniture store is huge. On the second floor, they walk around looking at beds, wardrobes and dressing-tables. Emma is feeling overawed, spending so much money and choosing new furniture. They settle for two wardrobes in light oak and Emma chooses a dressing-table to match. It has three decent-sized drawers and a tall

oval-shaped mirror, which pleases her. They inspect the beds and choose one with a headboard in the same shade as the light oak. Downstairs they wander past the three-piece suites.
'We can't afford them, can we?' Ron asks. Emma shakes her head. 'Over there. Fireside chairs. We will need two,' she says. Then in the far corner, she spots some small Formica-topped tables with chairs to match. 'What about sunshine yellow? It's a lovely bright colour.' Ron doesn't mind. 'The table will fit in the corner of the living-room for us to sit at for our meals and there are four chairs for when we have visitors.' They smile at each other; a happy couple spending their hard-earned savings.

When speaking to the priest, the following Sunday, Emma senses that he would have liked Ron to have more instructions, before being received into the Church, but on hearing that they will be moving shortly, agrees to their request. He arranges for him to have conditional Baptism and make his First Confession on a Saturday night later in the month.
'Then you go to Holy Communion on the Sunday,' he explains to Ron. On the way home, the couple mull over the conversation.
'Are you happy about it?' queries Emma.
'Of course, I am. Otherwise, I wouldn't have asked him.'
'We need to tell your parents at some point. Shall I, next time I write?'
'Yes, you can, but not until I've been received.'
'I'll write to mine at the same time.'

Emma accompanies Ron on the Saturday evening. He is not worried as he feels prepared and has quite enjoyed the discussions that he has had with Father Rodger. They enter the church and the priest greets them, but before going through the rituals, he introduces two parishioners and explains that he has asked them to be witnesses, seeing as Emma and Ron have no family nearby. It is a happy moment for Emma because she knows her husband has made this choice of his own accord. The following day, they leave the flat for early Mass, after an early cup of tea as allowed by recent easing of the rules on fasting. At Holy Communion time, they join the line of parishioners walking towards the altar-rails and on arriving, they kneel alongside others. Emma feels for Ron because, although she is used to putting her tongue out to receive the Host, she thinks it may be embarrassing for him, but he doesn't seem to mind. She finds it strange that no-one else apart from the priest, knows that this is Ron's first time and a special occasion for them both.

'Perhaps the two parishioners, who were there on Saturday evening, are in church,' she thinks, 'but apart from them, no-one here is aware of this milestone in our lives.' After Mass and on their way out of the building, Father Rodger congratulates Ron. The two witnesses, standing beside the priest, step forward and give Ron a religious congratulations card. This acknowledgement of the special event pleases Emma immensely. Hand in hand, the happy couple saunter back home to breakfast.

The day arrives for Ron and Emma to go into Stockport to pick up the keys to their new home, after both having taken a day's holiday from work. They have been packing what little possessions they have and have put them in a pile with the boxes of wedding presents ready to be transported. It is too early to get up but Emma cannot sleep and is tossing and turning, thinking about their cosy flat and the daunting task of taking on a mortgage. She finishes work mid-November and is trying to make a mental list of things to buy before her wages cease, such as baby clothes and a cot and highchair. She also realises that there will be extra monthly bills to pay once they move.

'Will we manage on one salary when my job has ended?' she questions herself, anxiously.

Autumn 1961 / Winter 1961

'Can this really be ours,' Emma says to Ron, as she approaches the front door of number thirty-one, Longmeadow Avenue. Her cheeks are glowing in the cool evening air and her hazel-coloured eyes are shining. Damp black curls cling to her forehead. It has been a brisk walk covering over five miles from the attic flat with only one stop, sitting on a wooden bench for ten minutes. 'I just need to rest before we go inside,' she adds, sitting down on the grass in the small, front garden. 'It seemed a good idea yesterday but I didn't realise how far it would be, when I suggested walking here.'

Earlier in the day, after picking up their keys, they had taken a bus back to Heatonburn and on entering the flat, had rescued their pram from the front room downstairs.
'We will put the pram in the hallway and carry everything down. It won't take long,' Ron had said. Their idea was to fill the pram with boxes and then walk to their new home, Ron pushing the loaded pram and Emma wheeling his bike. His chair, still in pieces, was also placed in the pram. Before leaving, Ron wanted to go to the shops for some screws and nails to take with them.
'I'll cook dinner and we can leave later, when it's a little cooler,' Emma had said. 'You go for your shopping while I clean the flat. Then we can have an early start tomorrow because the furniture is being delivered in the morning.' Emma remembers them both laughing as they set off on their long walk with the bike and pram. 'Who would do something like this?' Ron had questioned. 'We must be crazy.' Emma thought it hilarious.
'Not many people move their goods and chattels by walking miles with a bike and a second-hand pram full of their belongings,' she'd said, but they'd done it and now they have arrived.

Ron is smiling as he puts the key in the lock.
'We've made it and we can catch a train back,' he says. Then turning around, he kisses his wife who has picked herself up and is standing behind him. 'It is quite different from the terraced house on the cobbled street where I grew up,' he comments, pushing open the door. He takes his bike into the front room and helps Emma with the pram. Once inside the empty house, he turns again to his wife and putting his arms around her, hugs her tightly. Hand in hand, they explore the rooms, their footsteps echoing as they

walk across the wooden floorboards through the front room and into a small living-room. Emma gazes upwards.

'Look,' she says. Hanging from the ceiling is a pulley with four wooden slats on which to dry clothes. 'We had one at home. They are so useful.' Then she sees the garden. 'What a length,' she exclaims, 'and fields beyond. It reminds me of our farm.' They both gaze out of the window, overwhelmed that this is going to be their home.

'They've left an old wireless,' Ron says. 'You will enjoy that. This is much better than I thought we'd get. All that saving has paid off.' They wander into the kitchen which is small, but there is an old cooker for which they are grateful. On opening the door to the narrow room off the kitchen, they are delighted to find that the previous owners have left the three-quarter bed.

'She said she'd leave it and she has left some blankets and they look like they've been washed,' states Emma. 'They will do for us until we buy some. That bed will be so useful when we have company.'

'Expecting someone?' asks Ron. Emma nods.

'I bet Miriam and Jacob will be down in the summer holidays. It will be somewhere different for them as we didn't go on holiday when we were all at home. Your mam and dad will come, you know.' They have a quick look upstairs before leaving the property and walking up the long road to make their way to the railway station.

Next morning, Ron and Emma are up bright and early. They enjoy their last breakfast in the flat and pack their suitcases with any remaining possessions. As they leave, their landlady appears and wishes them well. After a quick walk to the railway station and onto a train for the short journey, followed by another walk, they arrive at their new home and realise that they need food.

'I'll walk to that little row of shops that we spotted yesterday when walking back for the train,' Emma says. 'You stay here and wait for the furniture van. You can show them which bedroom to put furniture in. The rest goes in the living-room.'

By the end of the day, the furniture is in place and the bed made up with brand new sheets and pillow-cases plus the blankets that were left behind. Emma sets out their tea on the yellow table in the living-room, using new cups and saucers and plates.

'I asked Father Rodger about the nearest church,' she says. 'There is one in Hazeltrees within walking distance. We can set off early tomorrow morning to give ourselves plenty of time.' After clearing the pots and washing up, they each retire to a fireside chair. Ron lights his pipe as Emma has bought some tobacco for him. She reads the newspaper that she purchased at the shops while Ron is engrossed in a book about aeroplanes. Later, in bed, both very tired, they snuggle up and talk gently about this latest move and reminisce about how much they have achieved.

'I called at that row of shops,' Ron says on Friday, when walking into the kitchen. 'I bought a shovel and firelighters. You can cross them off your list. Thank goodness they left us some coal but we will need to order more when I find out where to get it.' Emma is pleased and thanks him. Each evening, she has been adding to a list, items that they need for their new home.

'Josie was talking to me today, at work,' she says, when they are eating eggs, chips and beans. 'She is fancying a trip out to the boating lake at Fairhaven near Lytham St Anne's, on Sunday, to see The Lights at Blackpool. They will pick us up early afternoon if we'd like to go. I said yes. Is that okay?'

'It's fine by me. I have some good news, too. You know my foil and mask that I use, when I go sword-fencing. A lad at work is interested in going, but hasn't the equipment. I don't intend using them anymore. We are doing a swop. I'm giving him mine and he has a twelve-inch television that he is giving me, as he is getting a bigger one.'

'You mean that we are going to have a television? That's great.' Emma knows how much Ron loves watching films et cetera. She is delighted for him.

'His dad will drop it off at the weekend. Maybe one day, we will have a coloured television,' he says, wistfully. 'They are being made now.'

'That's not a problem. It's a television. I didn't think we'd be able to afford one. It will be fine.'

'I'm going upstairs now to work on the chair,' says Ron. 'I don't think that I will be making a dining-room suite. We will just have a chair.' They both laugh.

Sunday afternoon is a cooler day but the weather is fine when Basil and Josie arrive. After the pair have a quick look around the house, they all pile into Basil's car. It is a lengthy ride to Lytham St Anne's, but entertaining, with Josie full of her usual exuberance and anecdotes. Wandering around the town, they come across a large boating lake.

'Fancy taking one out?' Basil asks Ron, watching the yachts gliding across the water. Ron jumps at the idea.

'I haven't been on water since I was on holiday at the Norfolk Broads with a group of mates. You two coming?' he asks the girls.

'I'm certainly not,' replies Emma, patting her rounded stomach. 'Not with this little one.'

'I'll stay and keep you company,' says Josie. The two lads leave their coats with the girls before approaching a wizened, little old man sitting in a shelter beside a small heater. They pay him and he gives them two tickets and points them in the direction of the yachts moored alongside the lake. Arriving, they are allocated a yacht and they glide off very slowly across the waters that are a little choppy because of the rising wind.

At first, Josie and Emma, chatting and watching, think the lads are doing nicely, but begin to get concerned when the lads appear to be losing control with the yacht seemingly having a mind of its own.

'They'll turn over if they are not careful,' says Josie, as they both watch, holding their breaths.

'It's going. It's going. Oh, no!' shouts Emma. The yacht dips over and Ron ends up in the water, followed by Basil. They haul themselves back into the yacht and steer it to the moorings. The lads, with big cheesy grins, walk back to join the girls, water dripping from their trousers. The old man is watching.

'Come and dry out,' he calls to them. They walk into the shelter and stand close to the heater. Soon, steam is arising from the wet clothes. The girls wait outside, laughing.

'I'm glad I didn't go with you,' Emma says to Ron, as he comes outside and takes off his jumper, before putting his coat back on.

'I'll be okay now. My trousers are still damp, but I have dried my shoes a bit and taken off my socks.' He shoves them into his pocket.

'Now onto Blackpool for The Lights,' says Basil. 'Sorry, there is no heater in here. I will have to upgrade this car, I think.'

'Don't worry about me,' says Ron, laughing to hide his embarrassment. 'I will slowly dry out on the way.' Nothing else untoward happens, but the accident is talked about with much glee, most of the way.

November arrives. By the middle of the month, Emma is finding the early start and fast walk to the train station, followed by another walk through the streets of Manchester and a long day at work, very tiring. She can't wait to finish.

'At last. Only one more day,' she thinks, on leaving work one Wednesday, as she finishes the next day, the thirtieth of November. When she arrives at Piccadilly station, the train is crowded. She pushes her way through the standing passengers but there are no vacant seats. She makes her way to the guard's van which is empty apart from one bicycle. There is nowhere to sit. She slumps to the floor and sits on the hard surface. She is weary. After the twenty minutes ride, she struggles to her feet and makes her way to the exit. 'Just the walk home now,' she thinks.

After her last day at the office, Emma eventually arrives home laden with chocolates and some baby clothes, from her colleagues. She was surprised that one guy didn't even know she was pregnant and thought she was transferring to another office.

'The maternity skirt was a great buy,' she thinks, after his comments. With loose fitting tops, her figure is showing no sign of a bump, just a thickening out.

'Plenty of stuff there,' says Ron, eyeing the bags that she is putting on the small table.

'Yes, they have been generous to me. I am so glad to be finished.'

The next morning, Emma is up early as usual and decides to walk to morning Mass as she has the whole day to herself to do as she pleases. Her plan is to tidy the house later.

'That was a mistake,' she thinks afterwards, because she has an unexpected visitor just after she returns home.

'I was wondering how you are doing. I'm Maureen Macklin, Ben's mam. He has spoken quite often about Ron and told me about you moving in. I thought I'd call and see your new home seeing as you have no family around to visit. You have finished work, I believe.' Mrs Macklin, with shoulder-length, peroxide-blonde hair, is smartly dressed in a thick, brown overcoat and high-heeled, brown shoes. She has a beige scarf tucked around her neck and is wearing matching fur-trimmed gloves. Emma's embarrassment is when she shows her the spare bedroom upstairs, with the floor covered in wood shavings left by Ron after finishing late. He is busy making shelves for his books and for the wireless.

'Mam and dad will bring more of my books when they eventually visit. I want the shelves ready,' he'd explained. Emma apologises to Mrs Macklin for the mess.

'Don't worry about that,' she replies, but Emma can see that she is quite surprised. Emma doesn't like to explain that she'd promised Ron she would clear the mess this morning, as he was tired last night, but that she's been to Mass instead and intended tidying up later.

The following Monday, after her midday meal, Emma walks out down their road and takes the left turn into Hazeltrees, passing the little row of shops, known as The Boulevard. It is a good twenty minutes before reaching the small town. Her first call is at a doctor's surgery where she registers them both, before asking if it is possible to see a doctor. It is almost half-an-hour later when she is finally called to see a doctor.

'I've just moved,' she explains, 'and I am seven months pregnant with my first baby. I thought I ought to come as I need to book a midwife.' The doctor checks her over and says that everything is fine.

'I'll see that you are allocated a midwife and she will contact you. Are you thinking of a home birth?'

'I am,' states Emma. 'My mam had all seven of us at home on the farm.' The doctor raises his bushy eyebrows. He is thick-set and rather stocky, with thinning brown hair.

'Did she indeed!' he exclaims. 'Mothers-to-be can have their first in hospital but they are encouraged to have their second at home, if all goes well with the first. It is a shortage of beds, you see. You have a choice with this one. We'll see how things go. Nurse Jameson will explain more.'

'I want to be at home,' Emma replies. The doctor scribbles on his note-pad.

'I will see you again in a month,' he says.

On the way home, she stops by The Boulevard and notices that there are items for sale in a shop-window. She scans the many hand-written notices and is pleased to see that someone has a four-foot bed and mattress for sale in good condition and can deliver. Another notice offers a wooden drop-sided cot; and a wooden high-chair, with tray, that converts into a push-a-long. She makes a note of the telephone numbers and then walks to the end of the row of shops where there is a telephone-box. Sorting out some change, she enters and dials. A few minutes later she comes out smiling, especially as the sellers offered to drop the items off when Emma explained that they had no transport.

'Another little job sorted,' she thinks. 'I can't wait to tell Ron.' They'd discussed the previous evening about a few items that they needed to get, with Emma's final wages. Ron is happy for Emma to manage their finances knowing she is good with figures. She has warned him that they might have to penny-pinch, living on one wage.

It is five-thirty when Ron arrives home and Emma has a cooked meal, all prepared. She knows he loves sausages and mash and she has opened a tin of beans. Over their meal, she tells him of her shopping expedition.

'Well, not exactly shopping,' she explains. 'I've registered us with a doctor and I stopped by those little shops at The Boulevard. I made some phone calls as there was a four-foot bed for sale where all those notices are displayed. It is coming tomorrow. They even have a few blankets that they'll throw in with it. Also, I'm buying a second-hand cot and high-chair. Now we'll have somewhere for Martha and her little ones to sleep, when they come in January. Can you bring your woodwork stuff downstairs tonight, please? You can use the front room as it will be ages before we can afford to put anything in there.'

'Yes, I'll do that. Are all Martha's children coming?' asks Ron, imagining what it might be like with three under-fives staying for days.

'They will have to, as Joe can't run the farm and look after them. Martha will cope and you will be at work most of the time,' she states, reassuringly. 'Don't worry. It will be fine.' They settle down to watch television because, not having watched one for months, they are enjoying their evenings catching up on programmes. Ron particularly likes the architectural ones, those about Roman times and war-time films.

The following day, not only do a man and his son arrive with the bed and take it upstairs for her, but another visitor turns up as they are leaving.

'Mrs Harding?' the woman asks, walking towards the front door.

'Yes.' Emma notices her blue uniform inside her unbuttoned grey coat.

'I'm Nurse Jameson, your midwife. May I come in?' She is elderly, short and stocky with grey, curly hair framing her wrinkled and weather-beaten face. Beneath her bushy eyebrows, her deep-set blue eyes peer out, scrutinising Emma. 'You don't look seven months pregnant,' she says, as Emma leads her through the bare-boarded front room, empty apart from Ron's woodwork equipment stacked tidily in one corner.

'My baby is due on the sixteenth of January. Would you like a cup of tea?'

'Yes, please; milk but no sugar.' They enter the living-room and Emma goes into the kitchen to make a drink while the nurse, after removing her coat, sits herself down on a fireside chair. 'I like to meet my patients in familiar surroundings,' she says, as Emma comes through with cups of tea. 'We'll book your next appointment to see me at the surgery.' She continues with general information before finally telling Emma about ante-natal classes. 'They are held weekly in Hazeltrees. I think you will benefit from going and you will meet other expectant mothers. This is the address,' she adds, passing a printed card to Emma.

It is a dull November morning when Emma arrives at the hall where the classes take place. She tentatively walks in and is greeted by a young, blonde-haired lady, who appears to be in charge.

'You can stay for this class. We are a couple of weeks into the course but you will manage quite a few sessions before your due date. It will be too late for you to book the next course.' Emma notices other ladies, each sitting on a mat, awaiting the rest of the class. She picks up a mat and joins them.

'Hello. Your first visit?' asks a young woman. She has just arrived and is still standing, holding her mat. Emma nods. 'It's fun. My baby is due in March, but I joined this course, as the next one runs past my due date. I'm Jacqui, by the way.'

'Emma.'

'When are you due?'

'Two weeks into January.'

'You hide it well.' Jacqui is as tall as Emma, with long, brown hair tied back in a bun, but with some loose strands hanging around her neck and shoulders. She is a pretty girl with her high cheekbones and twinkling light-brown eyes. Emma finds her vivacious and talkative.

'Ladies. Let us begin. First, go into your relaxing position.' The session continues and at the end, Jacqui tags along with Emma. 'We live nearby, on the way into Hazeltrees, an end-terraced house. Any time you are passing, call in. I don't have family down here. I come from further up North.'

'So do I,' exclaims Emma. 'How weird is that. Give me your address and I will write it down. This is mine,' she adds, scribbling on a piece of paper that she tears from her shopping list. They part company with promises to meet.

Two days later, Emma has just finished hanging out some washing when she hears the doorbell ring.

'Hello. My name is Maire, Irish, you know,' says the lady, standing there. 'I live up the road. Father Wilfred asked if I would pay a visit as he said that you are new to parish and don't know anyone. I have called a couple of times but with no answer.'

'Come in. How thoughtful of him. I'm Emma. I just finished work recently. That will be why I wasn't at home.' Maire follows Emma through the empty front room and into the living-room. 'Would you like a cup of tea?' Emma asks, while studying the lady who is a little shorter in height than herself. Maire has light-brown, short-cut, wavy hair and a few freckles sprinkling her round-shaped face. 'A soft, gentle, kind face,' Emma thinks.

'Yes please, with milk.' Emma returns with the tea and explains why she has moved to Hazeltrees. They share information on their husbands and Maire joyfully enthuses over her three young children, the youngest just having started primary school. Three-quarters of an hour later, she finally stands up, to leave. 'If you have any problems, come and see me,' she states. 'We must meet up again.'

'It has been lovely talking with you,' responds Emma. 'Thank you for coming.'

Ron is delighted that Emma is finding friends.

'I called to see Jacqui today,' she tells him, one Thursday evening. 'She is funny. She has begun decorating their living-room and wants it done for Christmas. The place is a real mess. She has certainly set herself a task. I met her husband, Patrick, a dark-haired, good-looking bloke. He works in a nightclub as a DJ and plays the piano. Jacqui says she is planning on having a party on Christmas night and we can go if we don't go back home to family.'

'Are you wanting to go home for Christmas?' asks Ron.

'I'd like to, but we would have to try to visit both sets of parents. We can have Christmas Day with yours, if you like. There are always plenty at our house. I'll check with the doctor though, as I have an appointment to see him next week. I'm going to start writing Christmas cards now that we are into December. I want to include a letter to Faith, in reply to her last letter. She is getting serious with her young man. I do hope that it turns out well for her, this time.'

'Come in,' says Jacqui, on opening the door to Emma who is calling in on her way to the doctor's. She has smudges of paint on her faded orange jumper which looks like it has seen better days. Her slacks are also smattered with paint. Her slippers are threadbare in places. 'Don't mind my old rags,' she says, laughing as she speaks. 'These are my work clothes. What do you think?' she asks, waving her arms in the direction of the walls of the living-room. One wall is finished and Patrick is carefully papering the first strip of the next wall.
'The walls are so uneven,' he says. 'Getting the pattern to match is nearly impossible.' He steps off the ladder and goes to put a kettle on.
'Are you really going to get it finished in time?' asks Emma, thinking that they have a daunting task ahead of them.
'We will, even if I have to stay up half the nights,' Jacqui replies. 'I usually go with Patrick to the Club. It is a really busy time for him, but I think he will have to go without me. You two must come one evening, maybe in January before the baby comes.' Emma says she'd love to.
'I must go,' she states, after finishing her tea. 'I have a doctor's appointment. Good luck with the decorating.'

'What did the doctor say?' Ron asks, over their evening meal.
'He doesn't want me travelling so near to my due date. First babies can be so unpredictable, he said.' Emma is a little downcast but accepts that she ought to take the doctor's advice, even though in herself, she feels absolutely fine.
'I'll write tonight to both sets of parents and let them know.'
'We'll be able to go to Jacqui's on Christmas night. So, it won't be too bad,' replies Ron, knowing that Emma is used to family at Christmas and will find it hard with only the two of them.
'I've finally finished your mam's cardigan. I will have to post it tomorrow along with your dad's waistcoat.' Emma is delighted with her knitting: a light-brown waistcoat for Ron's dad in a small chequered pattern and a pale lilac cable-patterned cardigan for his

mam. 'I'll call at Jacqui's on the way and tell her that we will be there on Christmas night.'

Now that she isn't going away for Christmas, Emma decides to make a Christmas cake. She knows that Ron loves them. She takes her recipe book *Home Recipes with BERO Flour* and finding the recipe on page fifty-six, she copies down the ingredients.
'It was a great idea,' she thinks, 'my mam giving me this book. It has loads of recipes in that I can try out.' Emma had been baking for years but at home it was her mam who always made the Christmas cake. She writes out a shopping list and as usual, tries to estimate what each item will cost: one shilling and six pence; nine pence; four pence; one shilling; two shillings and six pence; five shillings, et cetera. With only one wage to live on, she is very methodical and careful with their money. Some of the ingredients she hasn't bought before and she makes guesses at the prices. After walking to Hazeltrees and buying all the items on her list, she finds she has over-estimated some items and buys tobacco for Ron, having noticed the previous evening that his packet was almost empty.

On arriving back home, she begins making the cake. Emma is in the throes of baking when Maire stops by, on her way to the shops. 'You look very busy,' she says, eyeing all the ingredients set out on the table, plus mixing bowls and the Christmas cake tin. I have been wondering what you are doing for Christmas. Are you going back home?' Emma shakes her head, explaining that the doctor doesn't want her travelling so far, at this late stage of her pregnancy.
'I'm sure I will be fine, but I have to follow his advice,' she says, dejectedly.
'Why don't you come to us for Christmas dinner? I have family coming later in the day, but there is just me, Kevin and our three little ones for dinner. Come and join us. We'd love to have you.'
'Thank you. That will be lovely. I'll tell Ron tonight.' Hours later, she removes the cake from the oven and is pleased with the results although she thinks that she has overcooked it a little.

The day before Christmas eve, a parcel arrives and Emma waits for Ron to come home, before opening it.
'It's from your mam. Oh! She has wrapped one up for baby,' she states, emotionally. They put the presents on the table to be opened

on Christmas morning, before reading the letter. … *I hope you like the knitted garments for baby. Every stitch comes with a kiss….*
'That is so sweet. I think I'm going to cry,' Emma says, her eyes filling up. Receiving the present, reminds her that she hasn't iced the cake and she begins her task.
'What are you doing?' Ron enquires, walking into the kitchen and seeing Emma with a knife, gently slicing thin layers off the cake.
'I need to ice it. I'm just cutting off the burnt bits.' She places the cake on an upside-down plate. Following the instructions from her recipe book, she proceeds to make the icing and although thinking it seems very thin, carefully layers it onto the cake. The icing is too runny. It thins out on top and flows over the edges and down to the plate. Emma adds more icing-sugar to thicken it and has another go but it is still too runny. She empties the remainder from the packet and after mixing it in, tries valiantly to cover the cake but the icing is lumpy and looks a rather botched job and she starts to cry. 'I'm becoming an emotional mess,' she thinks, wiping her eyes with a handkerchief. Ron returns to the kitchen and seeing Emma upset, puts his arm around her. 'I'm no good at this. I've done something wrong,' she explains.
'It will taste delicious, I'm sure. I love Christmas cake and the icing will be fine. Anyway, it looks like lumps of snow. Where are those things you bought to put on it? They will look authentic on the snow.' Emma smiles at him, knowing that he is trying to cheer her up. She dries her eyes. She has bought a little Father Christmas, a robin and a tiny fir tree. The cake looks much better with the three placed strategically on the bumpy snow.
'I must have read the instructions wrongly. Maybe next year, it will turn out better.'

Darkness comes early but it is a lovely moonlit night when Emma and Ron walk down the road together to go to midnight Mass. They take their time, hand in hand, talking about the New Year and their expected baby. Next morning, they lay awake, enjoying lingering in bed, knowing they have nothing to do, delighting in the thought of Christmas dinner out and a party at Jacqui's in the evening. Eventually, wandering downstairs, they open presents, including theirs to each other: chocolates for Emma and tobacco for Ron. They'd agreed not to buy much as money is tight since Emma is no longer contributing to the finances.
'That is a great jumper, Ron. You could wear it today if you want. New pyjamas for you, too,' Emma comments, watching her

husband open his presents from his parents. Ron takes off his well-worn jumper and puts on the new one; his favourite colour: air-force blue. 'It fits a treat. Keep it on. You look good in it,' she adds, before opening her presents. Emma's gifts are a floral full-length nightdress and a pale pink, chunky, wool jumper with collar that has a short zip fastener from the neck. Her mother's Christmas card arrived earlier in the week, with a short letter explaining that when they are next down, they will buy something that the couple need for their home.

Around eleven-thirty, Emma wraps up a bottle of wine for Maire and Kevin and sweets for the children as she doesn't want to go empty-handed.

'Happy Christmas,' Maire says, greeting them at the door. She is wearing a bright-red blouse and grey cardigan with a darker, grey skirt. 'Come in.' Emma looks around, noticing how festive it looks in the living-room, especially the tall pine Christmas tree, covered in baubles and twinkling lights, standing in one corner. Coloured streamers hang across the ceiling and there is an assortment of presents wrapped in glittery red paper, under the tree. A cheery Father Christmas sits on the sideboard, grinning at everyone. His reindeers and sleigh are trailing across, behind him. The pleasant aroma of cooking floats through from the kitchen. Three children are sitting on the carpet and glance up at the visitors before continuing exploring their presents. Kevin walks in and offers the couple a drink. He is a quietly-spoken Irishman, a little taller than Maire and slightly built, with short, brown hair, light-blue eyes and clean-shaven.

'It's very homely,' Emma thinks, like Christmas at Bankside farm with her siblings. She is missing her family at such a festive time.

They all sit around the table and tuck into an array of vegetables plus chicken, followed by Christmas pudding and custard.

Afterwards, presents are exchanged, with toiletries for Emma and aftershave for Ron. 'I didn't know what to get you,' Emma states, apologetically.

'You needn't have brought anything, but the children will enjoy a few extra sweets and we'll enjoy the wine, won't we, Kevin.'

After the pots are removed to the kitchen, Kevin washes up while Maire chats to her guests.

'Can I help?' asks Emma.

'No. Kevin likes to do this on Christmas Day. He has always done it. He thinks I deserve a rest after all the cooking although he also helps with that. She smiles and continues chatting, talking about her life in Ireland and how she met Kevin. Matthew, the youngest child, wants Ron to admire his new set of cars and wooden garage. He is a chubby-faced five-year-old with freckles and a mop of brown hair. The older two are engrossed in a board game. Noticing that the clock on the wall shows it's almost three o'clock, Emma decides it is time to go, as Maire's extended family are due to arrive, shortly.

'We have had a lovely day, thank you. I thought it would be a quiet Christmas Day with just the two of us but it has been very enjoyable,' Emma says.

The couple set off hand-in-hand, covering the short walk to their house in two minutes. On arriving home, they have a drink of tea and Emma rests awhile, while Ron lights his pipe, puts his feet up and relaxes by watching television. Later, they watch the early evening news, before setting off on foot to go to Jacqui and Patrick's.

Jacqui greets them at the door. She is wearing a full-length flowing garment, in delicate chiffon material, displaying all the colours of the rainbow.

'You look great,' says Emma, 'very flamboyant.' Jacqui's hair, with streaks of dyed, blonde strands enhancing the brown, is piled high on her head. 'So fashionable too,' she continues.' Jacqui gives one of her radiant smiles.

'Come into the mad house,' she says, taking their coats. Food is spread out on a table at the far end, with a choice of chicken legs, sausages, pickles, cheeses, crisps, sandwiches and much more. Patrick is behind a makeshift bar, serving drinks. He waves them over.

'Just a squash for me, please,' Emma says.

'I'll have a beer,' adds Ron. The place is swarming with people. There are neighbours from next door, plus friends from Patrick's Club who have descended upon them in droves. There is noise and laughter.

'He just threw out a general invitation one evening at the Club,' says Jacqui, by way of explanation.

'You finished it,' Emma says in amazement, looking at the walls and noticing that the last couple of strips are barely dry.

'I was up most of the night,' explains Jacqui. 'We finished an hour

before the first guest arrived. I'm shattered but will keep going for
another few hours.'

'Let's have a sing-a-long,' shouts Patrick, now a little worse for
drink and swaying over to the piano. He plays well and the room is
filled with the noise of alto and baritone voices.

'This is why we asked neighbours,' laughs Jacqui. 'Better to have
them with us than complaining about noise.'

At eleven-thirty, Emma and Ron say farewell and leave the party
that is still in full swing.

'I don't know when they will all go,' says Jacqui, standing at the
door to see her friends off. 'I may just crawl into bed and leave
Patrick with them.' After expressing their thanks once more at
having a wonderful evening, Ron takes Emma's hand and they
slowly make their way home. It is an incline on the way and
Emma is very tired. They crawl into bed and soon Ron is snoring,
but Emma is awake.

'Just settle down,' she whispers, speaking to her baby who has
decided it is playtime and is kicking Emma in her ribs.

After the festive season, Ron is back at work while Emma is filling
in the days, counting down to her due date. She still hasn't a carry-
cot and keeps scrutinising the *For Sale* notices in shop-windows.
The day before New Year's eve, on a bitterly cold morning, she
wraps up well and walks to The Boulevard shops.

'At last,' she thinks, seeing that there is a carry-cot for sale. She
notes the address which, luckily for her, is a street nearby. On
arriving, she is shown a cream carry-cot, very basic, but it is
collapsible and the young woman offers her the wooden stand to
go with it.

'I've a baby bath if you need one,' she says to Emma. 'It fits on
the stand and the stand folds, if necessary.'

'Yes, please. I can take them now,' Emma says, finding her purse
and handing over the cash. Delighted with her purchases, she
walks slowly back home, stopping every so often to give her arms
a rest as she is carrying the carry-cot and stand with one hand and
the bath with the other. 'So many things for one tiny baby,' she
thinks.

Back home and after a bite to eat, she washes the carry-cot and
places it in their bedroom on the stand. Then wiping down the
baby bath to freshen it up, she puts it alongside the carry-cot and

places inside it, baby soap, powder, cotton-wool, a jar of Vaseline and safety-pins et cetera. She has a pile of terry and muslin nappies in the corner of the bedroom plus three cream-coloured, flannelette, full-length baby nighties with long sleeves and tiny pink flowers embroidered on the front. They are folded up alongside three baby vests. There is also a crepe, beige-coloured, rolled-up bandage that she has bought, to wrap around the baby's tummy when the umbilical cord is cut. The nurse at the classes explained about the need for the bandage.

'This baby is taking over and hasn't even arrived yet,' Emma thinks, smiling to herself.

The couple spends New Year's eve at home watching television on the tiny screen and wait to let in the New Year before going to bed. Long after Ron is asleep, Emma is still awake as the baby appears to be playing football, its legs kicking inside her. She is excited but apprehensive about what is to come. Her last salary at the end of November has been spent. She knows she will have to budget carefully.

'Even though I have friends, I have no family close by. It is daunting what lies ahead. Will I be able to manage the budget, the home and our baby?'

Edna Hunneysett

Winter 1962 / Summer 1962

A week before her due date in mid-January, Emma wakes up in the
early hours.
'Something is happening. Are these contractions?' she wonders.
They are irregular and not strong, but not knowing quite what to
expect, Emma gets up and creeps quietly downstairs and makes
herself a cup of tea. She watches the clock on the wall and times
the contractions but there is no pattern to them, just discomfort and
movement. After two hours, she is still experiencing them and
when Ron appears, she tells him.
'Should we call the midwife?' he asks.
'When you are ready for work, if I am still having them, you can
ring her when you pass the phone box at the end of the road, just
so she knows what is going on. I might wander up to Maire's later.
Don't worry. I will get someone to ring you at work if there is any
news.' An hour later, Nurse Jameson arrives.
'What is happening, then?' she asks.
'I'm not sure, but I have been having contractions. I hope we've
done the right thing, calling you,' Emma says anxiously, knowing
how busy the Nurse can be.'
'I was in the area anyway. Let's go upstairs and we will see what's
going on.' After examining Emma, the midwife reassures her that
she is not in labour. 'The head is well down. It might be a week or
sooner. Babies are so unpredictable. If you are worried, give me a
ring and leave a message.' She knows how anxious, first-time
mothers can be.

After the midwife leaves, Emma sets too and cleans the house. She
wants everything ready just in case. Then she writes a letter to
Martha updating her on the baby. The days drag but an hour at the
classes helps to pass the time and afterwards, she visits Jacqui's
where they have a good laugh reminiscing over the Christmas
party. Maire calls in on the Friday afternoon and Emma explains
about her false call to the midwife.
'I'll pop in again next week. If you need me, just come, or if it is
evening, ask Ron to come for me.'
'She is such a kind and gentle person,' thinks Emma.

The following week, in the early hours of Wednesday morning, the
day after Emma's due date, she is having contractions. This time,
she stays in bed and dozes. Ron sleeps on, beside her. He has taken

a week's holiday in the hope that something might happen. Getting up around eight o'clock, Emma paddles downstairs, careful not to catch her feet in the frayed carpet. She walks across the bare front room boards and goes through the living-room and into the kitchen. She isn't hungry but makes a pot of tea and butters a slice of bread. The contractions are strong and regular and she knows instinctively that it is happening. The baby is coming. She is nervous but calm.

'Anything?' asks Ron, appearing in the doorway. He asks this, each morning.

'Yes. It's pretty definite, I think.' His face lights up.

'Shall I go and ring the midwife?'

'No. Not yet. They explained at the classes that it can go on for hours. I will time the contractions. When they get to ten minutes apart, then we will call her.'

'I'll walk down to the post office and send Martha a telegram if you like. It will give her time to plan coming.'

'That's a good idea.'

While Ron is out, the midwife calls unexpectedly. Emma explains about the contractions.

'You are over your due date. I'm surprised you have gone this long as the head was well in place a week ago.' After examining her, she confirms that she is in labour. 'First babies usually take a while. I'll make up the bed while I'm here so that all is prepared. I'm expecting this baby to arrive today, if all goes well. I have a busy schedule but I will try and call back around dinner-time. If things get too uncomfortable, get your husband to ring me.' Emma recalls being told at one of the ante-natal classes, about the contractions changing at the pushing stage, later in the labour.

'Do you know what telegrams cost?' Ron says, on his return. Emma shakes her head. 'It was about three shillings. It's half the price if it's for the next day, but I thought it was urgent.'

'You did right. Martha will need time to organise and find out train times. When you think that a letter costs three pence, or four and a half pence. It is a special occasion, though, isn't it?' She makes them both a drink and Ron settles down and lights his pipe before reading the paper that he has just bought. The pale, grey smoke wafts up to the ceiling.

'It's a waiting game,' he thinks, trying to concentrate on his reading. 'Are you all right?' he asks, ten minutes later, noticing

Emma paddling up and down and stopping to breathe heavily at regular intervals. He watches her as she glances at the clock.

'They are really strong. I'm trying to breathe like they said. The midwife said she might call in around dinner-time, but I think you should ring her.' Emma is beginning to struggle with the strength of the contractions and they seem to be speeding up. Shortly after Ron leaves, Emma hears the doorbell ring.

'Ron came and said you were in labour and that he has gone to ring for the midwife,' Maire says, stepping inside. Immediately she can tell by Emma's expression that things are moving fast. Emma starts groaning. The overwhelming contraction lasts longer and she feels her back is being torn. She is finding it difficult to breathe deeply like they were taught. Barely has one contraction subsided than another engulfs her, even stronger and longer. She moans as she breathes.

'I want to push,' she exclaims, suddenly. 'Oh, God, help me.' Maire is very apprehensive but leads her upstairs.

'I think you should get into bed.'

'Yes.' Then all is calm before another urge to push overtakes Emma. Maire holds her hands and Emma grips them tightly at each pushing pain. It becomes a rhythm and Emma even manages to smile. 'Another,' she says and squeezes Maire's hands as she moans while trying to lick her parched lips. 'I need a drink.' Maire lets go of her hands to go to the bathroom but another pain engulfs Emma. 'Don't leave me,' she cries. In the middle of the pain, Maire hears the doorbell ring but continues talking gently to her, encouraging her to push hard and then relax. 'It's coming,' Emma says. 'The baby is coming.' Maire sees the midwife's car going back down the road and feels panic arising.

There is a commotion downstairs and the midwife rushes up followed by Ron as they hear Emma cry out again. Ron, walking back home, had flagged the midwife down and she'd turned around. Maire steps back, very relieved. Seeing the midwife taking over, she quietly goes out of the door. Ron hovers in the back ground, not sure what to do. The midwife breaks the water bag. 'Don't push,' she instructs. 'Just pant. That's good.' Emma half sits up and watches, praying for her baby to be all right. The baby's head is out but the cord is around its neck and the baby's face is turning a blue colour. The midwife unhooks the cord and instructs Emma to push hard. Out comes the baby. Immediately, the nurse cuts the cord and clears its air passages. 'You have a little girl.' Tears of joy run down Emma's face. The baby gives a little cry.

'Is she all right?'

'She is. You go and put a kettle on and bring us a cup of tea,' the midwife says to Ron, who has been hovering around, feeling helpless. He smiles at Emma as he leaves the room. 'She weighs seven pounds,' the nurse states, looking at the scales. 'She is a healthy baby. You can hold her when I have sorted you out.' She wraps the baby in a sheet and lays her in the carry-cot, before approaching the bed. 'Now, I want a gentle push to expel the afterbirth. Then I can remove the padded sheet. Have you draw-sheets?'

'They're in the airing cupboard on the landing. They are not new as my mam sent me them. They are made from old sheets.' Emma knows about using a draw-sheet from when her mam gave birth at home, a half-sized sheet placed on top of the bottom sheet to protect it. Her mam also sent some plain, flannelette pieces of cloth to wrap the baby in, made from an old sheet.

After making Emma comfortable, the nurse busies herself bathing the baby in the cream-coloured baby bath. Emma loves the fragrant smell of Johnson's baby powder. It was on offer when she bought it, as otherwise, she would have bought a cheaper brand. Emma watches the midwife wrapping the crepe bandage around the middle of the baby's tummy to keep the cut cord protected, until it dries up. Then the midwife folds a muslin nappy very neatly into a triangle and deftly puts it on, followed by a terry one, fastening it with a safety-pin. Emma notices that she doesn't use the rubber pants that go over the nappy.

'I'll be using them when I start changing the baby,' she thinks, remembering the times that she'd watched Martha and realising the importance of them. Later, with baby settled in Emma's arms, swaddled and sleeping, the nurse sits for ten minutes enjoying the cup of tea, before collecting her bags and putting on her coat.

'I will be back tomorrow. Baby will sleep. If she is disturbed, just give her sips of boiled water.'

After she leaves, Ron joins his wife and they gaze at their baby girl.

'She looks just like your dad,' says Emma. 'A chubby round face and no hair to speak of and you can see those heavy eyebrows shaping already even though practically hairless.'

'She is beautiful,' says Ron, taking her from Emma. He is amazed at this little girl.

'Our baby girl, our little Karen Ann,' states Emma, emphatically. They chose the name, months ago.

'I'll go and send telegrams to our parents. My mam will be anxious to know,' says Ron.

'Call in at Jacqui's and tell her, will you, please,' Emma requests. 'Also, can you buy a bucket while you are out? I need one to soak nappies in everyday, before I wash them. Ron has another walk out while Emma and baby sleep. In the evening, they have a visitor. Maire, carrying flowers, a card and baby clothes, enters the bedroom, having been ushered upstairs by Ron.

'How are you?' she asks. She peeps at the sleeping baby. 'She is beautiful. I wished afterwards that I'd stayed.'

'You were quite wonderful,' says Emma. 'I'm sorry I put you through it.'

'That's okay. You did really well. I know you are expecting your sister, but meanwhile, let me know if there is anything I can do. I will drop by tomorrow at dinner-time with a cottage pie. That will save Ron worrying about what to cook.'

'Thank you. That's so kind. You have been such a help already.'

The following day, Jacqui arrives, flamboyantly dressed, as usual, in a flowered smock over her baggy, bright red trousers and armed with fruit, chocolates and flowers.

'I thought you should be spoilt,' she says. 'Just look at this little darling,' she gushes, picking up Karen and cuddling her. 'She is beautiful. Come on then. Tell me all the details. I need to be prepared,' she says, patting her big bump. They are still in the throes of talking motherhood and babies when the midwife arrives and shoes Jacqui away.

'She needs rest,' the midwife states. 'I am sure you will have talked long enough.' Jacqui smiles and gives Emma a wave, as she leaves the bedroom.

On the morning of the third day, Emma awakes and bursts into tears as the midwife walks in.

'Postnatal blues. It is common,' the midwife says, dispassionately. 'It will soon pass.' Nurse Jameson is in her early sixties and has come out of retirement to help because midwives are in short supply. She has dealt with hundreds of young emotional mothers and their tears tend to wash over her. They have a chat about the baby and feeding. 'Your baby will only take small feeds at first. I think that you will need a breast pump to express some milk. That will ease your discomfort.' Ron brings tea and biscuits and after the nurse has seen to Emma and bathed the baby, she sits down, pulls out her cigarettes and lights up.

'Aren't you worried about getting cancer?' Emma asks. She is feeling more cheerful but is surprised seeing the midwife, smoking.

'If I'd been getting cancer, I would have got it by now. I'm a bit long in the tooth to give up them up.' Ten minutes later, when leaving, she gives Emma advice. 'You can get up and wander downstairs, you know. We don't keep mothers in bed for days like we used to. You bath your baby when it is convenient for you. In the evening might help in settling her. Don't be feeding her every time she whimpers. You will wear yourself out. Every four hours is fine. You might find that a little boiled water in between often helps. I'll call in briefly to check on you tomorrow, but all seems well to me.' As she leaves, Ron walks in and hands Emma a letter, before asking about what they can eat.

'Walk out and get fish and chips if you like,' Emma suggests.

'A good idea,' he replies as he isn't confident at cooking. The letter is from Martha, posted first-class, the day after receiving the telegram. On reading it, Emma is delighted with the news that Martha wants Ron to meet her and her children at Piccadilly train station, on Saturday afternoon. Martha explains that Joe went to the village for her, to telephone about train times.

Next morning, after feeding the baby around seven o'clock, Emma finds something to wear, a little difficult as she cannot fasten her skirt and doesn't want to wear the maternity one. She rummages around and finds a baggy pair of trousers, worn in early pregnancy and they are comfortable. After dressing and having breakfast, she organises the sleeping arrangements. Her plan is for little Alan to sleep in the cot while Sandra and Brian sleep in the double bed with Martha, unless she wants to sleep downstairs in the small bedroom. Emma is very excited as she is looking forward to days with her sister. She knows that they will have plenty to talk about. Ron is up and about and she gives him a shopping list.

'It's rather a long one, I'm afraid,' she says, apologetically. He comes back later, laden with shopping. Meanwhile the post arrives. She opens congratulation cards, plus a parcel containing a lovely set of matinee coats from Ron's mam. After feeding Karen, she hand-washes the nappies and after rinsing and wringing them out as tightly as she can, hangs them on the Pulley to slowly dry, the weather being no good for drying outside.

'I'll bath the baby tonight,' she thinks, so that Martha and her children can watch. After dinner, Ron leaves to catch the train into Manchester and Emma curls up in bed and sleeps, with their daughter asleep in her carry-cot.

Two hours later, Emma is disturbed by crying and realises it is over four hours since the baby's last feed. She quickly gets out of bed and picks up her daughter.

'Mammy slept too long, didn't she,' she says, as her little one suckles contentedly. There is noise downstairs and then Martha appears in the doorway carrying twelve-month-old Alan, followed by Sandra and Brian. They crowd around the bed watching the baby feed.

'What a journey,' exclaims Martha. 'I'll get Joe to bring me by car next time I visit. Ron has been great. It was such a joy to see him walking down the platform towards us. I brought Alan's pushchair as I didn't think you'd have one. How are you?'

'I'm fine, thank you. Lacking in sleep, but otherwise, we are okay. I have made your beds. You can sleep with your children or downstairs on your own.'

'I'll stay upstairs and crawl in with them as they might want me in the night, being in a strange place.'

'It is lovely you being here. I've been so looking forward to seeing you. I think she has had enough. Do you want hold her?' After putting Alan on the floor, Martha takes the baby and bends down to show her to him while the other little two crowd around. Two-year-old Brian soon loses interest and begins wandering around the bedroom.

'She's tiny,' says Sandra, a chubby three-and-a-half-year-old.

'So were you, once,' her mam says, smiling at her daughter.

Martha is practical and efficient and organises the household. She has brought cot sheets which she intends leaving.

'They double as wraps for your baby. You can keep your good baby blanket for best when you take her out.' She encourages Emma to sleep while she can. 'You won't find it so easy when I've gone as you will be busy washing and shopping and being up in the night. Take advantage of me being here.'

On Monday, Emma shows Ron more congratulation cards, after he
returns home from work.
'Apparently, your mam put the announcement in the Evening
Gazette. Angela has enclosed the cutting in her letter. She says that
she is happy that Des is already more than half-way through his
two years call-up and that it is passing quickly. There is a lovely
card and letter from Joan, who made my wedding-dress, plus
another card from your friend Dan. He is now engaged to Barbara.
I'm pleased for her. Even Mrs Black, my landlady, has written and
enclosed a postal order. How kind is that.' The next day, the
postman brings more cards including one with a gift voucher from
her aunty Marjorie and uncle Abe. 'Lots of thankyou letters to
write, but I'll wait till Martha goes,' Emma thinks, 'as she won't
be here for long.' Emma is hoping for a card or letter from her
mam, but so far, not a word.

It is a week after the birth of the baby when the doorbell rings and
a lady is standing there, holding a large bouquet of flowers.
'Mrs Harding?'
'Yes, that's me.'
'Flowers for you, love, through *Interflora*.' The lady hands them
over and Emma goes inside the house to show Martha. She reads
the printed, small, white card, fastened to the wrapping.
'From mam and dad, with love and congratulations,' she says,
reading it out loud, but with little enthusiasm.
'They're lovely,' says Martha, looking at the lavender-coloured
irises and red and white chrysanthemums, plus greenery.
'Yes, they are,' Emma replies, placing the flowers on the table and
going into the kitchen for a vase, but she feels disturbed. She
thinks that it is easy to order flowers when shopping in Whitby.
Deep down, she knows that she would sooner have had a few lines
from her mam. 'It must have cost them, too, when they can't really
afford to buy them,' she muses.
'You know, Emma,' Martha begins, sensing a kind of
disappointment. 'When I told mam that I was pregnant, she said
she wouldn't be babysitting and was just letting me know. We've
seen her struggle when we were growing up. She does her best but
with not having had her mother around when she had us lot, maybe
she sees things differently. Dad's mam died when he was twelve.
So, she wasn't there for mam, either. We didn't have grans to spoil
us. We just have to be here for each other.'
'I know, says Emma, 'and they must have been thinking of me,'

she adds, consoling herself. The next day, Maire calls in and
brings biscuits and chats to Martha as Emma is asleep in bed.
Jacqui also makes a visit and is ever the friendly, chatty person,
even with Martha's children. She has sweets for them.
'I'm the eldest of seven,' she tells Martha. 'I'm used to playing
mother to little ones. I was second mother in our house.'

Ron and Emma have already asked if Martha and Joe will be
godparents. Martha writes to Joe to explain that they can have the
ceremony on the Sunday as Baptisms are at twelve noon. *Emma
says that apparently, they just invite anyone to turn up*, she writes.
*We don't know how many Baptisms there will be, but hopefully
you can get here on time...* The week passes quickly. Joe arrives in
good time on the Sunday, looking very smart in his brown small-
chequered suit and with his thick thatch of hair neatly combed. He
has a quick cup of tea before they leave for church.
'Are you sure you can take us all?' asks Ron, wondering how they
will fit into the little red Fiat.
'We can if each adult takes a child,' says Joe, 'apart from me, of
course.' They all squeeze in. Martha is next to Joe, with Alan;
Emma takes Karen; Brian is on Ron's knee; and Sandra squeezes
in between Emma and Ron. When they arrive, they notice two
other couples with babies, accompanied by lots of family and
friends. The priest calls the new parents and the godparents to the
front of the church. He takes particulars from each of them before
proceeding with the Baptisms. Although some prayers are general
for all three parties, he calls each couple up separately for the
moment of pouring of water on the baby's head. They remain in
the front benches for the anointing; for the rite with a white piece
of cloth; and for the lighting of the candle. Emma and the other
new mothers are invited to stay back for a blessing, something
Emma thinks, used to be called 'Churching'. She'd heard it was to
do with cleansing and that you couldn't go to Holy Communion
until you'd been churched but she wasn't sure if that was true. She
stays back with the other two mothers and tells Ron that it is a
special prayer of thanksgiving, plus a blessing.

'We're going shortly,' Martha says to Emma when they arrive
back at the house. 'Joe wants to get away. He has milking to do.
We will have a cup of tea and sandwiches and then we will leave.'
While Emma prepares the food and feeds the children, Martha
packs their belongings and puts them in the boot of the car. Sandra

and Brian are excited about going home and can't contain their glee. Little Alan is happy to be on his dad's knee, sharing his sandwich. After farewells and kisses for the children, Emma watches as they drive off and stands at the door until they are out of sight. She feels like crying but knows she will have to get over it. She misses sharing her ups and downs with Martha. With the baby sleeping and the house very quiet, Emma settles down and writes a number of thankyou letters, before writing a long letter to Faith in reply to her letter received at Christmas. Faith is getting married in February but having a quiet wedding with close family only. Emma sees Ron take a box from the top shelf of the bookshelves and is curious.

'What's that?

'There's a scrap heap outside the office with all sorts of metal bits, springs, screws, bolts and suchlike. I'm going to try and make a robot. I didn't like to bring it out when Martha was here as I didn't want her kids getting them.' Emma smiles at him. 'I don't like waste and I like inventing things and it's all free,' he adds.

'I think it is great how you are always thinking up things,' she replies. 'You're never bored, are you? Will the robot move when you have made it?' Ron grins widely.

'Maybe not, but I can try.'

Karen soon settles into a routine and Emma, when not walking out, puts her in the pram in the garden for her morning sleep. The baby usually objects by crying, but having been told that fresh air is good for babies, Emma leaves her and eventually Karen settles down. She bumps into Margo one morning while out walking to the shops. Margo is an older, heavily-built mother-to-be who was at the ante-natal classes and is still awaiting her baby's birth. She is smartly dressed in a light-brown coat, trimmed with fur. Her elegant, black, leather boots are also topped with fur and she carries a swish crocodile-skin shopping bag. Margo peeps at Karen while Emma stands there feeling embarrassed, wondering what Margo will think of the second-hand pram with its patched corners.

'She's very cute, isn't she?' she says. 'How did it go?'

'It was okay. The instructions learnt at the classes about breathing when in labour, came in very useful.'

'Any stitches?'

'No, I didn't need any.'

'Good for you.'

'I hope all goes well,' Emma says, before she continues walking.

On the way home, she meets a neighbour who lives next door but one, who stops to speak. Emma has noticed her often, sitting in the bay window at the back of her house, busy, but with what, Emma doesn't know. The lady is short and stocky and is pushing a black Silver Cross pram, still looking as if it is straight from the manufacturers with not a mark or scratch on it and certainly no patched corners.

'Hello,' she greets Emma, with a gentle smile. 'I see you sometimes hanging out the washing. You know a lot of Irish songs. I hear you singing. Are you Irish?' Emma laughs.

'No, but we used to sing a lot at home in the evenings. There are quite a few of us. How old is your baby?' she asks, peeping into the pram.

'She was eight weeks, yesterday.'

'She's a little older than mine.' Emma pauses and then voices a thought. 'Would you like to call in for a cup of coffee, one day? I have no family in the area.'

'Thank you. I'd like that. I don't have many visitors. We can compare notes and talk babies.'

'We can have a good chat. That's for sure. I see you in your bay window at the back of the house.'

'Yes, I'm making curtains on the machine. It is my sewing area.'

'Is next Wednesday afternoon, around two o'clock, okay? I'm Emma, by the way,' she adds, laughing, when realising that they don't even know each other's names.

'Doris,' her neighbour responds, pushing her mousy-coloured hair away from her eyes. It is short and thick and hangs in a fringe. They each say goodbye and go their separate ways.

The two mothers meet as planned and enjoy a couple of hours sharing their stories on family and their babies. When meeting up for the third time, Doris tells Emma that she has been talking to another new mum, who lives further down the road.

'She'd like to join us. I hope it's all right with you as I said she can come next week to my house. She has a little boy who is two years old. She will bring a few toys for him to play with. She is called Janice.' Doris waits expectantly for a response.

'I don't mind at all. It's lovely getting together.'

Emma is enjoying the Wednesday afternoons. She decides at her next turn, she will make a rainbow cake, as the young women are not only providing a drink but also a snack. On the Tuesday, she sets to, making the mixture, before separating it into three portions, to add cocoa powder to one and pink colouring to another. Then she scoops a spoonful of each portion into a tin lined with greaseproof paper, using all the mixture.

'Oh, bother,' she thinks, on hearing the doorbell ring. She is wearing her baking pinny and has brushed her hair away from her eyes twice. 'I've probably got streaky marks on my face,' she thinks, as she walks to the door.

'Hello,' says Maire. 'You look as if you are baking. I won't stay if you are busy.'

'No. Come in.' Emma explains about the Wednesday afternoons. 'Can I join you?' asks Maire. 'I'd love an hour off. I would need to leave early to pick up the children at primary school.'

'Yes, of course. You can sample my rainbow cake,' Emma replies, placing the cake in the oven. 'That's Karen, awake. It is feeding time. I'll just put the kettle on. We can have a cuppa while I feed her. I am thinking about topping her up with a bottle as I'm not sure she is getting enough from me.' Maire is good for Emma and reassures her that she is doing well with Karen.

After their evening meal, Ron lights his pipe before taking Karen to hold her awhile, while Emma washes up. He saves his tobacco for leisure times at home and uses it sparingly as he knows that tobacco is quite expensive and has to be budgeted for, but even so, he runs out at times. Having finished the pots, Emma goes into the living-room.

'There is tobacco in my bag that I bought today, if you want more,' she says. She tries hard to make sure that he always has some, especially after Jacqui's comments one weekend, when visiting.

'He never seems to have any tobacco in that pipe of his,' she'd said, but Emma reassured her that it is only occasionally that he has none and suggested that she must have called in, the weekend before payday.

'I'll take Karen up,' she says to Ron. 'I saw Jacqui today, by the way. She is funny. She thought it hilarious when she called last weekend and saw one of your slippers with its toe cut out. Apparently, you told her that you were making a Roman sandal when she asked you why one of your slippers was toeless.' Ron grins at Emma.

'Yes, she did comment at the time. I didn't do a good job, if it wasn't recognisable as a Roman sandal,' he adds, ruefully. 'Maybe I'll leave things like that for the ladies to work on. I'll stick to wood and drawing.' They smile at each other as Emma leaves to take their baby to bed. Then letter-writing time as she wants to thank Faith for the wedding photograph. Faith is wearing a well-cut, cream, knee-length dress and matching stylish small hat while Mitch is sporting a dark-coloured suit with cream tie. 'I'm so happy for her,' thinks Emma.

Emma regularly visits the Mother and Baby Clinic to get Karen weighed. She has been told that breast-fed babies put on less weight than those who are bottle-fed and that Karen is doing fine. However, it bothers her that her baby doesn't seem to be putting on as much weight as the other babies. Consequently, she decides to top up with bottles at some feeding times even though her baby has already cut out one night feed and appears contented. Within weeks, she is completely on the bottle and is starting to have tastes of baby food and Emma is able to cut out another feed. In the earlier weeks, Karen had some evening colic but she now settles well at bedtime and Emma is finding life easy and enjoyable.

At the end of March, after going a week over her due date, Jacqui finally gives birth to a little girl. Emma has been calling regularly when going to the shops in Hazeltrees. She is delighted to find her friend in good spirits even though she has had a difficult labour. 'All well worth it,' Jacqui says, cuddling her baby. 'You forget as soon as you hold the baby. She is quite wonderful. We haven't a name for her yet. Just think. You and I will be able to spend time together, going to the park and having picnics with our little girls. It will be such fun.'

'It will be,' thinks Emma, while walking back to her house, 'but that won't address my problem, well, not exactly a problem, more a desire.' It was on the previous Sunday, after having been to church and then had dinner that Emma wanted to take her baby out and visit someone. 'But who?' she'd asked herself. She was longing to show her little girl to people, but with no family within a reasonable journey time, she couldn't think of anyone. She'd explained her thoughts to Ron and he suggested visiting Mrs Maughan at Heatonburn, from whom they rented the flat, as he couldn't think of anyone else.

'She's a motherly sort of person. We can take Karen on her first train journey. It is only a short run.' Emma thought this a good idea. On arriving at the flat, Mrs Maughan had made them very welcome and fussed over Karen. As pleasant as it was, Emma realised, on the way home, that what she'd really like is to visit her mam and dad or Ron's parents or Martha and Joe. This is what is on her mind.

'Having a baby seems to have made me a little home-sick,' she thinks. 'I have some lovely friends. It's just the weekends.' Her thoughts tail off as she arrives home.

Jacqui now visits a couple of times a week and they share the joys of motherhood with babies Karen and Daphne, the name chosen by Patrick and Jacqui after much deliberation, as they'd found it difficult to agree on a name.

'Are you going home for Easter?' Jacqui asks.

'No, but Ron's mam has written to say that they coming down with his brother Clive and Nancy, who is expecting in July.'

'You are going to be busy planning meals, are you.'

'Looks like. It will be good to see Ron's parents, though. I think they are very excited about their first grandchild.'

'I certainly am going to be busy,' thinks Emma, later in the week, wondering what her in-laws will make of her cooking. She needs to plan a meatless day for Good Friday, as is the rule of the Church. As much as she likes to go to the Holy Week services, she realises that it may be difficult as she doubts that, apart from Nancy, their visitors will be interested in going and she'll feel bad about leaving them.

Ron's parents, with Clive and Nancy, arrive on Maundy Thursday in a taxi and there are greetings all around. Karen is introduced and everyone takes a turn, holding her. Although a special day in the calendar of the Church, Emma decides that she will give church a miss, as she feels it will be impolite to walk out just after their guests arrive. She is right in thinking that Nancy may be interested in going on Good Friday because, while Clive and his parents stay at home with Karen, she joins Emma and Ron at the afternoon service. Nancy walks slowly because of being pregnant and when they arrive, the church is full, but Emma sees an empty seat at the back for Nancy while she stands with Ron nearby. 'Mass again, on Easter Sunday,' Emma thinks. 'It will look like we are always going,' but Ron's parents make no comment, as they are more than pleased to be spending time with their first grandchild.

Easter Sunday, being late in April, is a beautiful sunny day and quite warm. The family spend time in the garden with Clive larking about and having fun with his dad.
'You'd think he was still a lad,' says Nancy, watching him pretend to climb on his dad's back.
'Clive,' shouts his mother. 'Stop it. You are too heavy.' The yellow Formica-topped table and the four chairs are brought out and everyone enjoys afternoon tea with the sandwiches prepared earlier by Ron's mam. Emma brings out her rainbow cake and proudly displays it in the centre of the table.

Garden picnic: Ron and Nan

'Who's walking out for a pint, later?' Ron's dad asks. He is used to his Sunday evenings at the British Legion club, which he and his wife attend with their friends. Nancy doesn't want to go and offers to babysit.
'You all go,' she says.

Later in the evening, the five of them wander down to The Rising Sun and relax over drinks. It is a noisy evening with guest artists. After a couple of hours, Emma is ready for bed.

'I'm leaving now,' she says. 'You all stay and enjoy yourselves. Here is my key as Nancy will let me in.'

'I'll walk back with you,' says Ron. Clive and his mam stay and Emma and Ron enjoy a walk together in the cool of the evening. 'They are going on Tuesday,' says Ron. 'It has been great having them but it will be nice to be on our own again.' Emma agrees and holds his hand as they amble back home.

Throughout May and June, Jacqui and Emma meet up regularly and walk to the small park, taking sandwiches plus baby orange juice for their little girls. Karen sits on the grass propped up with cushions from the pram. She explores the green blades with her fingers and tries to touch a fast-moving beetle, but it scuttles away into the long grass and disappears. Daphne is too young to sit up unaided, but Janice, sitting on a blanket, props her between her splayed legs and the baby happily plays with a coloured rattle, gazing around and smiling. She already has more hair than Karen who is still almost bald.

'It will grow eventually,' reassures Jacqui. 'They are all different.'

Later that evening and in bed, with Ron asleep beside her, Emma is thinking.

'I am going to have to tell people, no matter what they might say…'

Summer 1962 / Autumn 1963

'I have something to tell you,' Emma says, hesitantly, one
afternoon in late June, when sitting on the grass at the small park
with Jacqui and their little girls. Her friend looks at her, waiting
expectantly. There is a pause.
'Spill it out then.'
'I think I'm expecting again.'
'What! Are you sure?'
'I am. I'm late this month and I missed last month's and I'm
feeling queasy in the mornings like I did with Karen but not so bad
up to now, although I have been sick, once or twice.' A silence
follows.
'How do you feel about it?' Jacqui eventually asks.
'Quite honestly, I'm happy, as Karen is easy to look after.'
'Does Ron know?'
'Yes. He enjoys his job and says if I'm happy, then it's fine by him
as I do most of the baby stuff. We haven't told anyone else yet.
I'm going to wait until I'm three months and then go to the
doctor's.' They each pick up their little ones and give them a
drink. Karen has pulled off her sunhat and Emma puts it back on.
Jacqui realises that Daphne has filled her nappy and proceeds to
change her.
'Time to go, I think,' says Jacqui. 'Patrick is coming home early
today and I need to have his meal ready before he leaves for the
Club.'

At the next Wednesday afternoon session, Emma thinks about
telling the others her latest news, but decides that she will wait
until the baby's date has been confirmed. She is already wondering
about what extras she'll need.
'Another cot,' she thinks, as she is walking up the road from
Janice's house after the usual get-together. 'I will have to start
saving each week until I have enough to buy second-hand one.
Apart from that, I will need more nappies, but I have plenty of
first-size baby clothes, mostly in white, which will be fine even if
it's a boy.' She is feeling excited about having another little one. 'I
will need a pram seat for Karen so that I can take them both out.'

After much deliberation, Ron and Emma decide to go on the train
to visit their families in late July and tell them in person about
Emma being pregnant again. She has been to the doctor's and was

given the twenty-sixth of January as her due date.

'I'll write and let them know we are coming,' she says to Ron.
'We can stay at your mam's as she'd like that and, hopefully, we'll
have a day at Bankside to show Karen to my family. We can visit
Clive and Nancy too and see their new baby as it should have
arrived by then.'

Very early in the morning, the day before they are planning to
leave, Emma hears the doorbell ring. She creeps quietly downstairs
in her pink, cotton pyjamas and opens the door, wondering who on
earth can be calling at this hour. Standing there are her parents.
She is surprised and delighted. They walk in.
'We thought we'd come and drive you up as it will be a much
easier journey than on the train with a carry-cot,' says her mam.
'We left very early to avoid the traffic,' adds Tom. 'It makes
driving easier for me. You and Ron and the baby will easily fit in
the back of the van.'
'We'll have a cup of tea and then have a lie down if you don't
mind. It's been a very early start,' Mary states. Emma goes to put
the kettle on. Then she disappears upstairs as she can hear Karen
making noises. Ron is fast asleep. Taking her baby, she goes back
down to find that her mam has made the tea and they are having
some bread and marmalade.
'Here she is,' Emma says, handing the baby to her dad. She is so
happy that they have come. The three of them sit quietly, talking.
'It's a lovely house, you have,' says Tom. 'It's a good size garden
too,' he adds, looking out of the window. 'You've done well, the
pair of you.' Any doubts about Emma being happy and Ron
looking after her, have been blown away. He can see their
daughter is very content.
'I have some news,' Emma says. 'I'm expecting again; due next
January.'
'A bit like your dad and me, then,' says Mary, encouragingly. 'We
had our first ones quickly.'
'They'll grow up together,' says Tom, totally nonplussed. 'There's
nothing wrong with a few little ones. Our Martha's doing fine with
her three.' Ron wanders in looking sleepy and more conversation
follows, before Tom and Mary go upstairs to catch up on some
sleep.
'Just use our bed, if you want,' says Emma.
'Aye; that'll be fine. We'll just lie on top of blankets,' her dad
replies.

There is another surprise after dinner. This time Ron answers the door. His parents are standing there and greet him with smiles. 'We thought we'd come down and help you travel back on the train,' his mam says, as they walk into the front room with its bare floor boards and no furniture. Ron is speechless. 'Aren't you pleased to see us?' she continues, wondering at his strange reaction. Emma walks through and Ron explains to her about his parents coming to journey back with them. The young couple look at each other, wondering what to say.

'It's lovely that you've taken the trouble to come all this way on the train, Mam. It's just that Emma's parents had the same idea and they've come in their van.' There is a prolonged silence.

'Well, we can't go straight back,' his mam replies. 'We're here now.'

'I'll make you a cup of tea. My mam and dad are in the garden with Karen,' says Emma, walking through to the kitchen. She goes outside and tells her parents. 'It's a bit awkward,' she says.

'We'll have to make the best of it,' replies Tom. 'Come on, Mary. We'll go in and say hello.'

The afternoon passes and everyone tries to be polite and pleasant but no-one seems relaxed. Karen is in the limelight and helps to lighten the atmosphere. Ron and Emma manage to get a few minutes alone.

'What are we going to do?' Emma asks him.

'Well, I can't let mam and dad travel back on their own,' says Ron, 'not when they've made such an effort to come all this way.'

'It will be easier taking Karen in the van,' suggests Emma.

'I'll tell you what. Why don't you go with your parents in the van with Karen and I'll go on the train with my parents. You can have a night at the farm and see all your family and maybe Joe or your dad will bring you through to Thorntees and we'll have a few nights at my mam's, as planned.'

'We don't really have a choice.' Emma states. 'We have to try and please both sets of parents. I think that's a good idea.' They smile and hug each other. 'We will have to sleep downstairs tonight,' she continues. 'I'll make the spare bed up for your parents and mine can sleep in our bed. They won't be fussed about using our sheets. I'll be leaving early in the morning with Karen, as dad likes to drive when there is little traffic on the roads. What a going-on.'

'And we thought we were the trouble,' jokes Ron, grinning at his wife.

Before the night is over, there is yet another surprise. On answering the door, Ron comes face to face with Ben, his work-mate, with a young lady whom he doesn't recognise.

'We thought we'd come by so that I can introduce you to my girlfriend, Jane,' Ben states.

'Come in,' says Ron. 'It's good to see you but before you go through, let me explain.' At that point, Emma joins them, having heard their voices. Ben, his dark hair neatly trimmed, introduces Jane. She is a bonny girl with thick, black, wavy hair, dark eyes and a chubby face and not unlike Ben in build, a little stocky. Emma explains about the holiday planned, the two sets of parents arriving and the dilemma it has given her and Ron. Ben and Jane think it hilarious and start laughing.

'You couldn't make it up,' Ben says, chortling.

'Come and say hello. We can do with some laughter,' says Ron. As the evening passes, Ron takes a photo of the gathering, but it seems to him that only the three young ones are smiling.

Emma and Parents with Ben and Jane

'It must be disappointing for your parents,' Emma says, as she snuggles up to Ron in bed. 'Coming all that way and then finding they won't have the pleasure of Karen, on their way home.'

'I know, but they'll have plenty of opportunities when you join us,' he replies.

'My parents are tired. They haven't had much sleep with having such an early start. It's not easy socialising with people you don't know well, either. It was great that Jane and Ben turned up.' Getting no reply, she glances at Ron and realises that he has fallen asleep. 'It's been a hectic day,' she thinks, as she closes her eyes.

It is a very early start next morning for Emma, Karen and her parents. On arriving back at Bankside, Emma spends her first night with Karen and next morning, visits Martha's, who springs some news.

'I've just learnt that I'm having another one.' Emma's eyes open wide.

'You are going to be busy. We'll have quite a little family between us.' Later in the day, Joe takes her through to Ron's family and after few days holiday, they return by train to Hazeltrees.

Emma's brother Mark, having borrowed their dad's van, turns up a day later, bringing twelve-year-old Jacob and Miriam, who has just turned eight. The holiday was arranged while Emma was at the farm on her short visit.

'You are getting tall, Jacob' she comments, looking at her youngest brother. 'You don't put weight on do you,' she says. He is very lean.

'I work hard and burn it up,' he answers, with his lop-sided grin.

'You don't mind sharing a bed, do you?' Emma questions, as they carry their bags upstairs.

'No,' replies Jacob. 'I'll just boot her out if she doesn't lay still.'

'No, you won't,' Miriam replies, defiantly. 'He won't, will he?'

'Of course not,' Emma responds. 'He is teasing you, but if he does, I will put him out in the back garden.' Miriam smiles knowingly at her brother, now she has Emma on her side.

'See!' she says. 'Emma won't let you.' Jacob gives her a gentle shove. They are good mates.

'There's a few things for you in that bag,' Mark says, when Emma comes downstairs. 'Eggs and bacon and cabbages and a few spuds. Dad thought they would help a bit.' She is delighted and unpacks the goods, before handing him the empty shopping bag. He hangs around a little while for a drink and bite to eat, but he is keen to get away.

In the garden: Ron and Karen

A lovely three weeks pass with Miriam enjoying playing with
Karen and helping to feed her. The two youngsters explore the area
and find a narrow beck beyond the fields at the back, with a rope
swing across it. They get to know the local children who
congregate there and spend hours playing around the beck. In the
evenings, they concentrate on cards with Emma and Ron, knock-
out-whist being a favourite game. Ron and Jacob play chess a few
times while Emma plays noughts and crosses with Miriam. When
Ron is at work, Emma walks to the shops and treats them to fish
and chips on occasions. They visit Janice too.
'We have a bit of money,' says Jacob, one Wednesday morning.
'Is it okay if me and Miriam walk to The Boulevard this afternoon,
when your friends come. We want to have a look around those
shops.' It is a novelty for them to be able to walk to shops. They
leave after dinner but after looking at the small row of shops, they
decide to walk into Hazeltrees instead to buy little presents for
their mam and dad.

It seems no time at all before Mark is back to take Miriam and
Jacob home.

'What a journey that has been,' are his opening words, on walking into the house.

'You look flustered. Has something happened?' Emma asks.

'I was driving along when this car overtook me at speed and the next thing is, it took a bend too quickly and ended up hitting a tree. Four lads about my age scrambled out, looking shocked and shaken. They were lucky to be alive. I pulled up, but other cars stopped and people went over to see if they were all right. I drove off. I'll tell you what; I drove slowly after that. I'll have a cup of tea. I'm still a bit shaken up.' Emma finds it very quiet after they leave. She goes out for a walk, pushing Karen in her pram, feeling a little sad. She loves her younger brother and sister and is coming to realise that she misses her family more than she expected to.

'Time to answer some letters,' she thinks. She wants to write to Angela and Des who are planning on a quiet wedding in the November when Des will be home for good from the forces.

The weeks pass and Emma is concerned that Karen, with her bottom-shuffling movement, is now trying to reach the door into the front room, which is usually left open, so that Emma can hear the doorbell ring.

'I think we need to consider getting a carpet for that room,' she explains to Ron, one evening. 'If Karen gets in there, she might get splinters on her hands and feet from the floor boards. She is forever pulling her bootees off. It doesn't have to be an expensive one or even a hard-wearing as we don't use that room and are not likely to for some time. I have been saving up for one.'

The following weekend, they go into Stockport on the bus, carrying Karen. They find a warehouse selling cheap carpets and choose a mottled blue.

'Can you fit it too?' Emma questions. The middle-aged well-built bloke, wearing brown overalls, assures them than he has a fitter who will do a grand job.

'Be with you Monday afternoon,' he says. They walk further down the street until they come to a furniture shop.

'Let's look in here,' Emma says to Ron. 'I want a drop-leaf table with chairs, to put in the front room. 'Then we can eat in there when we have company. It was such a squash using our little Formica-topped table when your mam and dad came with Clive and Nancy. We can put two of the chairs in the living-room when people come, instead of them sitting on those little tubular-legged kitchen chairs.' They find a medium-brown mahogany table in the sales, reduced in price, as it has a slight scratch, but hardly noticeable. The four dining-room chairs have seats covered in red imitation leather. Emma examines a sideboard that goes with the table and chairs. It has two cupboards, three drawers and two smaller compartments above, one of which has a glass sliding-door to display fine pottery and glasses.

'They are in the sale as a set,' the assistant explains, seeing Emma's interest. 'I can do you a good deal.' Ron can see his wife is keen.

'Can we afford them?' he asks, with concern in his voice.

'I can manage. Don't worry,' Emma replies. 'The sideboard will be so useful to put stuff in.' She pays a deposit and signs an agreement to pay the rest, over twelve months.

On the bus home, Emma remembers about the letter.

'It came this morning from Amy,' Emma tells Ron. I skimmed it but enough to know that she wants to come and stay with us. She left school in July and has been working at different farms doing jobs inside and outside. She doesn't seem to be able to find a decent job even though she has seven GCEs. Dad suggested she comes to stay and gets a job around here. He was talking about her when I went home overnight before coming to your mam's. I told him that she has a good chance of getting a job in Manchester or Stockport. Do you remember I mentioned it at the time?'

'Vaguely,' Ron replies.

'Well, she is coming. She gets into Manchester at two o'clock on Saturday and wonders if we'll meet her as she hasn't been before. She can have that downstairs bedroom. It is big enough for one and it will save us moving Karen into ours from the back bedroom upstairs. Amy won't be any bother. It will be fun.'

'It is fine, Emma. I like your Amy. She is always chatty.'

It is the day before Amy arrives, that Emma receives some sad news. Ron finds her with a letter in her hand and quietly crying. 'What is it?' he asks, coming close and putting his arm around her. 'It's Martha. She's lost her baby. There was a freak thunderstorm and while she was standing washing up in front of the little kitchen window, the lightning struck her. Luckily for her she was wearing rubber-soled boots which absorbed it, but it caused her to miscarry, a baby boy. You can tell at around twelve weeks, you know. They're tiny but formed.'

'I'll make you a cup of tea,' her husband offers, sympathetically. Emma continues reading. Martha tells her that Joe buried the baby, wrapped in a small sheet, in a private corner of the stackyard where no-one really ventures. *It was so small. My baby...,* she writes. Emma puts her hand on her tummy and cries gently. She can't imagine what it must be like to lose one. She feels a gentle fluttering and is reassured that her baby is alive. Later that evening, she takes pen to paper and writes to Martha, not knowing what to say except to express sadness, sympathy and a prayer.

The next day, as requested, Ron meets Amy at Piccadilly station. She walks in, smiling.
'She is growing into a vivacious young woman,' Emma thinks, as they catch up, over a cup of tea. 'Not as tall as me but just as slim and the same black, short, curly hair.
'I must tell you,' Amy says, 'that Mark wants to come down again for a few days with his mates. They really enjoyed their stay in the flat. He is hoping to arrive in a week's time and said to let him know if they can't come.'
'Is that all right with you?' Emma asks Ron. He nods. He is getting used to his wife's family coming and going. Emma then thinks about where they will sleep.
'The two brothers can go in the back bedroom in the double bed and the other two can camp downstairs, in the front room. We'll move Karen temporarily into our bedroom. I'll write to Mark and tell him to bring camp-beds and bedding for him and Keith. We have to walk past them to get into here and the kitchen, but they'll have to put up with that. It's good that we got that carpet laid and that we bought the table and chairs.'
'They won't mind where they sleep, Emma. Honestly, they just want a holiday,' Amy says, reassuringly. The next day, Amy ploughs through the jobs section in the local newspaper that Emma bought for her.
'I'll walk out later and buy today's paper,' Amy says.
'Let's both go and we can call in to see Jacqui, my friend,' Emma replies.

The days pass and Amy begins the task of writing to employers. On Saturday, the lads arrive. They are a cheery bunch and Amy, knowing them well from the village primary school and the local dances, enjoys their company. The lads spend a lot of time in Manchester as they love watching the motor-bikes.

'You should see them,' Mark says. 'They go round and round and get higher and higher and faster and faster till they're at the top.'
'It's amazing to watch,' say Keith. 'I'd be petrified.' Amy sits up late at night in the back garden talking with her brother and his mates, but Emma is concerned when she finds that her sister was up until two in the early hours, talking with Barney, after the others had gone to bed. He is a very charming nineteen-year-old and Amy is an extremely attractive and appealing sixteen-year-old. She decides to have a word with her.
'I know you feel responsible for me,' Amy says in response, but we're just friends. I've known him for ages. There's nothing going on.'
'That's okay, then. It's just, you know…' Emma doesn't finish the sentence.
'You don't need to worry,' Amy replies, reassuringly, smiling at her sister.

In no time at all it seems, the lads are packing up and going home.
'We've had a great time,' Barney states, as he walks into the living-room, followed by his brother Jed, who is carrying a bunch of flowers and chocolates.
'From us all,' Jed says. 'Thank you for putting up with us.'
'You've been no trouble. Well, maybe a bit noisy in the early hours,' says Emma, but she is laughing and they know she doesn't mean it. 'Come again.' Ron holds Karen while Amy and Emma stand with him on the doorstep, as they wave the lads goodbye.
'Now I'll start writing about these jobs,' states Amy. 'It has been fun having Mark here, but I need to find work. By the way, I've just remembered. I meant to tell you that dad has now got electrics put in and intends having mains water laid on and a bathroom where that small box-room is, off the landing. Tim has been helping him to dig a hole for the septic tank which will be needed when the toilet is put in. I don't know quite when that will happen but soon, he hopes.'
'That is good news,' says Emma, totally used to electric lights and a flush toilet. 'Mam will be pleased.'

It is another two weeks before Amy is invited to an interview.
'I've been here almost a month,' she says to Emma, one morning. 'I have two interviews next week. I'm looking forward to getting a job.' Her enthusiasm lasts until later in the morning when she receives a letter from their mam and her plans are scuppered. She

gasps, on reading it.

'What's the matter?' asks Emma.

'Listen to what mam writes.' *...dad and I think you need to come home and look after things as I'll be in hospital a while. It's major surgery. We're sorry to have to ask you but there isn't an alternative...* Amy's face drops. 'Just when I thought I'd be starting a proper job.'

'That is so hard,' says Emma, 'but you'll be doing a great job back home looking after everyone. Miriam will need you if mam is in hospital awhile. Does she say what the matter is?'

'No. She says that she will explain when I get home.'

'You can always come back if you want, when she has recovered. Keep me informed, won't you.'

'I'll write. I'll get the train back, tomorrow. I know the times as I checked them before I came.' The next morning, after breakfast, Amy puts on her coat and picks up her luggage. The sisters hug each other and Emma watches while Amy walks down the road until out of sight.

'Just you and dad and me now,' she says to Karen. Her heart feels heavy and she hugs her little girl closely to her. She misses her family. 'You're just emotional because you're pregnant,' she tells herself. 'Go and get the washing done.' Emma puts Karen down and walks into the downstairs bedroom to collect the laundry for washing. 'Hopefully, one day, we will have a washing-machine,' she thinks, as she pounds the sheets in the kitchen sink.

'I have some news,' Ron tells Emma after their meal, a couple of nights later. 'You know Ben. You met him that night when he brought his girlfriend. His mam has been having a sort-out and found a television enlarger that will fit ours. It will make the screen two inches bigger.'

'That's great,' enthuses Emma.

'Also, I don't think I've told you this, but at one end of our office there are four blokes who do technical illustrating. It is really interesting. I've asked our boss if I can have a go and he said I can and suggested that I take a course on it at Manchester College of Art, starting in January. Ben will take me on his motor-bike as he goes to night school.'

'Sounds good,' Emma replies. 'By the way, I mentioned to Janice, up the road, about going to the pictures on Friday night and she is happy to babysit. She has offered before.' Ron's eyes light up.

'We can go and see *The Great Escape* that has just come out this year. It's about prisoners of war escaping and there is a great motor-bike chase in it.' They look forward to this as it is a treat for them to go out and especially with knowing that Karen will be in good hands.

The young couple enjoy their night out but on returning home, are shocked to learn that President John Kennedy of the USA has been shot. After taking off their coats and saying goodbye to Janice who assures them that Karen has been fine, they sit down to watch the news.
'It is horrendous,' says Emma. 'It must be awful for his wife and little ones.' They are glued to the television for the next half-an-hour until Emma decides she needs to go to bed. Ron switches the television off and follows her upstairs. They are both subdued.
'A lovely night out, but coming home to that,' Ron says. 'It is so difficult to take in.'

The following evening, after both have watched more of the news about John Kennedy, they are ready to see something less intense. They settle down to watch the first episode of a new series called *Doctor Who*. Ron loves coming home to his television in the evenings, even such a small one but the enlarger helps.
'You might not enjoy it, but I've been reading about it and it sounds intriguing,' he says. Emma is knitting a matinee coat for the new baby.
'I don't know when Karen is going to creep or attempt to stand up. She is so content. I put toys in front of her and she plays happily,' she tells him. 'They said at the clinic that she is fine and all babies progress at different rates.'
'Sounds all right to me,' comments Ron, filling his pipe.
'I've had a letter from Amy. Mam has had her operation but she's not picking up. She will hate it in hospital. It's the reason why she wouldn't even go in to have any of us. Not that I blame her.'

Eventually Emma hears from Amy that their mam is back home after a three week stay in hospital, but was discharged because she wasn't getting better and it was decided that she might improve in her own surroundings. *Dad says that she has been pining away. She'll do better now, we hope*, writes Amy. Emma, after some thought, decides that she will buy a weekly paper with cryptic crosswords in and post it to her mam, as she knows that she enjoys doing them.

'I don't know what else to do, but she will realise that I am thinking about her, if I send one every week.'

Christmas comes upon them quickly. It is a time to include letters with cards and Emma has posted their cards two weeks ago except for those to be hand-delivered to the Wednesday group. She enjoys receiving updates from friends. Faith is expecting her first baby at the end of March. She learns that Des and Angela's plans were turned upside down when Des was told that because of the world-wide troubles taking place, he, like many others, would have to serve another six months. *It was awful*, Angela writes. *When Des explained about the wedding plans, he was given three days leave and we had one night's honeymoon in Edinburgh before he went back. The lads all complained that they'd done their time and didn't see why they should stay, as they weren't Regulars. It worked, as they were allowed to finish after a month. We are together at last…* Inside Dan and Barbara's card is an invitation to their wedding.

'I can't see us getting to it,' Emma says to Ron, later in the evening. 'It will be too soon after the baby's arrival and Karen isn't walking yet. We don't have transport. What do you think? He's your friend.' Ron ponders for a while.

'I think you are right. Just write and apologise, will you and explain why. We can send them a present.'

'Just the three of us,' thinks Emma, late on Christmas eve, 'but we will enjoy a visit to Jacqui's for Christmas dinner. Maire calls in with a card and to wish them a Happy Christmas on her way to Midnight Mass. They take Karen in the pram to church on Christmas morning and she is admired by a number of parishioners. 'It's different from walking over the moors in the moonlight,' Emma thinks, as they arrive back home to pick up little presents to take to her friend's. 'You look so pretty,' Emma says to her little girl as she is fastening Karen's coat, 'with your new dress that Nan sent you.' Karen's fair hair is finally growing and Emma, at first, brushed it into a cock's comb when it was washed, but now it falls loosely around her face. She is attempting speech and can say dada and mama, much to Emma's delight. Dinner is ready when they turn up at Jacqui's and there are crackers to pull. Little Daphne is an active baby and already creeping around. Later in the day, as some of Patrick's friends arrive, Emma and Ron leave. 'It was a delicious meal,' Emma says, and we've had a lovely day. I will catch up with you during the week.'

'It's too early,' Emma thinks, three weeks later, on experiencing mild contractions in the early hours. 'Probably a false alarm, like with Karen. You have another ten days to go,' she says to her baby, patting her tummy. The contractions continue and she gets up and makes a cup of tea. Luckily Ron is at home because it is a Saturday. At breakfast time, he decides to ring the midwife.
'I think we should, to see if everything is all right,' he says, before leaving the house to walk to a telephone box. He hasn't forgotten the last time. Nurse Jameson arrives before he returns.
'We don't want a last-minute panic,' she says, remembering what happened at Karen's birth. 'Let's have a look at you.' Emma picks Karen up and they go up to her bedroom. 'It is not a false alarm; you're on the way. In a rush to get out, this one,' she adds. 'I'll sort out a few calls, but I will soon be back. I am not taking any chances this time.' She returns late morning and after examining Emma, settles herself down with a cigarette and a cup of tea. Emma is excited but calm. She writes a hurried note to Martha knowing that she will let the family know.
'Can you post it, first class,' she says to Ron. 'Then hopefully she will get it on Monday. We need to let your mam know, but a letter will do this time, after baby is born. Telegrams are too expensive.'
'I'll ring work on Monday and ask for holiday entitlement until she arrives,' he says. 'I warned them that this might happen.'

It is almost two o'clock when Emma finally gives birth to a baby boy and she notices that he has plenty of black hair.
'No stitches needed,' states the nurse. 'He weighs seven pounds, twelve ounces; a decent weight.' When he is bathed and dressed, Ron brings Karen in to see him but she is not particularly interested.
'He has your family's lean look about him,' says Ron to his wife, 'and dark hair, too. He'll be a handsome little fellow. Is it Samuel James, then, like we planned? He will probably get Sam or Sammy, you know.' Emma nods. She is exhausted. It wasn't a difficult labour, but still hard work.
'The second phase was much quicker than last time with not many pushes,' she thinks. 'Will you take Karen downstairs as I need to sleep,' she asks her husband, after the midwife leaves. She curls up in bed and closes her eyes.

Sam is a hungry baby and Emma tries to satisfy him, breast-feeding. He cries more than Karen used to and she is already giving him drinks of boiled water between feeds. The feeding every four hours message is glued to her brain. She is glad when Martha arrives on Wednesday afternoon. This time Joe brings her in the car with their three little ones. Her sister immediately comes upstairs to see the new baby, bringing her children with her.

'What a journey,' she states, as she sits on the bed and takes baby Sam into her arms. 'The kids are not good travellers. Alan was sick. The weather is sleeting. I hope it doesn't snow before Joe gets home. The good news is that we've brought our washing-machine. We bought it second-hand when we got electricity put in, last year. It is big and cumbersome and oil has been leaking out of it into the car. Ron and Joe have brought it in.'

'You did well to bring that,' says Emma.

'I remembered all the washing last time,' answers Martha. 'You look tired.'

'I am. He is not a calm baby like Karen or maybe he is a hungry one. Ron tries hard but it's not the same as a woman taking over. I've bought another second-hand cot that Alan can use if you like. It took me weeks to save up to buy it. We watch the pennies now. You might want to sleep downstairs. It is up to you. I'm so glad you are here.' Ron joins them, carrying Karen. They are still chatting when Brian, now turned three, is bored and starts wandering around the bedroom. Spying the glass of water, he picks it up and then starts coughing. With each cough, he jerks the glass and water sprays everywhere. Ron grabs the glass with his spare hand, still holding Karen in the other. The sisters start laughing. Wrapping Sam up tightly in the flannelette sheet, like a cocoon, Martha lays him in the carry-cot.

'I'd better go downstairs and take these three with me. I'll make Joe a cup of tea and a sandwich as he needs to get back for milking time. Cows don't like waiting.'

'Do you mind if I have a sleep. I've had a bad night. Just help yourself to whatever.' Emma smiles as Martha leaves the room with her little brood. 'It is good to have her here,' she thinks, closing her eyes.

An hour later, Emma awakes to the sound of the baby making snuffling noises but she leaves him sleeping. Martha brings her a cup of tea and a cheese cracker and sits on the edge of the bed. 'I have news for you,' she says. 'I'm expecting again, due early

July.'
'You'll have your hands full.'
'I know. I have three lovely little ones but I always wanted children. I love my babies. Sandra starts school in September. They grow up so quickly.'
'How is mam doing?' Emma asks.
'She has been very weak for some time, really poorly, but is starting to pick up. It has been a long haul. Amy is doing a great job looking after them all and I think she will be carrying on with that for some time yet. I doubt you'll hear from mam though, but she will be thinking of you. She doesn't want you worrying about her.'

The weekend soon arrives and Emma is up and about, but with three extra children in her house, there is a lot of noise. Martha has done a brilliant job running the home but has told Emma that she will be going back when Joe picks her up, mid-week.
'Thanks again,' says Emma, as once more, she is waving them off. She sheds a few tears as she re-enters her home with Karen, Sam being fast asleep upstairs. She has found that he sleeps better away from the noise as he was constantly being disturbed by shouts and shrieks of the children playing. Over the next days, he cries between feeds and Emma also realises that she cannot catch up on sleep when he sleeps as she also has Karen to look after. 'It is so different with your second child,' she thinks. 'I used to do my housework while Karen slept. Now I have to do it while watching her and I don't get a rest. It is so much harder.'

It is mid-February and the couple plan on having Mark and Amy as godparents for Sam at his Baptism. Emma writes early in the week to invite them to come the following Sunday. On Friday, she receives a letter from Amy. *We can't come,*' she writes. *Sorry, but we're completely snowed in. You know what it is like in February when the snow comes down. Mam is up and about but very weak and I'll be here for a while, yet...*
'We'll just have to go on our own,' Emma says to Ron, when telling him on Friday evening. 'We can stand proxy for them. You are allowed to do that. It might be weeks before they can get down.'

The little family of four make their way to the church for twelve noon, the following Sunday. Sam is in his warm leggings and top and wrapped in a shawl and blanket. On arriving, Emma counts the babies.

'Seven including our Sam,' she whispers to Ron as they sit together with their two children, the smallest party there. Emma explains to the priest that they are standing proxy because the godparents can't come. After the seven Baptisms, which take some time, there is the Churching for the mothers. Emma leaves Ron, with Karen on one knee and Sam on the other, while she joins the other mothers for the thanksgiving prayer and blessing. A bitterly cold wind is blowing as they set off home and she pulls Karen's hood well down as the snow is falling. Her little girl is perched on the pram seat with only her face, red and shiny from the cold, visible, as she is well wrapped up in an all-in-one bright red suit, a Christmas present form Nan and Grandpop.

'The sooner we are home, the better,' says Ron, as they make their way through the falling snowflakes. The sky is darkening and a storm is brewing.

Although Emma is coping, she is worried about Sam who never settles for long. She goes to the clinic and, leaving the pram outside, carries her children inside, as Karen isn't walking yet, although she can move around fast with her bottom-shuffle. Baby Sam weighs eight pounds, six and a half ounces, which means he has gained only ten and a half ounces in over five weeks. The young nurse attending the weigh-in, consoles Emma by saying that some babies don't put on weight as quickly as others, but Emma is not re-assured. The next day, she goes with her babies and visits the doctor's surgery. After listening to her concerns, the doctor asks her about feeding.

'I'm breast-feeding,' she replies, 'but he wakes up between feeds and I give him water. Sometime he takes two ounces of water.'

'And you have had him weighed?'

'Yes. He was seven pounds, twelve ounces when born. Yesterday, five weeks and three days later, he weighed eight pounds, six and a half ounces. It's here, on this card.' The doctor looks at the blue card issued by Cheshire County Council, Maternity and Child Welfare Centre. It is a record of Sam's birth and weight et cetera, plus added details from the clinic in Hazeltrees. He gazes at Emma with his piercing blue eyes.

'You have tried breast-feeding,' he says, 'but with these two to look after, you have your hands full and my guess is that you don't rest. This baby is starving. Stop breast-feeding him and put him on full-cream milk. If he doesn't settle down in a week, bring him back, but I think you will find that he will be much easier to deal with and you won't be as tired.' Emma is on the verge of tears. She feels an inadequate mother.

Stopping breast-feeding so abruptly means the milk mounts up before it starts to eventually subside and Emma goes through the pain. Full-cream milk has caused Sam to be constipated and she struggles watching him strain so hard but within a couple days, the problem is resolved. Luckily, apart from that, he is much more contented and sleeping better. Karen is little trouble as she sleeps all night and has a good routine. There are always nappies to wash and as they haven't a washing-machine, Emma washes daily, by hand, but now she is getting more sleep and Sam is less demanding for feeds, she is beginning to enjoy her little family and visit her friends again. The mothers haven't met since before Christmas and although Maire doesn't always come and Janice has a little part-time job which means that she is working sometimes, Emma and Doris begin again meeting weekly.

'You've run out of coal?' Jacqui states, in surprise. 'Not like you.' Emma has called in while out shopping.
'I know. I have used more than we expected with the weather being so bad and I'm just waiting for the new order to arrive. I had to wait till payday to put the order in.'
'We can put some in the shopping-tray under my pram. I've plenty of spare. You haven't got room in yours with all that shopping. I'll walk back with you.' Jacqui fills up her tray with hunks of coal and they set off, pushing their prams up the incline, out of Hazeltrees. 'I hope no-one asks why I am carrying coal like this,' Jacqui says and begins laughing. 'The things we do. I never thought my baby pram would end up a coal-carrier.'
'What it's like to have a good friend,' replies Emma. They smile at each other.

Spring is on its way and Ron's parents intend coming for Easter. Meanwhile, Ron is going to college and studying technical illustrating. He has been moved into that section at work and is enjoying it more than being a draughtsman.
'I think I will get a little extra job for a few weeks, as I want a lawn-mower for after Easter,' he says, one evening. 'That hand-pushing one that the previous owners left is not much good. Would

you mind?'

'Not at all, but what will you do?' says Emma, surprised at this suggestion.

'There is a job going for an insurance collector Friday and Saturday nights. I thought I might give that a go.'

'Well, if you are happy doing it, it is okay by me. I can knit or watch television or read in the evening.'

Ron visits the office in Hazeltrees on the Saturday and is given a local area, but a week later, when talking to Emma, he tells her that it is not for him.

'It is time consuming and tiring, walking around the houses and flats with little reward, but on my round, I saw a vacancy for a bar job in The Rising Sun. It is just Friday and Saturday evenings. I could try it.'

'You do so well,' his wife says.

'Thanks. I'll go down one night this week and have a chat with the manager.' Ron is taken on the following weekend. When he finally arrives home, late on the Friday, he is tired but exhilarated. Emma is waiting up for him.

'How did it go?'

'It went well. It's easy enough and I got some tips. It will only take a few weeks and I'll have enough for my lawnmower. I will be working over Easter and probably an extra day on the bank holiday Monday.'

'I'll have a word with Janice,' says Emma, 'and see if she might babysit when your parents are here and we can then come down and see you. She won't mind as I babysat for her last week.' Ron does another weekend at the pub, delighted with his earnings, while Emma prepares for his parents' visit.

'You have another job?' his mam asks in surprise, when Ron explains on their arrival, his weekend schedule, but before he has time to reply, his dad chips in.

'You won't be going to see Manchester United on Saturday, then?'

'I'll go with you on the train but I'll come back as I have work at night. You'll get back all right, won't you?' His dad nods. He doesn't often have the chance to see a top team playing. He loves his football, unlike Ron who has no interest in it. His parents are happy to visit The Rising Sun with Emma on the Sunday evening. Ron looks very smart as he wears his suit. Emma is proud of him but his mam is a little concerned at him having to do two jobs.

'It's only for a few weeks,' her son explains. 'Honestly, Mam, I quite enjoy it.'

Emma, Karen, Nan and Sam

Life runs along smoothly for the couple. Emma has received a letter from Faith apologising for not writing sooner. *You know what it is like when you have just had a baby. Imelda is beautiful. I enclose a picture of her in her Christening gown...* Faith writes. Emma looks at the photograph which looks like it has been taken professionally. The gown is long and lacy and quite exquisite. 'Maybe it is passed down from his family,' Emma thinks. 'I'm glad for Faith. I'll write a long letter to her.'

Within weeks, Ron has bought his lawn mower, an electric one. He informs the manager on his last shift that he no longer wishes to work at weekends and they part on amicable terms.
'If you ever want to earn a few pounds again, just get in touch,' the manager tells him.
'That was nice of him,' says Emma, when Ron tells her. 'You obviously did a good job.'

The following day, after Sunday dinner, while they are in the garden watching Karen happily playing in the sandpit with spoons and plastic bowls and Sam asleep in the pram, Emma approaches the subject of a holiday. She hasn't seen her parents for almost a year and is thinking about maybe paying them a visit. 'I will try and get a collapsible pushchair for Karen. We can carry Sam by taking turns. I am sure Joe will pick us up at the station. It will be lovely staying with Martha and I can use her nappies and suchlike. She will be able to put us up.'

'What about your parents?'

'We can visit them but I don't think my mam will want us around for long, although she will be happy to see us. She is back on her feet now, according to Amy in her letter and Amy has a job further afield and lives away. Martha's children will help amuse our two. What do you think?'

'Go ahead and organise it. I will need to book it in, at work. Try for a week towards the end of July.' Emma is thinking excitedly, about spending time with her family on Joe and Martha's farm, when she hears someone shouting and goes to investigate. She is delighted to find Jacqui with Daphne at their door.

'It's lovely to see you. Come on through. Daphne can have fun in the sandpit.' Janice is wearing a bright multi-coloured top and flared cotton skirt in red. 'You look cool and summery,' Emma says. 'I'll bring out juice for the little ones and make us a cup of tea. After saying hello to Jacqui, Ron leaves them to go inside and, taking out his box of metals bits, he settles down, lights his pipe and continues trying to making a robot.

Soon it is into July and Emma is looking forward to their holiday. 'What is the matter with you?' Emma wonders one morning as Karen isn't interested in her food and seems lethargic. 'She's been off colour for a few days,' she says to Ron, watching him putting on his jacket and picking up his bait box that contains his sandwiches for his midday meal. Karen is hot and sleepy all morning and doesn't want her dinner. Emma is anxious.

'Something is wrong,' she thinks. Jacqui visits later in the day. 'I think she is sickening for something,' Emma sys to her friend. Karen is hot and restless and will only take drinks.

'Daphne is out of sorts too, too,' says Jacqui. 'They must be going down with something.'

Garden: Ron with lawnmower

After a restless night, with Emma in and out of bed, seeing to a whimpering Karen and giving her drinks, morning finally arrives. Ron picks up Sam and carries him downstairs. He is a lively six-month-old.

'Nothing wrong with you, little fellow,' Ron says, getting his bowl and putting in two Weetabix. Emma appears, carrying Karen.

'Can you ring the doctor's when you get to work, please,' she asks Ron. 'Karen is poorly and she is coming out in little red spots all over and she is running a temperature. She' has hardly eaten, these last two days. I am worried.' It is late morning before the doctor arrives, a different one from her usual doctor. This one is tall and thin with greying hair and clear blue eyes. Very gently, he takes Karen from Emma and examines her.

'She has the measles,' he says, speaking in a quiet voice. 'I will give you medicine for her to keep her temperature down. Try and give her plenty of fluids and she doesn't want bright light on her eyes. Her appetite will come back as she recovers, but it will take a few days. She will probably sleep a lot at this age.' Emma thanks the doctor as he leaves. In the evening, with Ron at home, she goes to see Doris, to tell her that she will be missing the Wednesday meet-up for a week or two. The days pass and Karen spends most of her time in the pram either propped up with a cushion or sleeping. It is another week before she is on the mend and Emma is tired. Day after day, watching her little girl languishing in her pram with no energy or appetite has been a worrying time. 'I guess Daphne has the measles too,' she surmises, realising that she hasn't seen Jacqui for two weeks.

In the evenings, Emma has been organising their holiday by writing letters. They plan to take the train to Middlesburn where Joe will pick them up. Martha is delighted that they are coming and Emma is looking forward to helping her sister whose baby arrived two weeks ago. She has purchased a collapsible pushchair for Karen, who still isn't walking and shows no inclination, seemingly happy with her speedy shuffle-bottom movement. The pushchair comes in useful walking to the station and down the long platform at Piccadilly. On arriving at the farm, Emma carries Sam into the farmhouse kitchen and plonks him on an easy chair which is old and worn but very comfortable.
'My, he's a big lad,' states Nurse Readman, who has just been checking in on Martha and new baby. 'How old is he?' she asks.
'Six months.'
'You feed him well.'
'He is a hungry baby,' Emma tells her. 'He has two Weetabix for his breakfast.'

The next day, Emma and Ron walk to Bankside to visit her parents and introduce Sam. Miriam is delighted to see Karen. Apart from a second visit with the children, Emma spends the days happily helping Martha while Ron sometimes accompanies Joe by riding on the trailer and giving him a hand with work. The two sisters find time to idle on the grassy bank at the back of the farmhouse watching their little ones and enjoying the summer sunshine. Edmond is a contented baby and Martha catches up on sleep when Emma takes charge of the children. It is a happy relaxing time for them all.

The day before they leave, they visit Tom and Mary to say goodbye.
'Your dad is up the fields with Jacob. He will be in shortly,' her mam says, as she makes them a cup of tea. Miriam is soon entertaining Karen, while Ron holds Sam. The door opens and Jacob walks in with Tom, who looks pale and shaken. 'What's

On the farm: Joe and Ron

up?' Mary asks. 'You look awful.'

'I'll have a mug of tea,' he replies, sitting down in his wooden chair in the corner near the fireside. He says hello to Emma and Ron and then explains. 'That brake on t' tractor was never any good. I parked tractor and trailer on t' field near where it drops down a sharp incline. I was putting bales of hay in t' trailer when tractor started moving. I think brake jarred, with me throwing them in. Jacob spotted tractor moving and yelled for me. I ran and jumped on t' tractor to pull at steering wheel but it suddenly turned and threw me off. Tractor's side-wheel and trailer-wheel ran over me where I landed.' He pauses. He is shaking.

'I thought dad was dead,' Jacob says, his lip trembling. 'He just lay there for a while.' He is fighting tears as he speaks.

'Lad's a bit shook up,' Tom says, taking a sup from his mug of tea. Mary is aghast.

'You are lucky you are walking,' she says.

'Aye; I'm a bit unsteady. It feels like I've been hit by a bus.'

'Shouldn't you go and get checked out?'

'No. I'll be all right.' He looks at Jacob. 'Maybe you should go back with Emma and Ron. You need a break. It'll take your mind off it and help you get over t' shock, being away for a few days.'

'That's a good idea,' Mary says. 'Is that okay with you, Emma?'

Emma nods.

'Miriam was coming anyway. Joe will run us to the station at Middlesburn. We'll pick you up in the morning,' she says to Miriam and Jacob.

'What happened to the tractor?' queries Mary.

'It went nose down into the beck at bottom and hit other side. I'll ask Jack to come and pull it out.' There is a silence except for Karen giggling with Miriam. Emma and Ron hang around for a while talking to Mary and Tom. 'Have you got an aspirin?' Tom asks his wife. 'I'll take a couple. I have to get cows in shortly for

On the farm: Sandra, Karen, Ron and Brian

milking. Mark will help me if he gets in from work in time.'

'We'll be going, Mam,' says Emma. 'It's about teatime and then bedtime for these two.' They say their goodbyes and leave, quite subdued about what has taken place. 'Not a good ending to a holiday,' Emma thinks.

The journey back passes quickly. Jacob recounts the accident again. He is finding it difficult to forget. Over the next week, he goes with Miriam to meet with the youngsters at the beck where the swing rope is and to renew the friendships. He slowly stops talking about his dad and enjoys his stay. Ron discusses birds with him as Jacob loves the bird book that they'd bought him for Christmas.

'I used to shoot spuggies,' Jacob tells Ron. 'I mean sparrows, with my bow and arrow. Our Tim made it for me, but since I've read about different birds, I don't shoot at them anymore. I listen to their singing and try and identify them either by their tweeting or by their colouring and size. It's really interesting.' Miriam plays with Karen a lot, encouraging her onto her feet to stand at the fireside chair and take slow steps, when holding hands. She carries her around and plays with her in the sandpit. Sam is a happy little fellow, content with cars and bricks. He is forever falling over from his sitting position on the grass and Miriam keeps propping him back up with cushions.

In the garden: Miriam, Emma, Sam, Karen and Jacob

One morning, Miriam tells Emma that she isn't feeling well. She has lost her appetite but tries to remain cheerful. In the night, she wants a drink and her temperature is rising. It is another day or two before the spots appear. She lies in bed, hot and restless. Then she is listless and sleeps.

'I want her checked out,' says Emma to Ron. 'She is really poorly. Will you ring the doctor when you get to work, please?' Later in the day, the doctor arrives, the same one who visited when Karen was ill. He goes upstairs with Emma and examines Miriam, while Jacob watches the little two.

'She has a bad attack of measles. Give her plenty to drink. What about you, young fellow?' The doctor says to Jacob, when back downstairs.

'I think I had them when I was little, before Miriam was born.'

'That's good news, then,' the doctor replies, smiling at him. 'You will be able to help with these two. If the little lass is not any better after a few days and you're worried, give us a ring,' he tells Emma, on leaving. Miriam picks up slowly and Jacob helps a lot with carrying her meals upstairs or minding the other two. Mary writes in response to Emma's letter and expresses her sympathy. *Mark will drive down and pick them up at the weekend. I think you've had them long enough*, she writes, but Emma has enjoyed their stay, in spite of the measles. She knows that she will miss their company and their help.

'Never mind,' she tells herself. 'I'll go and visit Jacqui, after they leave.'

Emma has something on her mind that she hasn't told anyone yet and wants to share her news with Jacqui, but when she arrives, her friend is full of her own news.

'We are moving. Patrick wants to live further out into the countryside. I'm afraid we will be gone by Christmas. You can always come and visit us.' Emma tries to cover her disappointment.

'I'll miss you,' is all she says.

'We must keep in touch,' Jacqui says. 'Having our first babies together has bonded us. We'll write. Let's enjoy today. Daphne is standing at furniture now. How is Karen doing?' They spend a happy two hours with the little ones before Emma leaves, but on the way home she dwells on the sad news. She has found Jacqui a real comfort and support as well as a good laugh.

'I'll just have to get along without her,' she decides. 'No good being miserable, but I didn't even get to tell her my news. She won't be around anyway. Who shall I talk to now? Who will understand?'

Autumn 1963 / Summer 1964

'How far on?' asks Maire, when Emma blurts out her news on meeting up a few days later as she is walking home from the shops. 'Have you been to the doctor?'
'No, I don't need to. I know I'm pregnant. I've known for weeks. I will go eventually.' Maire is quite concerned.
'You'll have your hands full. When is baby due?'
'Sometime in March. I've worked it out. I'm not worried.' Emma feels she is on the defensive because of having another baby so soon after the others. Having told Maire, she also tells Janice and Doris when they meet up on Wednesday afternoon, but they aren't sure whether to congratulate her or not. They don't comment. Although she is more tired in the evenings, she is not feeling nauseous and gets through the days quite happily with her two little ones. Karen is walking around furniture and taking a few steps. 'We can buy her a doll's pram for Christmas,' Emma thinks. 'She will love pushing her dolly around in it.' Later in the evening, she tells Ron that Angela has written to say that she has given birth to beautiful baby boy with a mass of ginger hair who looks just like his dad. 'I'll buy a card next time I'm in Hazeltrees. I am so pleased for them.'

One Sunday afternoon, before Jacqui leaves, she invites Emma, Ron and the children to tea. There are half-filled boxes lying about and empty shelves where Patrick kept his books. After Emma tells Jacqui about being pregnant again, Jacqui congratulates her and the two mothers reminisce about their time together since they first met at the ante-natal class.
'You will be busy, but our mams both managed with seven. I'm sure you will be fine,' Jacqui says, encouragingly. 'You must come and visit us in our new home. You can pick them up, can't you, Patrick,' she says to her husband. 'It's not too far, about an hour's journey. You won't mind.'
'Of course not,' he replies. 'We can't wait to get into our new house.'
'He will do that after we've settled in and before you have this next little one. You won't have time afterwards,' Jacqui adds. An hour later, they say their farewells. 'Don't forget. You are coming to see us,' she states, from the doorstep, as they leave. 'We will see you soon.'
'She's great, isn't she,' Ron says, as they walk back home. 'She is

so friendly and welcoming.'
'She is. She didn't bat an eye-lid when I told her about the baby. I
will miss her.'

Expecting a third baby gives Emma lots to think about. She is
potty-training Karen, so as to cut down on the nappies to wash,
knowing there will be plenty more when the baby arrives. She is
reading the adverts in the shop-window, every time she goes, as
she wants to pick up a second-hand washing-machine. Sam is
crawling everywhere.
'He crawled outside after me today,' she tells Ron, one evening. 'I
was hanging washing out as it was a good drying day, although
quite cold. The next thing, Karen is telling me that he is eating
coal. Her speech is coming on, you know. She is quite a little
talker. I rescued Sam from the coal-bunker and fished small lumps
of coal from his mouth. The wooden door doesn't shut properly.
He looked like he had a black moustache. He does take some
watching.'

Emma enjoys the Wednesday meetings and the children love the
change of toys at Janice's or Daphne's. Going to the baby clinic is
a bit of a chore and she doesn't visit often, as Sam is thriving. She
has made sure that he has had his smallpox injection at three
months, like Karen; his triple vaccination at four, five and six
months; and later, his polio one. Since then, she has visited very
intermittently, but was told the last time, that Karen needs her
shoes building up a little. Emma now has the chew of catching a
bus into Stockport to go to the clinic at the hospital. She puts Sam
in the pushchair and Karen walks very slowly beside her.
Sometimes, Emma alternates by putting Karen in the pushchair
and carrying Sam, but he is heavy. Getting on the bus is difficult
when trying to fold the pushchair and hold Sam and somehow hold
Karen's hand. The news isn't good when she finally arrives at the
hospital.
'Even her welly-boots?' she says, in dismay, to the nurse.
'I'm afraid so, especially if she wears them a lot. Bring them next
time when you pick up these shoes.' Karen is wearing her little red
welly-boots as she only had one pair of shoes. 'We will notify you
when the shoes are ready. You'll be done by Christmas,' the nurse
tells her, cheerfully. The nurse was right, but it takes another two
trips to the hospital.

'I am so glad that I don't have to go anymore for a while,' Emma
says to Ron one evening, a week before Christmas, when
describing her last visit. 'I have decided to try putting Karen in a
bed in the New Year, so that she won't think I'm just giving her
cot to the baby. I want her to feel special in a bed. I saw a pram for
sale in the pram shop in Hazeltrees earlier in the week. I meant to
tell you but forgot with thinking about my journey to the hospital.
The pram is extra-long. I figure that when the baby comes, he or
she will be in it, with Sam on the pram seat and Karen can sit in
the bottom end as there will be room. It is the only way that I will
be able to take them out together. It even has a shopping bag at the
front and a basket-type tray underneath, for shopping. It is light-
brown in colour, very smart and with a good discount on it. I guess
it is too big for most mothers, but it will be ideal for us. What do
you think?'

'You go and buy it, if you need it,' answers Ron. 'You know more
about these things than me. Have we decided what to buy for Sam
and Karen, for Christmas?' They chat about presents. Emma has
made a cake and is determined to make a better job of icing it. She
goes to Midnight Mass alone and Ron attends on Christmas
morning. They find it easier to go separately rather than the long
walk with the children. They spend a quiet Christmas Day with
their little family.

January arrives and Emma discusses with Ron about plans for a
joint birthday party for Karen and Sam, as there is only a day
between their birthdays. She suggests that it takes place on a
Wednesday, two days before Karen's actual birthday so that Janice
and Daphne can come with their offspring. Sam isn't aware of
what's going on but Karen is quite excited at receiving presents
and being sung to. Maire calls in with little gifts. There are lovely
cards from Jacqui, who includes a short note to say that Patrick
will pick them up the following Sunday at one o'clock. *That's so
we can have plenty of time together. Have an early dinner and
hopefully you'll stay for tea, before Patrick brings you home*, she
writes. Emma explains to Karen about their forthcoming trip and
that she will see Daphne again but isn't sure how much her little
girl understands. Birthday cards arrive for the little two from both
families and from Ron's parents, a gorgeous winter dress in pink
for Karen and blue, hand-knitted, short trousers and jumper to
match for Sam. Later in the evening, Ron has some news for
Emma.

'I've been talking to Ben at work and he knows someone who gives driving lessons. I think I might book some as we will need to buy a car at some point.' Emma's eyes light up.

'That will be great. You do that.'

'I know we can't afford many, but I can start.'

'With you getting an increase in wages at the end of January, we will manage to pay for some,' Emma says, enthusiastically. 'I never thought about us getting a car.'

The following Sunday, after church and an early dinner, the family await the arrival of Patrick. The two children are dressed in their new winter clothes and Karen is excited about a ride in a car. On arrival, the couple are given a grand tour of the house. Jacqui explains that it is more spacious than their old one and has four bedrooms. There is an open view through the living-room window, beyond their garden, that looks over green fields. Emma points out the sheep to Karen.

'It's lovely,' exclaims Emma. 'Plenty of room for more babies,' she says, grinning at Jacqui. The friends have lots to chat about and the little ones play with Daphne's toys. Jacqui has thoughtfully bought a few second-hand cars for Sam to play with. He enjoys watching an adult stacking up the wooden coloured bricks for him to knock down and the girls laughing. Patrick and Ron are deep in conversation over work, while each enjoying a beer. The day passes quickly and then more goodbyes. 'I don't like farewells,' says Emma, hugging her friend. Jacqui watches from the front door step with Daphne in her arms, waving until the car disappears from sight.

The weeks leading up to the baby's due date are very wearisome for Emma. Six weeks before, the nurse at the clinic tells her that the baby's head is down and baby can arrive anytime.

'It may not,' she adds, 'but just to be aware.' Ron asks a couple at church if they can pick up Emma if she walks to the end of the road because she is finding it tiring, walking the distance. The couple show concern and willingly help. Ron does the weekly shop on the Saturday. He is finding it hard keeping Emma cheerful as she soldiers on, dragging her weary body around. Luckily, they now have an old second-hand washing-machine and it eases the workload for her.

'Is this baby ever going to come,' she says despairingly, to Ron one evening, after the little ones are in bed. She is resting her feet on a chair. 'I can't even get comfortable in bed and I'm forever going to the toilet. All the nurse says is that it will come when it is ready. Sam was early but this one seems happy to stay where it is.'

On the expected arrival date of the baby, Emma has the fire burning fiercely as it is a cold March morning. She hears a loud noise, almost a roaring noise.

'What is it?' she thinks. Then she looks over to the fire and realises the chimney is alight. 'Oh, God,' she screams. She gathers up her two children and runs outside in a panic. 'Help,' she cries, to no-one in particular. She can see the black smoke bellowing from her chimney. A tall, well-built man from three doors away, walks up to her.

'I'm George. It's okay. I have phoned the fire brigade.' Elsie, her neighbour from next door, approaches.

'You come with me,' she states. 'Have a cup of tea. You need to sit down, in your condition.' Emma gratefully goes into her house. She is shaking and feels weak. The children are quiet but want their mam. She hauls one up onto each knee, with what little room there is, as her baby bump is large. Elsie places a hot cup of tea on the table next to her and gives a biscuit to each of the children.

Meanwhile, Ron is walking home from the shops, laden with bags of shopping. Just before he turns into their road, a fire engine screams past him.

'Wouldn't it be awful if it was going to our house,' he thinks. As he turns the corner, he realises that it has stopped somewhere in the vicinity of their home. He races down the road as best he can with the heavy bags and gasps when he sees that it is outside their house.

'Don't worry,' George, the neighbour, says, as Ron approaches him. 'Your family are safe next door.' A fireman comes out and speaks to Ron.

'It's all done now, but you need your chimney sweeping regularly. Don't let it get in a state like that again.' Ron thanks him and also George, who has been watching. He collects his family from next door and they walk back in. The carpet is pulled back. The fireside is dirty. Black soot with remains of water is evident. Emma bursts into tears.

'Don't cry, mammy,' says a little voice. Karen is gazing up at her, looking bewildered. Ron starts to clean up and Emma finally begins putting the shopping away.

Later in the day, when they have recovered somewhat, they sit down to have a cup of tea.

'Can you go and ring that couple and tell them that I'm not going to church tomorrow,' Emma asks her husband. 'I'm too shaken up and weary.' Ron gets up and puts coats on the two little ones. 'Come with daddy. We will have a little walk.' Karen smiles as she takes hold of her dolly's pram and Sam climbs onto the pushchair. 'You get a nap,' Ron says to Emma. 'You need a rest. I'll keep the children out for a little while and make the phone call.' The next day, Ron goes to church, following which, the family spend the day quietly at home, still recovering from the shock of the fire.

Ron hates leaving Emma on the Monday morning but has to go to work. Each night when getting into bed, Emma thinks that maybe she will go into labour. Each morning, she wakes up, disappointed. No baby and another day to get through. It is mid-week when the doorbell rings and Emma, half-asleep on a chair, while keeping watch over her children, wearily drags herself to the door.

'Hello,' a young woman says cheerfully, greeting Emma with a big smile. 'I'm Joanne, your midwife.' She is tubby, round-faced, with blonde, short-cut hair. Her blue eyes have lashes coated with thick, black mascara. She steps inside and after a short chat, they go upstairs, Emma carrying Sam with Karen coming up behind. 'Time you had this baby,' Joanne says, on examining Emma. 'It is ready to drop. You are overdue and top of my list. Ring as soon as you go into labour. It might be a quick one.'

The days continue. It is on Saturday evening, after having put the children to bed, that Emma asks Ron if he will say the rosary with her. They take out their beads and begin praying. Half-way through an *Our Father*, she experiences her first contraction. 'At last,' she thinks. She stops praying and smiles at Ron. 'I think you'll need to go and phone Joanne, shortly,' she says. 'She said to let her know as soon as I start.' He hugs his wife; the relief evident on his face. The contractions are strong and only ten minutes apart.

Not long after Ron makes the call, the midwife arrives. She examines Emma, before preparing the bed.

'Are the little ones asleep?' she asks, as Emma is paddling around and breathing heavily; the pains are taking hold. Emma nods. 'We will go down and have a cup of tea,' says Joanne. 'I'm staying, as I don't think it will be long before baby arrives.' In the living-room, the nurse watches as Emma paces up and down with each contraction.

Eventually, after another examination upstairs, the midwife suggests that Emma stays on the bed. Emma is moaning and beginning to shout as she breathes through long and painful contractions. Ron has come up, on hearing his wife shout out and sits by the bed, holding her hands.
'I need to push,' she yells, before striving with all her might to heave the baby out. She runs out of breath but the baby keeps pushing. She grips Ron's hands even more tightly and pushes again. Then she yells as the baby comes out in one long swoop. She lays back and gasps. 'It's over, thank God,' she thinks. Ron is rubbing his hands.
'I thought you were going to break them,' he says. 'Only joking,' he adds, looking at the expression on her face.
'That was a sharp, short labour. Two hours from start to finish and another one crossed off my list,' says Joanne. 'A fine, plump, baby boy you have here. Eight pounds, six ounces, but I thought he would weigh heavier. He looks a healthy little chap.' She is pleased, as she recently qualified and is enjoying totting up her numbers of deliveries.

On Monday, Ron is concerned to find a rash all over his torso and instead of going to work, he visits the doctor.
'Some kind of nervous reaction,' he tells Emma, later. 'The doctor has put me on sick for a week. I explained about the chimney fire and these last weeks with you struggling. By the way, I posted your letter to Amy, with a first-class stamp. Do you think she will come?'
'I think so. We will just have to manage until she gets here. With it being Easter weekend, she will have four days off.' They muddle through the week with broken nights and busy days.

On Good Friday, early afternoon, Amy walks in. She greets the little ones and gives them sweets, before peeping at the baby.
'I can only stay the long weekend,' she says to Emma. 'I said I'd try and come. I'll have a hold of him when you've finished feeding him. Has he a name?'
'Aaron Peter.'
'I like that,' she says, taking him from Emma and cooing over him.

'He is a chubby little fellow.' Emma is overjoyed at seeing her sister.

'You don't know how pleased I am that you have come.' Then it is non-stop chatter. Amy is full of news about a young man she is going out with. 'You seem serious,' Emma comments. Amy chuckles.

'He certainly is, but he is a few years older than me and I'm not eighteen till next month. He will be worried about asking dad.'

'That serious!' exclaims Emma. 'How long have you known him?'

'I met him last August.'

'I can see why dad might be worried.'

'Now, you get to bed and I'll take over. We will talk later.' Amy enjoys her weekend, enabling Emma to have plenty of rest, while she does the cooking, the washing and minding the little two with Ron's help. There are goodbyes and hugs when Amy leaves on Easter Monday.

'I will write,' she says, 'and let you know about me and Andrew.'

'At least Ron is still off,' thinks Emma, wandering back into the house, but the following morning after he leaves for work, Emma is feeling disconsolate. She struggles through the rest of the day and has an early night knowing that she will have broken sleep with feeding Aaron. The next afternoon, she puts her three children in the pram and walks up to Janice's house. As Janice opens the door, Emma begins to cry. Janice takes the pram around to the back of the house and leaving baby Aaron sleeping soundly, helps Sam and Karen into her kitchen.

'Come on. What is it? What's the matter?' she asks, as she passes Emma a cup of tea.

'I just miss them all. I just miss my family. I haven't seen mam and dad for months or Martha.'

'Maybe you should think seriously about moving further North to be nearer to them all,' suggests Janice.

'I can't do that as Ron's work is here.'

'Have a talk to him. He might be able to find work up there.'

'He loves where he works.'

'You are probably very tired but you will pull through. You always do,' Janice says, trying to console Emma. 'That will be Doris,' she adds, hearing a knock at the door. Doris arrives with her little one and after she has a peep at Aaron and comments on how cute he is, the conversation turns to discussions over plans for the summer holidays. Eventually, Emma makes a move.

'Ron's parents are coming at the weekend,' she says. 'I'd better go and start planning for that. Thanks for the tea.'
'Call in again, anytime, if you feel in need of a chat. I don't mind. Don't be sitting on your own, crying.' Janice says, as she sees Emma out.

The letter from Ron's parents arrived that morning to say they are coming down on Friday for a few days. Emma has planned to have Aaron baptised on the Sunday and Maire has agreed to be a godparent, as well as Tim, Emma's oldest brother, but there is some doubt as to whether he can make it on Sunday. His letter arrives Friday morning to confirm that he cannot come.
'You can stand proxy,' Emma says to Ron. 'We'll just take Aaron, as your mam and dad will mind the other two. I don't want any fuss.' After the Baptism, they return home to find Ron's mam has taken the trouble to iron a tablecloth.
'I thought you might be having people back,' she says.
'No. Maire has gone home. We had no plans. Thank you for bothering, though,' Emma says. The table cloth, the wedding

Nan and Aaron

present from Hannah Black, is folded up and put away.

'My dad had a chat with me tonight, after you went to bed,' whispers Ron, much later, as they snuggle up in the smaller bed downstairs.

'What about?' asks his wife. She can hear the snuffled breathing of their baby in the background.

'He gave me a little talk on the birds and the bees.' Emma can see he is smiling.

'Did he really?' she says, in amazement.

'He did.'

'What did you say?'

'I kept quiet; it was embarrassing for both of us. My mam had gone to bed but I suspect she'd asked him to do it. They are trying to help, but it's none of their business how many kids we have. I suppose that they are thinking the best for us.' The young couple find it rather amusing, his dad giving Ron the talk and still smiling, they drift off to sleep, holding hands. Over the next few days, Ron's mam tries hard to help and minds the children while Emma sleeps, although Emma doesn't really like doing this as she feels her little ones don't know their Nan. Emma is tired and not much company; it is not the best of visits and she doesn't mind when Ron's parents leave.

A week after the parents leave, there is a letter from them.

'Your mam is telling me that if we have a row, we should make up. She thinks we'd been arguing when they were here. I'm going to write and tell her that we don't row. I know I wasn't myself, but I was tired. Aaron was two weeks old when they came.'

'She means well,' says Ron. 'Be careful what you say. I wouldn't like them to be upset.'

'You are right, but I do find it annoying. I will put it to her, gently.'

'I've finally booked six driving lessons, by the way. We did discuss it if you remember. It means I will be out another evening, as the classes in tech drawing start again next week, as well.'

'Don't worry. I'll be fine. It is great what you are doing. It will be so useful to have a car, now we have three children.'

Emma is trying each day to be positive and cheerful, but admits to herself that she is struggling and decides to put Aaron on the bottle and stop breast-feeding. She feels that this way, she may be less tired. Within a week, Aaron has cut out a feed, is taking the bottle well and is happy and contented. This pleases her and helps her to do away with her guilty feelings about not feeding him herself. The downsize is that both her other two want a bottle like the baby and she ends up giving them water or juice in baby bottles, when Aaron has a feed, so that they don't feel left out. 'Not sure if I'm doing this right,' she thinks, ruefully, 'but it helps keep my little family content and that is important.'

One Saturday evening in May, Ron finally decides that it is time to time to converse with his wife about his concerns that have bothered him for weeks.

'I've been thinking and we need to have a serious talk,' he says. 'I haven't told you before as there was enough going on, but work is slowing down and there are rumours of moving some of us to another part of the country.' He stops speaking as he sees the shocked look on his wife's face.

'Where to?' she asks.

'I don't know which site but I don't want to go and leave you here and then return at weekends which is what would happen. Alternatively, it will mean uprooting us and moving. I am wondering if I should look for another job and stay here, or I can look for one nearer Middlesburn and move there. We'd be much nearer to our families and you'd be able to visit during the day maybe, or they may come and see us more often. I know that you miss them a lot.' Emma's eyes fill up. She can hardly believe what he is saying.

'Are you sure?' she asks. 'I thought you loved working near aircraft.'

'I have enjoyed it, but I think this is a better option than been sent further afield. I have more experience under my belt and I'm studying again. I should be able to get a job. What do you think?'

'If you are happy with that, I think it is a great idea.' She pauses. 'Just think. We will be able to visit the farm and maybe stay over. It will be lovely for the children to spend time with their cousins.' She pauses, before continuing. 'We can visit Abe and Marjorie again and Angela and Des. I haven't seen their baby yet and he will soon be a year old. You can visit Hadrian's Wall more easily too, especially if we get a car.'

'Let's sleep on it,' Ron says, 'and we can talk more tomorrow.' In the middle of the night while Emma is feeding Aaron, she ponders over Ron's suggestion.

'We will have to sell the house,' she thinks. 'Where will we stay until we buy another one? What happens to the furniture?' The questions keep coming. 'You sleep, little fellow,' she says, putting Aaron back into his carry-cot. 'I need to sleep too,' she thinks, but it is a while before she can stop the many questions racing around in her mind.

The following evening, after further discussion, the couple decide to go ahead and move north. The next day, Emma takes her three little ones in the large pram to Hazeltrees and visits the Halifax Building Society. She doesn't like leaving the pram outside and it is awkward getting it inside. Sam is restless and wants to get out of the pram seat. She gives him and Karen some sweets while she explains to the assistant about wanting their house to be put on the market. As she passes Jacqui's old house on the way home, she recalls the happy times spent with her friend.
'But life moves on,' she thinks. 'Maybe when we have settled again, we can visit her.' At home, Emma tries to clean and dust, but with difficulty, as she seems to have so little spare time in her busy days.

Correspondence increases between Emma and Ron's mam. His mam offers to send the weekly newspaper with jobs advertised. Meanwhile, Ron continues with his evening classes and driving lessons. On his free evenings, he tackles the window ledges where the paint is peeling, only to discover that the wood is rotting. He fills the gaps with putty and paints over it, hoping for the best. It doesn't take long for the surveyor, when looking around the house, to dig his pencil into the putty and it was rather embarrassing for Emma, she tells Ron, when relating the visit. The weekly newspapers keep arriving and the jobs section is thoroughly searched.

One Saturday morning in June when the sun is shining and Emma is hanging out the washing, Ron joins her, waving an envelope.
'I have an interview,' he says, excitedly, but his wife is running towards the sandpit.
'Not in your mouth,' Emma shouts to Sam as he reaches to his mouth with a large pebble. She removes it from him and returns to her washing. Baby Aaron is asleep in the pram and Karen is building sand-castles. Ron realises that she is distracted and that it is not the best time for a discussion.
'I'll give you a hand and I will fill in the application form when they are in bed,' he says. 'Haven't we a viewing at eleven-thirty?'

'Yes, we have and I need to tidy up.'
'I'll mind the kids. You go in.'

It is well after tea and the children in bed before Ron takes the application form from the letter and fills it in, while Emma is ironing.
'Who's it for?' she asks.
'It's a firm at Stockbridge, a town near Thorntees and not far from where mam and dad live. The job is for a Piping Draughtsman and the pay is slightly better.'
'I do hope you get it. I'm beginning to get excited.'

Within a week, Ron is invited for interview. He arranges to take two days off and plans to stay overnight with his parents.
'You will be all right, won't you?' he asks Emma. 'I don't like leaving you on your own.'
'I'll be fine. You will only be away one night.'
The two days seem long as Emma copes with their two-year-old, their one-year-old and new baby. Maire calls and Emma gives her the news.
'I will write,' says Maire. 'Probably not often, but I want to keep in touch with being Aaron's godmother.' Emma visits Janice and Doris and explains that she won't be coming on Wednesdays any more.
'It's a good move for you, I think,' says Janice. 'You will see so much more of your family. My brother is interested in your house, as he is moving into the area. Can he come one day next week and view it?'
'Yes, he can. We have had a few viewings but nothing definite.'
'I'll let him know and tell you which day he can make it.'
'This is good news,' thinks Emma. 'I just hope Ron gets the job.'

Ron thinks that the interview went well, but it is another week before he hears from the firm.
'I've got it,' he announces, on opening the letter. He grins from ear to ear and Emma throws her arms around his neck.
'That is so good,' she says, happily. 'We can move. Do they give you a starting date?'
'Yes. Beginning of August, as I have to give a month's notice where I am. Write and tell mam, will you and ask if we can stay there for a few weeks. We can move up in July as I have some holiday due. We can start house-hunting before I begin the new

job.'

'Will she have room? It's only a two-bed.'

'I know. We will all have to sleep in one bedroom. I can't think what else to suggest. We can rent, but that costs and I'm sure mam won't mind.' Emma writes and makes the request and asks if his mam can get hold of a cot for Sam and a bed or put-you-up for Karen. Aaron will sleep in the carry-cot.

Janice's brother keeps his appointment to view their house. He is delighted with it and makes them an offer, suggesting that they tell the Halifax that they have found a private buyer because that will save them money. Emma and Ron are worried about this. It is the first time that they have sold a property and they are unsure about the legality of it all. They are pleased that he wants to buy it, but decide to go through the proper channels. A letter comes by return of post from Ron's mam, saying that she will be happy for them to stay.

'That is a relief,' says Emma, on reading it and telling Ron. 'We now need to decide on a moving date and then I will order a removal van. I need to give the Post Office a forwarding address for letters. I must start packing. I'll see if I can get some cardboard boxes from the shops, the ones that they would normally be throwing out. I can collect a few at a time and do the packing while you are at work.'

'Look what one of the blokes has given me,' says Ron, walking into the house two weeks before he leaves. He steps over boxes before reaching Emma who is busily sticking them up with packing tape. He hands her a large stiff brown envelope. She stands up and takes it from his hand. 'Go on. Open it.' She pulls out a large caricature image of a robot pulling a cart driven by a bloke and behind him a small mountain of boxes and hanging in with them, a lady and two small children. Emma starts laughing. 'That's us, I suppose. They've left Aaron off.'

'I guess we're supposed to imagine him tucked away behind some boxes,' says Ron, grinning.

'It's very cleverly done. Makes us look a bit poor, though,' his wife replies, 'but I think we do all right.'

'I like it. He is very talented,' her husband replies, putting his arms around her. 'We will get a car, one day. You'll see. You do an amazing job with the money.' He kisses her and they wander through to the living-room to be greeted by Aaron who smiles at

A colleague's farewell image of the family move

them from his pram while Karen and Sam, seeing their dad walk in, rush to him.

'I'll write and tell your mam that I'll have the pram delivered to their house, but the rest of the furniture can go in store,' Emma says, later in the evening. 'Maybe I can put necessary clothes et cetera, for the children, in the pram and that way we won't have to carry so much with us on the train. I hope it will fit in the narrow passage at your mam's house as I really need it with us while we are there. We can fill our suitcases and they can be delivered to your mam's, too.' She stops abruptly as it suddenly hits her, the enormity of what they are planning. 'Can we do all this?' she asks him, tearfully. He puts his arms around her and hugs her tightly.

It is finally happening. Ron makes one last tour of their home, gazing at all the boxes piled up. He checks that the back door is locked and stepping out of the front door, turns the key. Emma is waiting, holding the handles of the pushchair. Sam is not happy and is showing his annoyance at being strapped in. The carry-cot is on the pavement with baby Aaron inside, asleep. Next to it is a large shopping bag with food et cetera, for the journey. Karen is holding Emma's hand and looking worried, not understanding what is going on. Ron takes the keys to Doris who has offered to let the removal men in, later in the morning. She will lock up and return the keys to the Halifax.

'Right,' he says, picking up the carry-cot with one hand and taking Karen's hand with the other. Emma lets go of Karen's hand. She picks up the shopping bag and wheels the pushchair slowly down the pavement with Sam still wriggling and trying to get out.

It is slow progress but the couple have allowed plenty of time to catch the train into Manchester, where they will change platforms for a train to Darlington and another change to Thorntees. A car pulls up beside them and a lady gets out.

'Hello,' she says. 'Are you going far? You look like you can do with a lift.' It is Joanne, the midwife, cheerful and friendly. Emma explains the situation. 'I can't fit you all in. I will take the carry-cot, the shopping bag and you and the little girl,' says Joanne. 'That just leaves you to push the little lad to the station,' she adds, speaking to Ron. 'Will that help?'

'Yes, it will. Thank you ever so much. It is very kind of you,' Emma replies.

'Come on, then. Let's get you into the car.' As the car pulls away, Emma waves to Ron, but she can see Sam crying. He is not happy.

It is more than an hour later when they are finally settled on the train to Darlington, having struggled on and off the train into Manchester and then, a good walk down a platform to their waiting train to go north.

'We have made it,' Emma says, holding Sam at the window as the train leaves the built-up area and makes its way across the countryside. The family have eaten their sandwiches and Emma has seen to Aaron who is sleeping, contentedly. Sam refuses to go to sleep and insists on standing up to gaze out of the window, fascinated by all that he is seeing. Karen is sitting beside her dad, enjoying nursing her favourite dolly and looking at the pictures in a story book. Emma sees the green fields and the haycocks and an idling tractor.

'Look, Sam. Sheep! See those cows.' She glances at Ron and gives him a radiant smile. He reaches over and kisses her.

'You happy?' he asks.

'Very,' she says. 'We are going home.'